**Mecklermedia's Official
Internet World™**

net.profit:

**Expanding Your Business
Using the Internet**

**Mecklermedia's Official
Internet World™**

net.profit:

**Expanding Your Business
Using the Internet**

Joel Maloff

IDG Books Worldwide, Inc.
Foster City, CA • Chicago, IL • Indianapolis, IN • Braintree, MA • Dallas, TX

Mecklermedia's Official Internet World™
net.profit
Expanding Your Business Using the Internet

Published by **IDG Books Worldwide, Inc.**
An International Data Group Company
919 East Hillsdale Boulevard, Suite 400
Foster City, CA 94404

Mecklermedia	**Mecklermedia Ltd.**
20 Ketchum Street	Artillery House, Artillery Row
Westport, CT 06880	London, SW1P 1RT, UK

Library of Congress Catalog Card No.: 95-077592
ISBN 1-56884-701-7
Printed in the United States of America
Second Printing, January, 1996
10 9 8 7 6 5 4 3 2
Distributed in the United States by IDG Books Worldwide, Inc.

Published in the United States

ABOUT IDG BOOKS WORLDWIDE

Welcome to the world of IDG Books Worldwide.

IDG Books Worldwide, Inc. is a subsidiary of International Data Group, the world's largest publisher of computer-related information and the leading global provider of information services on information technology. IDG was founded more than 25 years ago and now employs more than 7,500 people worldwide. IDG publishes more than 235 computer publications in 67 countries (see listing below). More than fifty million people read one or more IDG publications each month.

Launched in 1990, IDG Books Worldwide is today the #1 publisher of best-selling computer books in the United States. We are proud to have received 3 awards from the Computer Press Association in recognition of editorial excellence, and our best-selling ...For Dummies™ series has more than 18 million copies in print with translations in 24 languages. IDG Books, through a recent joint venture with IDG's Hi-Tech Beijing, became the first U.S. publisher to publish a computer book in the People's Republic of China. In record time, IDG Books has become the first choice for millions of readers around the world who want to learn how to better manage their businesses.

Our mission is simple: Every IDG book is designed to bring extra value and skill-building instructions to the reader. Our books are written by experts who understand and care about our readers. The knowledge base of our editorial staff comes from years of experience in publishing, education, and journalism — experience which we use to produce books for the '90s. In short, we care about books, so we attract the best people. We devote special attention to details such as audience, interior design, use of icons, and illustrations. And because we use an efficient process of authoring, editing, and desktop publishing our books electronically, we can spend more time ensuring superior content and spend less time on the technicalities of making books.

You can count on our commitment to deliver high-quality books at competitive prices on topics consumers want to read about. At IDG, we value quality, and we have been delivering quality for more than 25 years. You'll find no better book on a subject than an IDG book

John J. Kilcullen

John Kilcullen
President and CEO
IDG Books Worldwide, Inc.

WINNER
*Eighth Annual
Computer Press
Awards 1992*

WINNER
*Ninth Annual
Computer Press
Awards 1993*

IDG Books Worldwide, Inc. is a subsidiary of International Data Group, the world's largest publisher of computer-related information and the leading global provider of information services on information technology. International Data Group publishes over 235 computer publications in 67 countries. More than fifty million people read one or more International Data Group publications each month. The officers are Patrick J. McGovern, Founder and Board Chairman; Kelly Conlin, President; Jim Casella, Chief Operating Officer. International Data Group's publications include: ARGENTINA'S Computerworld Argentina, Infoworld Argentina; AUSTRALIA'S Computerworld Australia, Computer Living, Australian PC World, Australian Macworld, Network World, Mobile Business Australia, Publish!, Reseller, IDG Sources; AUSTRIA'S Computerwelt Oesterreich, PC Test; BELGIUM'S Data News (CW); BOLIVIA'S Computerworld; BRAZIL'S Computerworld, Connections, Game Power, Mundo Unix, PC World, Publish, Super Game; BULGARIA'S Computerworld Bulgaria, PC & Mac World Bulgaria, Network World Bulgaria; CANADA'S CIO Canada, Computerworld Canada, InfoCanada, Network World Canada, Reseller; CHILE'S Computerworld Chile, Informatica; COLOMBIA'S Computerworld Colombia, PC World; COSTA RICA'S PC World; CZECH REPUBLIC'S Computerworld, Elektronika, PC World; DENMARK'S Communications World, Computerworld Danmark, Computerworld Focus, Macintosh Produktkatalog, Macworld Danmark, PC World Danmark, PC Produktguide, Tech World, Windows World; ECUADOR'S PC World Ecuador; EGYPT'S Computerworld (CW) Middle East, PC World Middle East; FINLAND'S MikroPC, Tietoviikko, Tietoverkko; FRANCE'S Distributique, GOLDEN MAC, InfoPC, Le Guide du Monde Informatique, Le Monde Informatique, Telecoms & Reseaux; GERMANY'S Computerwoche, Computerwoche Focus, Computerwoche Extra, Electronic Entertainment, Gamepro, Information Management, Macwelt, Netzwelt, PC Welt, Publish, Publish; GREECE'S Publish & Macworld; HONG KONG'S Computerworld Hong Kong, PC World Hong Kong; HUNGARY'S Computerworld SZT, PC World; INDIA'S Computers & Communications; INDONESIA'S Info Komputer; IRELAND'S ComputerScope; ISRAEL'S Beyond Windows, Computerworld Israel, Multimedia, PC World Israel; ITALY'S Computerworld Italia, Lotus Magazine, Macworld Italia, Networking Italia, PC Shopping Italy, PC World Italia; JAPAN'S Computerworld Today, Information Systems World, Macworld Japan, Nikkei Personal Computing, SunWorld Japan, Windows World; KENYA'S East African Computer News; KOREA'S Computerworld Korea, Macworld Korea, PC World Korea; LATIN AMERICA'S GamePro; MALAYSIA'S Computerworld Malaysia, PC World Malaysia; MEXICO'S Compu Edicion, Compu Manufactura, Computacion/Punto de Venta, Computerworld Mexico, MacWorld, Mundo Unix, PC World, Windows; THE NETHERLANDS' Computer! Totaal, Computable (CW), LAN Magazine, Lotus Magazine, MacWorld; NEW ZEALAND'S Computer Buyer, Computerworld New Zealand, Network World, New Zealand PC World; NIGERIA'S PC World Africa; NORWAY'S Computerworld Norge, Lotusworld Norge, Macworld Norge, Maxi Data, Networld, PC World Ekspress, PC World Nettverk, PC World Norge, PC World's Produktguide, Publish& Multimedia World, Student Data, Unix World, Windowsworld; PAKISTAN'S PC World Pakistan; PANAMA'S PC World Panama; PERU'S Computerworld Peru, PC World; PEOPLE'S REPUBLIC OF CHINA'S China Computerworld, China Infoworld, China PC Info Magazine, Computer Fan, PC World China, Electronics International, Electronics Today/Multimedia World, Electronic Product World, China Network World, Software World Magazine, Telecom Product World; PHILIPPINES' Computerworld Philippines, PC Digest (PCW); POLAND'S Computerworld Poland, Computerworld Special Report, Networld, PC World/Komputer, Sunworld; PORTUGAL'S Cerebro/PC World, Correio Informatico/Computerworld, MacIn; ROMANIA'S Computerworld, PC World, Telecom Romania; RUSSIA'S Computerworld-Moscow, Mir - PK (PCW), Sety (Networks); SINGAPORE'S Computerworld Southeast Asia, PC World Singapore; SLOVENIA'S Monitor Magazine; SOUTH AFRICA'S Computer Mail (CIO),Computing S.A.,Network World S.A., Software World; SPAIN'S Advanced Systems, Amiga World, Computerworld Espana, Communicaciones World, Macworld Espana, NeXTWORLD, Super Juegos Magazine (GamePro), PC World Espana, Publish; SWEDEN'S Attack, ComputerSweden, Corporate Computing, Macworld, Mikrodatorn, Natverk & Kommunikation, PC World, CAP & Design, Datalngenjoren, Maxi Data,Windows World; SWITZERLAND'S Computerworld Schweiz, Macworld Schweiz, PC Tip; TAIWAN'S Computerworld Taiwan, PC World Taiwan; THAILAND'S Thai Computerworld; TURKEY'S Computerworld Monitor, Macworld Turkiye, PC World Turkiye; UKRAINE'S Computerworld, Computers+Software Magazine; UNITED KINGDOM'S Computing /Computerworld, Connexion/Network World, Lotus Magazine, Macworld, Open Computing/Sunworld; UNITED STATES' Advanced Systems, AmigaWorld, Cable in the Classroom, CD Review, CIO, Computerworld, Computerworld Client/Server Journal, Digital Video, DOS World, Electronic Entertainment Magazine (E2), Federal Computer Week, Game Hits, GamePro, IDG Books, Infoworld, Laser Event, Macworld, Maximize, Multimedia World, Network World, PC Letter, PC World, Publish, SWATPro, Video Event; URUGUAY'S PC World Uruguay; VENEZUELA'S Computerworld Venezuela, PC World; VIETNAM'S PC World Vietnam.

For More Information...

For general information on IDG Books in the U.S., including information on discounts and premiums, contact IDG Books at 800-434-3422.

For information on where to purchase IDG's books outside the U.S., contact Christina Turner at 415-655-3022.

For information on translations, contact Marc Jeffrey Mikulich, Foreign Rights Manager, at IDG Books Worldwide; fax number: 415-655-3295.

For sales inquiries and special prices for bulk quantities, contact Tony Real at 800-434-3422 or 415-655-3048.

For information on using IDG's books in the classroom and ordering examination copies, contact Jim Kelly at 800-434-2086.

Internet World books are distributed in Canada by Macmillan of Canada, a Division of Canada Publishing Corporation; by Computer and Technical Books in Miami, Florida, for South America and the Caribbean; by Longman Singapore in Singapore, Malaysia, Thailand, and Korea; by Toppan Co. Ltd. in Japan; by Asia Computerworld in Hong Kong; by Woodslane Pty. Ltd. in Australia and New Zealand; and by McGraw-Hill Book Company (Europe) Ltd. in the U.K., Europe, the Middle East and Africa.

From Internet World Books

With INTERNET WORLD books, the first name in Internet magazine publishing and the first name in Internet book publishing now join together to bring you an exciting new series of easy-to-use handbooks and guides written and edited by the finest Internet writers working today.

Building upon the success of *Internet World* magazine and in close cooperation with its staff of writers, researchers, and Net practitioners, INTERNET WORLD books offer a full panoply of Net-oriented resources—from beginner guides to volumes targeted to business professionals, Internet publishers, corporate network administrators, and web site developers, as well as to professional researchers, librarians, and home Internet users at all levels.

These books are written with care and intelligence, with accuracy and authority, by the foremost experts in their fields. In addition, the bundling of potent connectivity and search software with selected titles in the series will broaden their inherent usefulness and provide immediate access to the vast fluid contents of the Internet itself.

One key element illuminates all of these features—their focus on the needs of the reader. Each book in this series is user-friendly, in the great tradition of IDG Books, and each is intended to bring the reader toward proficiency and authority in using the Internet to its fullest as a complement to all the other ways the reader creates, gathers, processes, and distributes information.

The scope of INTERNET WORLD books is to serve you as Internet user, whether you are a dedicated "nethead" or a novice sitting down to your first session on the Net. Whatever your level, INTERNET WORLD books are designed to fulfill your need. Beyond this, the series will evolve to meet the demands of an increasingly literate and sophisticated Net audience, presenting new and dynamic ways of using the Internet within the context of our business and personal lives.

Alan M. Meckler
Chairman and C.E.O.
Mecklermedia Corporation

Christopher J. Williams
Group Publisher and V.P.
IDG Books Worldwide, Inc.

Credits

IDG Books Worldwide, Inc.

Group Publisher and V.P.
Christopher J. Williams

Publishing Director
John Osborn

Acquisitions Manager
Amorette Pedersen

Editorial Director
Anne Marie Walker

Production Director
Beth A. Roberts

Manuscript Editor
Peggy Watt

Design and Illustration
Benchmark Productions

Composition and Layout
Benchmark Productions

Mecklermedia Corporation

Senior Vice President
Tony Abbott

Managing Editor
Carol Davidson

Copyeditor
Angela Miccinello

Proofreaders
John Harmon
Margaret A. Hogan

About the Author

Joel Maloff is the founder of the Maloff Company, a consulting firm specializing in business and the Internet and based in Dexter, Michigan. Representing his company, Joel travels extensively, conducting speaking tours and hosting series of workshops. He has also written many magazine articles. He is often quoted in the press, including *USA Today* and *Business Week*.

$\mathcal{C}$ontents

Chapter Nine: Data, Data Everywhere, and Not a Byte to Eat! 135

Chapter Ten: Horsepower! Horsepower! Horsepower! 141

Part Three: Issues to Consider When Acquiring Internet Services 145

$\mathcal{P}$reface

The amount of information we create and consume has increased exponentially over the past decade, yet our ability to effectively exchange this information between locations is like trying to force an elephant through a drinking straw—the image and the effectiveness are equally unsatisfactory! Our methods of intercommunication—fax, telephone, personal visit, or data transfer over telephone lines—have not kept pace with our ability to create or consume information. If we are not careful, information can easily consume and control our everyday lives. Consider the thousands of messages hurled at us daily by billboards, television, radio, magazines, and newspapers. Then consider the telephone solicitors, junk mail, or personal contacts that occur. All of these are forms of communication, and we must increasingly learn how to manage them effectively or become immobilized by their volume!

One emerging solution to this dilemma could be the Internet (with a capital "I"). Internet has become one of the most talked about "buzzwords" in corporate communications circles throughout the world, and perhaps one of the most misunderstood communications techniques. The Internet also brings with it a myriad of lessons learned, technical approaches, and benefits to business users. Universities and government laboratories have been immersed in the Internet for years, and only recently—for reasons that will become clear in this book—have businesses begun actively exploring the Internet for purposes other than research or education.

I became Executive Director of CICNet (the Big Ten Universities research and education network) in 1987. As one of the National Science Foundation-funded networks, we were part of the Internet. As you become acquainted with the Internet, you will quickly see that the names of the service providers are pronounced, such as NEARnet, FARnet, or even MIDnet. The Big Ten network actually included other regional universities such as the University of Chicago or the University of Illinois at Chicago. For this reason, we were part of a group called the Committee on Institution Cooperation (CIC), and when CICNet was formed, we had a Board of Directors meeting to determine how our network name was to be pronounced. Our choices were Kick-Net (we did not want to be the Richard Nixon of networks), Sick-net (not a good choice for a high quality service provider), Chick-net (not a favorite among female Board members), or *Chic*-net (Midwestern hogs and corn did not lend themselves to a *chic* image). We chose to be pronounced See-Eye-See Net and received an award as the least creative name for a university network!

While acting as Executive Director at CICNet, I noticed that the information traffic on our eleven-node, T-1 (1.5 megabit per second) network was growing at a compounded rate of nearly thirty percent per month. When I asked the technical staff to help me understand which applications were driving this growth, they indicated "FTP (File Transfer Protocol), Telnet (Remote Log-in), and e-mail (electronic mail)." I explained that these were *tools* to do something—not the applications themselves. Was the growth simply from more and more users, or was it that the existing users were doing more "things"? Was it that people were conducting experiments remotely from their universities with the supercomputer located at the National Center for Supercomputer Applications

(NCSA) in Champaign/Urbana, Illinois, or simply sending recipes for onion dip to their old college roommates? We could see the smoke, but nobody could identify where the fire was burning! The process was as important—if not more so—as the end results to the university network administrators.

I joined CICNet after nearly fifteen years in competitive telecommunications, and one of my major objectives in moving to an academic environment was to understand how the networking techniques used in the Internet could be translated into the corporate environment. At CICNet, I began to define specific categories of usefulness for the Internet. This continued during my work with Advanced Network & Services (ANS) and at ANS CO+RE as Vice President of Client Services. My responsibilities at ANS were to understand the marketplace and design an effective marketing and sales organization. With the founding of The Maloff Company, Inc. in January 1994, I have been able to continue in my quest to help businesses take advantage of the innovations that have arisen as part of the Internet. The opportunities are particularly clear for smaller organizations.

As recently as ten years ago, small businesses' ability to compete in larger marketplaces was limited by available technology: Small firms had neither the in-house expertise nor the money to develop or buy the required technology infrastructure. In the 1990s, hardware prices have come down, and personal computers have become more common and easier to use. Companies of all sizes are using them to enhance business.

The same can be said about data communications, electronic mail, and the use of high-speed, high-volume data networks like the Internet. Originally, such facilities were restricted to those organizations that could afford them, plus the universities, government laboratories, and research facilities for which they were initially designed.

Today, access to worldwide networks is available to anyone with a computer and modem. This offers the potential for businesses of all sizes—from the single-person consulting shop to large industrial complexes—to move into the global marketplace. Dial-up network services best address the needs of businesses that do not require the high-speed dedicated resources needed by an EXXON, General Motors, and various other industrial giants. Smaller businesses can dial into a service provider to send and receive electronic mail, or use tools like Gopher, WAIS (Wide Area Information Servers), Archie, or WorldWide Web (WWW) to find specific information as needed.

In an economy where single-person offices and home-based companies are springing up like mushrooms, the Internet can open up the worldwide marketplace and allow small businesses to compete successfully. By using networking tools effectively, the entrepreneur can improve contact with customers, distributors, and suppliers while increasing cost-effectiveness. The Internet can truly serve as a great equalizer for both large and small organizations.

The purpose of this book is to explain how businesses of all sizes can benefit from both the "Big I" Internet and "Little i" corporate internetworking, identify the business issues involved in deciding whether to deploy such networking, and read actual case studies from organizations that have implemented these networks in a variety of industries. In addition, this book examines how the Internet can benefit organizations of all sizes.

A picture or an example is worth a thousand words. With the Internet, case studies are more useful to the corporate executive trying to find "the competitive edge"—or at least competitive parity—than any discussion about the nuances of e-mail, FTP, SNMP, Netnews, Archie, TCP/IP, or any of several hundred other acronyms. You need to know about these things about as much as you need to know about DTMF, relay stations, Feature Group B, and Signaling System 7 when you make a long-distance phone call! They are important from a "How do we make it work" perspective, but not from a "How do I take advantage of this in my business" standpoint.

In short, if you want to know how to configure your routing algorithms, set up Domain Name Service, or do a trace route, this is the wrong book!

On the other hand, if you want to know how the Internet or internetworking among your remote sites, clients or customers, and suppliers can be accomplished in a cost-effective, secure fashion, this book is written for you. Along the way, we will explain the alphabet soup, help you understand where it fits, and give you enough information to communicate with your own technical staff, consultants, or vendors.

A key principle of this book is this: If it doesn't reduce your expenses, increase your revenues, or in some direct, substantial way positively impact your bottom line, you probably aren't interested. This is the acid test we will use in evaluating the case studies.

The Internet and internetworking are neither magic nor sorcery. They represent an enormous wealth of information, information transport concepts, and resources. By exploring general categories of usage as well as specific examples, we hope you will be able to employ the Internet and internetworking within your own organization—and that your applications will appear in the next edition of this book!

Part One

WHY YOUR BUSINESS

NEEDS TO KNOW ABOUT

THE INTERNET AND

INTERNETWORKING

Chapter One

A BUSINESS PERSPECTIVE OF THE INTERNET

s the Internet a fad or a tidal wave? However you answer this question, it is quite likely that the Internet will have an impact on your business prosperity in the coming Information Age— whether you work with a Fortune 100 company or a home-based startup.

Consider the possibilities. If the Internet and the Information Superhighway are fads and you have invested time, effort, and money in "getting on," you will likely recover. Your costs simply are not that high, assuming that you exercise some

basic precautions. Perhaps most important is knowing what you want to do with these tools before you buy them, and what might be your alternative methods of intercommunication.

On the other hand, if you placed your bet on "fad" and it came up "tidal wave," you may have a difficult time catching up to your competitors who are now net surfing their way to bigger profit margins and expanded customer bases.

Myopia Can Be a Dangerous Business

Business history is filled with famous last words about oddities like the automobile, telephone, fax machine, and personal computer. All were thought to be fads. Why would anyone want to travel faster than forty miles an hour? I remember thinking a 20MB hard drive would last forever.

The computing and telecommunications industries have given rise to two famous examples of underestimating the potential of emerging markets. First, IBM has yet to recover from its mistakes in the minicomputer field, leaving the door wide open for the likes of Digital Equipment Corporation (DEC), Hewlett-Packard Company (HP), and Data General Corporation (DG). Consider how different the computing world might be if IBM had been more assertive in the minicomputer marketplace. Both customers and the marketplace changed, yet IBM didn't. Tom Peters, in *Liberation Management*, blames IBM's missed opportunity on an immense, inertia-laden, top-heavy organizational structure.

The best people in the world will frequently fail unless the dead weight of archaic vertical organizations are removed. IBM's mangement missed the boat on an enormous opportunity. They thought they knew what was best for their customers. In this case, their customers did not agree.

As a second example, AT&T did not think there was much of a market for the resale of private leased line circuits back in the late 1970s. Those decisions permitted the establishment of a new breed of fiber-optic long-distance carriers and long-distance resellers, including MCI, Sprint, and WilTel. The world of telecommunications would be substantially different today had those carriers not survived and prospered, yet one could argue that they were given that opportunity partly by the miscalculation of a competitor. It is important to consider the lessons of history.

Communication Is the Lifeblood of Business

Most businesses face the task of reaching customers and demonstrating the value of their products or services. This is critical to maintaining a positive cash flow and prospering. At the same time, nearly every organization is also charged with conducting its business as cost-effectively as possible. One important area that affects both the administration of excellent customer relations and the control of expenses is the communication of information—the lifeblood of business. How quickly and accurately organizations can access or accumulate knowledge is directly related to their success in the marketplace.

As Peters further points out, power in the marketplace is derived principally from skill at assembling the best interpersonal network of staff and outside help to take advantage of a "window of opportunity." The ability to apply knowledge quickly is, in turn, largely a function of

- the scope of an organization's people "network," including every internal and external resource

- the substantiality of the network, meaning the variety of partners brought to bear on a specific project and the strength of the relationships that can be employed when needed

- the interpersonal network's agility and expertise at quickly responding to changing circumstances

To achieve the maximum market power through networking, the "nervous system" must be open, flexible, efficient, and cost-effective. In many cases, the nervous system is evolving into or incorporating the Internet.

This book has a variety of intentions. Among the major themes are these

- What exactly is the Internet? How does it relate to traditional telecommunications? What about complexity and security issues? How does an organization decide if this is the right step for itself?

- The Internet and internetworking present opportunities for business that must be fully explored as they relate to your corporate plans. Failure to anticipate the potential impact that the Internet might have on your business could be very costly.

- The Internet is a viable business tool that, with proper planning, can provide significant and immediate financial as well as intangible returns to your business.

- The Internet may appear intimidating, yet it can be managed and used just like any other sophisticated business tool. It should not be feared; it should be understood and harnessed.

This book provides answers to these questions, pointers to other sources of information, and a start on your way to understanding the potential value of internetworking.

Few businesses can afford to buy a product or service simply because it is the latest technology (high "gee whiz" factor). It must either increase revenue or reduce expenses, and in either case new technology must contribute to an enhanced bottom line. This requires an analytical approach to the status quo and to the potential trade-off presented by Internet alternatives.

Categories of Business Use

To understand how the Internet might enhance business, this section discusses business functionality afforded by the Internet in terms of three distinct areas:

- **collaborative activities** (inter- and intraorganizational communications)

- **databases** (information sources)

- **rare remote devices.**

Each area offers fertile ground for innovation, cost reduction, and potential new business. Later chapters explore each of these areas in depth, including specific examples and case studies.

Collaborative activities

Communication directly between individuals or between computers serving different companies is a critical part of day-to-day business operations. Think about all of the ways in which you send or receive communication today. The newspaper you read this morning . . . the billboard you saw when driving to work . . . the conversation at your breakfast meeting . . . the memo, telephone call, or letter you received . . . the reports from your distant branches on sales performance or a technical development. All of these are forms of communication.

But are these the most effective ways to receive critical information? Are there better ways?

While "remote collaboration" has been traditionally useful in an academic environment, it also has tremendous value in the corporate world. Engineering drawings, large manual drafts, business plans, or statistical analysis can all be sent or received quickly and accurately using internetworking, even if the file is several gigabytes in size. Internetworking helps to speed the process and lower the costs associated with hand-carrying documents. "Lean and mean" was an overused cliché in the "greedy 1980's" yet it is clear that organizations that operate with a high degree of efficiency are also more likely to succeed. "Lean and clean"—maintaining high ethical and performance standards with a maximum of efficiency—may be the true secret for long-term success.

Lawyers, fire chiefs, architects, and musicians on the Net

Let's take a look at how actual businesses have applied internetworking in a creative manner.

One interesting example comes from the legal community. A law firm headquartered in Toronto coordinates work among offices throughout the world, but especially in the United Kingdom. This firm works collaboratively on cases. A staff person in London starts a project at 9 a.m. (3 a.m. Toronto time), and hands it off to a counterpart in Toronto at 7 p.m. London time (1 p.m. Toronto time). The Canadian group continues to work on the project until 7 p.m. (1 a.m. in London). Essentially, this law firm has found a way to keep an important project going for eighteen hours a day—without any undue stress or loss of productivity from personnel—simply by making the files available on a server and communicating with colleagues via electronic mail (e-mail).

Norman Data Defense Systems in Falls Church, Virginia, uses the Internet heavily to transfer large files and communicate with its offices in Norway and Malaysia.

David Dobbin of the Fulcrum Group in St. John's, Newfoundland describes an even more critical application. In Newfoundland (the entire population is only 600,000), there is a need to generate business outside the province and through affiliates to achieve maximum cost-effectiveness. For this reason, Dobbin uses the Internet to probe for new information sources or to identify and solicit potential partner organizations for his company's business planning and management services.

NaNoshka Johnson, CFO of Nosh Productions in San Francisco, California, has been using the Internet as a way to improve communications with the company's clients in Pacific Rim countries.

By communicating with branch offices, customers or clients, and remote facilities around the world, a company can keep information-intensive projects going around the clock and take maximum advantage of intellectual resources.

What is the value in new business added or current business saved? What is the value in raising your success rate on the projects that you choose to seek? The numbers, of course, are specific to each enterprise but may be substantial.

Finding ways to incorporate these techniques into your business may help reduce costs and could also increase your organization's competitive advantage (read "profits").

Shared data networks

Another emerging opportunity is the use of shared data networks or internet-working. Shared data networks provide a cost-effective way to connect company branches, suppliers, and customers in a private, secure manner rather than through a public shared network. Shared data networks perform like the Internet but do not offer general access. Previously, internetworking was accomplished primarily by using expensive point-to-point (leased) private lines. This meant that only a company's larger facilities could be connected together permanently, and that it was unlikely that customers and suppliers would share in this same network.

Today, more and more organizations are implementing "closed user group" internetworks to help them interact better with their branches, customers, suppliers, and/or colleagues.

For example, the International Association of Fire Chiefs has created an online service for members to discuss how to address issues as serious as people calling an ambulance for non-critical transport when they should be calling a cab. They might learn that another city has addressed this problem by passing an ordinance that imposes fines for abusing the ambulance system.

The software and hardware for the association's system are provided by Connect, Inc., a Cupertino, California company specializing in helping organizations set up virtual private networks for online information and electronic commerce. This network currently is accessed by dial-up long-distance telephone lines and connects more than 800 users, including fire chiefs, officials in related fields, and equipment vendors. By using local Internet service providers, it is possible for the association to reduce its current costs for access to the internetwork and even expand its reach internationally. Connect's Unix server already uses the Internet as a gateway to other e-mail systems, such as MCIMail or CompuServe.

Similar services are also provided to software vendors who use the Internet to communicate with their customers concerning software bugs and upgrades, as well as to companies like Domino's Pizza. Domino's has a closed user group network that sends news and documents from its headquarters in Ann Arbor, Michigan, to receiving clerks, drivers, and production workers in more than twenty-six distribution centers.

Sun Microsystems Inc. uses both private wide-area networking and the Internet as tactical communications links to its value-added resellers (VARs) and its own sales organization. Due to the detailed technical nature of questions posed by prospective buyers of computer workstations, salespeople must respond quickly and accurately to win the orders. According to Lisa Thorell of the market research firm Dataquest, Sun's field sales force exchanged real-time market intelligence, including competitive responses, via the Internet during the height of the workstation price/performance wars. Sun also publishes *Sun-Flash*, an electronic newsmagazine, that is transmitted across the Internet to more than 150,000 customers, business partners, and industry analysts.

Another interesting example of a "community of interest" group is a new six-node Internet link recently established by the U.S. government's intelligence agencies. The program, called Open Source Information System, is defined as unclassified data gathered from public sources. Open Source will link intelligence agencies, commercial data sources (e.g., DIALOG, Mead Data Central's Lexis and Nexis, Legi-Slate, WestLaw), and the National Technical Information Service.

There are other examples of closed user group networks (some using the Internet and some using proprietary network services like AT&T or Advantis):

- The Instrument Society of America (Research Triangle Park, North Carolina) has created an online network to serve its 50,000 members.

- The American Institute of Architects provides access to new information to its membership throughout the country.

- Billboard OnLine (*Billboard* Magazine) offers news and other important information to the entertainment and publishing industries.

- National Purchasing Corporation (Irvine, California) plans to establish a private electronic commerce network for its 6,000-company purchasing cooperative.

- The American Chamber of Commerce Executives (Alexandria, Virginia) offers an online network for members called ChamberNet.

Inter- and intraorganizational communications cover a wide area of activities but offer tremendous potential for increasing communications and effectiveness, both internally and to customers, suppliers, and others. These areas are explored in greater detail in Part Two.

Databases

Databases are electronically accessible information sources. Databases may be proprietary information repositories established by individual organizations, or publicly available resources free of charge over the Internet. Still more are available for a fee providing either abstracts or full documents from a variety of providers, including Dialog Information Service, Mead Data Central, Legi-Slate, Orbit, or BRS. Many organizations have shown substantial savings in personnel and early product introduction by electronically accessing useful information, such as patents or marketplace analysis from these service providers.

For example, Legi-Slate's online version of the U.S. Code of Federal Regulations keeps users current on changing U.S. federal laws and thus helps them avoid costly litigation. How much personnel time do administration departments or law offices spend manually conducting such activities? How many fines could have been avoided by more thorough use of these information sources? At first, these may not seem like communications costs, but the impact is quite real. Information is either originated or received. How effective that information is and how it is employed are critical to successful business operations.

The ability to seek out and find usable information in a timely and efficient fashion is essential to business. Knowing what customers want, where they are located, what they will pay, and who is competing for their business are key components of any business plan. Taking advantage of research that someone else has conducted or software that already exists may help you avoid "reinventing the wheel." Remember, "lean and clean." Take advantage of every opportunity to be the best in your particular areas of endeavor.

The Internet is rapidly becoming the "primordial soup" of information—it is what you do with the information that is important. Using the network to provide online databases and resources concerning your company (e.g., product and services catalogs, frequently asked questions, or technical white papers) can help you maintain more regular and efficient contact with customers and therefore help reduce "account erosion."

You have already invested the time and money to get the customer. How many do you lose due to poor communications? Do you know? Could better communications have helped you retain some portion of those lost? What is the value of the "retained" accounts? Implementing better ways to maintain contact with your sources of revenue is a business imperative.

Rare remote devices

Not every company has or needs supercomputers, particle accelerators, or astronomical observatories. You may not use CAT scans, NMR imaging systems, field sensors, printing presses, high-volume copiers, or optical disc reproduction systems. Perhaps you do need these kinds of resources, but they are too expensive.

By using wide area networking and the Internet, it is now possible to gain access to the benefits derived from some forms of expensive equipment: rare, remote devices. Any computerized device or system that is too costly or needs to be in a remote location yet is still able to transmit or receive important data is a candidate for a business using the Internet as an information conduit.

Improving efficiency and reducing costs

A company specializing in recreational vehicle (RV) rentals has ten rental locations throughout North America. Every day, each of these ten locations used "dumb" terminals to log onto a main computer system in the corporate headquarters through an X.25 dial-up value-added network. Annual costs were more than $200,000 for network access alone, operating at throughput rates of 4,800bps or less. The primary activity taking place on the system was the placing of orders—the number one source of income for the company. Yet, due to the traditional method of communications, if the system went down, the company would lose the data.

This company needed to reconsider how it was managing its mission-critical data. Because of the way its data communications had evolved over the years,

the company was spending a large sum of money for a highly inefficient method of communications. This extended even into the type of computer system used. When the company finally dissected their methods, it was found that the status quo was costly, inefficient, and needed to be modernized.

By implementing an upgraded, PC-based environment and using the Internet for connectivity, the company was able to improve the quality of the data transport dramatically *and* actually cut their costs in half! They "found" $100,000! In addition, many "lost" orders are now being turned into real dollars.

Printing and the Internet

Another interesting example involves the use of the Internet for printing services. Instead of going back and forth between a company's technical or marketing personnel and printing facility, print production processes (i.e., reviewing blue lines, making corrections, etc.) involving complete files can be transferred to the printer using file transfer protocol (ftp). This can dramatically reduce the turnaround time from days or weeks to delivery of finished documents the next day.

Dennis Geraghty, president of Greyden Press of Columbus, Ohio, uses the Internet as a business tool. Send him a file over the Internet and in a very short time, your finished printed materials are delivered to you.

In addition, Geraghty's company offers "one off" printing. Instead of ordering 5,000 copies of a document, dealing with where to store all the copies, and throwing away some portion when they become obsolete or damaged (spoilage), customers send files electronically and a specific printed quantity is delivered to the client's next presentation or trade show.

One-off printing offers substantial savings by avoiding inventory, storage, and spoilage costs. Cost savings may prove even higher if other elements are factored in. For example, consider the value of those storage shelves that are no longer needed. Also, since you can modify the files before they are "reprinted," business documents can be customized and updated to last longer. How much money are you spending on written materials (brochures, white papers, newsletters, training documents)? Would a 20 percent cost reduction be cause to investigate this application further?

A similar example of using the Internet as an information transport mechanism was reported in the September 1993 issue of *CD-ROM World*. One-Off CD Shops is a CD-ROM publishing service, headquartered in Calgary, Alberta, with large regional offices throughout North America. Each regional office supports a number of smaller local outlets. This organizational structure offers the agility needed to deal with technical innovations and permits the acquisition of special expertise, developed and shared across the network.

One-Off Shops is a full-service optical support bureau that distributes CD-ROM desktop systems and offers premastering and replication brokering services. When a job exceeds a particular site's expertise, its staff consults with another office and, occasionally, transfers some of the specialized work to another location. Communication between many of its facilities takes place daily through the Internet.

A Pioneer in Business Uses of the Internet

The final example in our opening look at business uses of the Internet comes from a company that encompasses a variety of functionality: access to information sources, access to customers and markets, and use of rare services.

How many companies choose their office locations based almost entirely on the availability of high-speed, robust connectivity to the Internet? Today, the answer may be a small number. Within the next several years, however, that number will grow substantially.

Midnight Networks, a three-year-old software development and consulting company, found the perfect answer to its needs in the Prospect Hill Office Park, located in Waltham, Massachusetts.

Midnight is a leading developer of software that is incorporated in the router technology of larger "name" vendors, including Cisco Systems Inc., Bay Networks, Inc., and Shiva Corporation. One of Midnight's main product lines is ANVL (Automated Network Validation Library), an automated test system for network products.

In 1992, when first looking to establish Midnight, Peter Schmidt and his colleagues recognized the need for broad Internet connectivity for their new venture to be viable. The best arrangement they could find was a 19.2kbps dial-up connection from regional network provider NEARnet. Given the need for Midnight's eight engineers to be online an average of twelve hours per day, NEARnet's fee was estimated at several hundred dollars a month. Even at those fees, which could be significant for a start-up company, the bandwidth was just not sufficient to meet Midnight's anticipated demands.

About this time Schmidt discovered Prospect Hill. With a 10mbps microwave connection directly into NEARnet and its 45mbps (T-3) connection into the NSFnet, Prospect Hill had the bandwidth that Midnight needed. More astounding was the price. Midnight Networks pays $300 per month for full ethernet access to the Prospect Hill Internet (PI-Net). This is equivalent to charges from many other Internet access providers for a local area network (LAN) dial-up connection!

Use of the Net and how it has paid off

Midnight uses several key Internet functions, including

- immediate access to "free" software that is then incorporated into Midnight's product offerings

- interaction with customer engineering staff

- communication of bug fixes

- sales of services using the Net as a vehicle for live demonstrations

- reduction of long-distance telephone (including fax) expenses.

Through its ability to gain access to freely available software on the network, Midnight spends five to ten minutes to save an estimated one week of development time. During the course of a year, this adds up to many person months of time and is roughly equivalent to another engineer. At today's salary structures, plus benefits, Midnight is spending $3,600 and receiving a return value of $60,000 to $70,000. That savings is from this application alone!

For Midnight, Internet access was "economically trivial" to justify. Nearly all of the people that Midnight works with are already connected to the Internet. This makes it easy to exchange files and software, as well as to have regular and

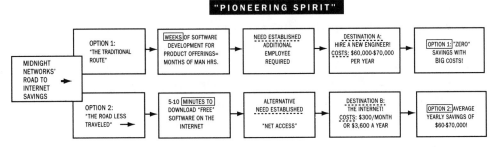

Figure 1-1:
Midnight methodically evaluated and identified the potential for online savings.

immediate feedback. This, in turn, helps cultivate and retain customers. Also, as the Internet becomes more popular and populated, Midnight has now found that their lawyers and less technical board members have gone online. E-mail has become a mainstay in the conduct of daily business, nearly eliminating the need for faxes and courier services.

How the Internet helps close sales

At an Interop conference in 1993, Midnight sold its products by taking prospects into a terminal room and accessing servers in Waltham. These demonstrations resulted in at least $50,000 in new sales at a show where Midnight didn't have a booth! Schmidt further suggests that having a booth at a trade show can, in fact, be inhibiting to potential sales because you cannot "walk around" to potential customers who have booths. When Schmidt needs connectivity at industry trade shows, he uses public terminals.

This approach doesn't work for everyone. When you consider that the cost to exhibit at a show with a reasonably sized booth, plus all of the required accoutrements, falls in the range of $75,000, the trade-off becomes quite interesting. After all, the purpose of most trade show exhibits is either positioning the company or actual show floor sales of products and services.

Midnight seems to have found a way around the standard approach to doing business. The company uses the Internet and its resources as a "sixth man," to borrow a basketball analogy, and as an instant replacement for a trade show booth and staffing.

Finally, for an eight-person office conducting business around the world, Midnight has an astoundingly low average monthly long-distance telephone bill of $150. Without the Internet to displace voice and fax calls, Midnight's costs would easily triple or quadruple.

When you add it all up, Midnight Networks could not live without the Internet. The Net's degree of access has directly resulted in identifiable benefits for Midnight of well over $100,000 per year. For a small company—or even a larger one—such an impact cannot be easily ignored. Midnight continues to discover new and innovative ways to use the Net to add value to its business.

Prospect Hill was a pioneer. Plans are under way for Smartnet to spread to Silicon Valley, and others like Prospect Hill will certainly follow. Landlords and developers take heed! A new market opportunity is at hand.

Conclusion

By understanding the nature of the information you exchange, you can explore the opportunity to reduce expenses or enhance your ability to earn revenues.

Traditional methods for handling large volumes of information have become inefficient. The only way to determine whether any better alternatives exist is to tear apart the status quo, examine it carefully, consider other ways of transporting information, and determine whether these methods work for you. New approaches may provide the competitive edge that businesses perpetually seek.

Chapter Two

INTERNETWORKING

TOOLS

AND RESOURCES

This book is intended as a guide for the business executive or manager who is considering the Internet as a tool. To that end, this chapter defines commonly used Internet concepts and terms, and provides pointers to other resources, should you require more detailed information. It is not designed to be a detailed primer on the various technical aspects of the Internet. Many quality resources can help you explore the nuances of the Internet from a technical viewpoint.

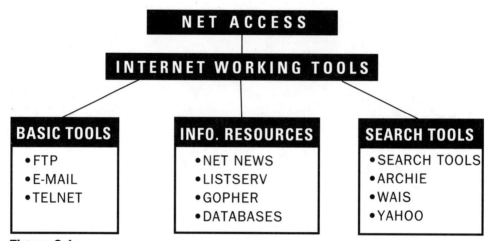

Figure 2-1:
The Internet's most frequently used tools and resources.

What Exactly Is the Internet?

Prior to 1990, the Internet was well known only to a relatively compact group of people worldwide. For those involved with the Internet back then, it was very difficult to explain to friends and family what they did for a living. Today, the Internet has made the cover of *Business Week* and *Time*, appeared on "NBC Nightly News," and is regularly covered by *The Wall Street Journal*, *The New York Times*, *The Los Angeles Times*, *USA Today*, and other mainstream publications worldwide. Yet, unfortunately, few people can tell you what it really means from a functional perspective.

In many ways, the hoopla surrounding the Internet is like a huge publicity campaign for a new movie. We hear about it all the time. It has wonderful stars and big name players, like Vice President Al Gore, former Lotus Development Corporation executive Mitch Kapor, Ray Smith from Bell Atlantic Corporation, and Bill Gates from Microsoft Corporation.

Everyone is telling us how great it is going to be. MCI's advertising features a little girl with a "down under" accent. AT&T tells us that we are going to be able to conduct business barefoot on the beach. Yet, nobody has really explained exactly what "it" is that we will be doing, or how the Internet can help us do "it." We seem to be waiting to find out if the movie we call "Internet" will be another *Ishtar* or another *Star Wars*. (For those who do not remember *Ishtar*, it's the movie that Dustin Hoffman and Warren Beatty would rather forget.)

So, let's see if we can provide a bit of illumination on this Internet-whatever-it-is.

First of all, the Internet is not a "thing." No single organization owns the Internet. Rather, it is a community, comprised of thousands of independent networks worldwide, linked using Transmission Control Protocol/Internet Protocol (TCP/IP). TCP/IP is nothing more than a common language that these networks have agreed to use as a uniform means of interacting electronically. Within TCP/IP is a series of functional tools that will be of use to you. The most important of these are electronic mail (e-mail), file transfer protocol (ftp), and telnet (remote log-in).

E-mail

E-mail comes in a variety of forms and flavors. You can already communicate with others on the Internet if you have an e-mail account with an Internet service provider. For example, if you subscribe to America OnLine (AOL), CompuServe, Prodigy, or GEnie, you already have e-mail capability and can communicate with others on the Internet through an "e-mail gateway." If you subscribe to AT&TMail, MCIMail, SprintMail, or Advantis, you can exchange e-mail with others on the Internet worldwide as well.

If you are not sure whether your e-mail provider is connected, ask! You can be certain this question has been voiced many times.

As described in Part Two, e-mail, although seemingly quite basic, is very valuable and can be used for many different business applications. Among its general functions are the capability to

- send a mail message to one person

- broadcast a single message to many people

- broadcast a message to a predefined group of individuals or companies

- transfer text files, binary files, spreadsheets, audio, or video

- distribute electronic information, such as newsletters, press releases, or announcements

E-mail is the workhorse of internetworking. During a normal day, I read messages of all types, including

- announcements of new conferences

- descriptions of new services to be offered over the Internet

- solicitations from prospective clients for my consulting services

- comments on magazine articles I have written

- comments from an attendee regarding one of my conference speeches

- confirmation of meetings

As you can see, this form of interaction lets me communicate with people worldwide without worrying about time zones or lunch hours.

Because I use a modem and dial into a local Internet access provider (IAP), my fees are $20 to $35 per month, regardless of whether I am communicating with London, Toronto, Detroit, or Dexter, Michigan. The Internet helps me communicate easily wherever I want. Thus, my ability to do business has expanded substantially.

There are many different e-mail and Internet access software programs available. Again, ask your access provider for a demonstration or assistance in getting started.

E-mail providers, like MCIMail, AT&TMail, or even AOL and CompuServe, provide the e-mail interface for you and take care of the gateway into the Internet. If you obtain dial-up Internet access from one of the many Internet access providers (e.g., Alternet, Performance Systems International, or Netcom), they will provide the e-mail interface as part of their service. Your organization will need to consider the e-mail issues when supporting multiple users in a local area network (LAN) environment.

Simply stated, as an individual, you need not worry about e-mail packages. Each one is different, however, and its ease of use may impact your selection of an IAP. Check with your service providers to see what kinds of interfaces they offer before you buy from them. Ask for a demonstration and try it out.

If you are supporting a network of users, it will not be cost-effective for each individual to have his or her separate dial-up account to an outside service provider. You will want to establish a single connection to the service provider so that anyone who needs access to it within your organization can be properly served. This is called a host or LAN connection. The type of connection that you require directly impacts the costs of Internet services and the extent to which others in your organization can reap its benefits.

The following boxed text shows a typical e-mail message. Someone wants to contact me to exchange information. Since this was sent to me at my AOL account, there is information at the bottom indicating what address it came

from and the time and date sent (slr@SEI.CMU.EDU Fri Nov 18 17:54:49 1994),
the Carnegie-Mellon University (computer) that sent the message, and the AOL
machine that received it, plus a few other pieces of data. This information can
be useful as a "time stamp," indicating when the message was sent and when it
was received by the mail host. It does not indicate when you actually logged on
and picked it up—that is your obligation to stay current with e-mail.

Sample e-mail message

```
Subject:  Your new book?
Date:     94-11-18 17:57:20 EST
From:     slr@SEI.CMU.EDU (Sheila Rosenthal)
To:       jmaloff@aol.com
Dear Mr. Maloff,

I am a librarian at the Software Engineering Institute, Carnegie Mellon
University, in Pittsburgh, Pa. One of the members of our Computer
Emergency Response Team (CERT) would like to know when your new book
will be released, so that we may request it for our library. She has a
copy of your paper below, and would like to read your book, once it is
published.


Author    Maloff, Joel
Title     The BUSINESS VALUE of INTERNETWORKING. (how the Internet
          can improve BUSINESS operations)
Source    Internet World v5 p34(5) July-August 1994
Abstract: The Internet provides an intercommunication environment that
can enable corporations to enhance their operations by INTERNETWORKING
with others. BUSINESS possibilities afforded by using the Internet
include lower expenses, larger revenues, and enhanced performance. Using
the Internet involves various costs, including those associated with
access services, telephone charges, hardware, software, network modifi-
cations, employee training, network management, and security. The
Internet can enhance BUSINESS resources by providing access to rare
remote devices, such as printing presses, CAT scans, supercomputers,
high-volume copiers, and other costly devices. Businesses can also take
advantage of the wealth of databases on the Internet. Especially help-
ful is the forum that the Internet provides to collaborate with other
companies.
```

```
Subject    Internet
           Communications Applications
           INTERNETWORKING
           Company BUSINESS Management
           Organizational Communications
```

For your reference, my address information is as follows:

Sheila L. Rosenthal
Software Engineering Institute
4500 Fifth Avenue
Pittsburgh, Pa. 15213
Phone: (412)268-7733
Fax: (412)268-5758
E-Mail: slr@sei.cmu.edu

Please let us know when your book will be available.
Thank you very much.

Sincerely,

Sheila L. Rosenthal, Librarian, Software Engineering Institute

```
——————————— Headers ———————————
From slr@SEI.CMU.EDU Fri Nov 18 17:54:49 1994
Received: from as0a.sei.cmu.edu by mail03.mail.aol.com with ESMTP
(1.37.109.11/16.2) id AA145159289; Fri, 18 Nov 1994 17:54:49 -0500
Return-Path: <slr@SEI.CMU.EDU>
Received: from iu.sei.cmu.edu by as0a.sei.cmu.edu (8.6.9/3.00)
id RAA23939; Fri, 18 Nov 1994 17:52:16 -0500
Received: from localhost.sei.cmu.edu by iu.sei.cmu.edu (8.6.9/3.00)
id RAA05032; Fri, 18 Nov 1994 17:52:15 -0500
Message-Id: <199411182252.RAA05032@iu.sei.cmu.edu>
To: jmaloff@aol.com
Subject: Your new book?
Date: Fri, 18 Nov 94 17:52:14 EST
From: Sheila Rosenthal <slr@SEI.CMU.EDU>
```

E-mail is a particularly useful tool and not difficult to learn. The most important aspect, however, is that it cannot work well if you (or someone authorized by you) fails to check messages on a regular basis. I check my e-mail at least twice a day, even when I am traveling. This permits me to keep on top of activities in my business and respond appropriately.

E-mail's "store-and-forward" nature allows you to compose messages on your laptop while in an airplane and then post them when you reach the ground and connect to the network. You can also download messages (copy messages to your hard drive or a floppy disk from a remote computer system) to read later.

E-mail can prove a powerful tool for increasing your efficiency, enhancing communications, and reducing current costs. Many of the actual tasks that are well served by e-mail are explored in Chapters Four and Six.

File Transfer Protocol (ftp)

Ftp can be a very useful tool, especially as data files become larger and more complex, even with compression techniques. For example, e-mail works quite well for communications of ten to twelve pages or less. E-mail systems do not work very well, however, for transferring large documents or large data files. Quite often when a large document is sent via e-mail, the document is truncated (shortened) and an incomplete version is received.

In addition, sometimes you will want to download or upload large files from or to resources on the Internet. In some cases, if you do not have ftp capability, you can request these large files be sent to you as an e-mail message. This is true for some forms of Internet documentation, known as Requests for Comments (RFCs). In other cases, where this e-mail response capability is not available, you will need service from an access provider that includes ftp.

Despite its name, ftp actually copies a file that you want to upload or download rather than transferring it from or to a distant computer. In this way, you can exchange large documents (book drafts, manuals, annual reports, financial statements) instead of sending them via courier or fax machine. Given that these documents were already created on a computer and saved as a file, why print them out when you don't need to? By sending them in their file format, your personnel can use the information without having to recopy or scan it into another computer program.

Here's how to access ftp:

1. **Log on** to your Internet service provider or connect into the Internet access from your company's LAN. A menu of actions or icons (symbols) for various services should appear.

2. **Select the action/icon** for ftp. If your service provider's interface is not menu driven, ask IAP for ftp instructions. In most cases, however, typing ftp and pressing Return should get you an ftp> response. (In reality today, you should have either a menu-driven or graphical interface to your service provider.)

3. **Enter the site address** (this is shown either as a name—**ftp.maloff.com**—or as a series of numbers—**121.24.5.64.7**) of the file server you want to reach. For example, if you were getting ready to travel and want to know what the weather is like where you were going, ftp to **bears.ucsb.edu**. Log in as **anonymous**, enter **cd pub/windsurf**, and type **get netweather**. You should then receive a message that the transfer was successful.

Unless you have Internet software (TCP/IP) on your PC, Mac, or workstation and a Serial Link Internetworking Protocol (SLIP) or Point to Point Protocol (PPP) account with your service provider, you still have one more step.

4. **Transfer the file.** When you downloaded the weather file, it came to your address at your service provider's machine. It hasn't reached your machine yet. You now need to use a standard communications protocol like Kermit or Z-Modem to transfer the file from your service provider to you.

This may seem complicated, but after a few tries it becomes quite easy. It is important to get help from your service provider because each operates a bit differently. Your service provider should have explicit directions on how to ftp. If IAP isn't forthcoming with the help you need, don't give up. Find another service provider!

More and more, Internet access providers are recognizing the need for easy-to-use services, coupled with superior help desk support.

Telnet

Telnet is the remote log-in function on the Internet. Telnet permits you to access computing resources remotely attached to the Internet, whether on the other side of the room or the other side of the world.

Telnet is easy to use. What you see once you get to the distant host will depend on the skills and intentions of the organization you have reached. Some will be easy whereas others may take more patience on your part and not suit your needs. It won't take you long to find a wealth of resources that you can use regularly.

Telnet can also be used for intracompany purposes. For example, with telnet, you can reach a computing resource in a client (computer workstation) located at one of your company's branch offices and do all the things that you could do if you were sitting there (change the master password files, diagnose problems, manipulate machinery, view medical images, or manipulate files).

Not all telnet-accessible servers are intended for public access. Increasingly many are protected by "firewalls" and other security measures designed to prevent unauthorized intrusions. The examples shown here are publicly accessible, and therefore useful for demonstration.

Telnet can be used to find scientific, language, business, and research data from Europe. The European Commission Host Organization (ECHO) offers this data in eight different languages. To retrieve this data, once at your access provider's menu or at the command line (if it does not have a menu), access or type telnet and type **echo.lu** and log in as **echo**.

To find more information on foreign legal systems, particularly those in Hispanic countries, telnet to **locis.loc.gov**, the U.S. Library of Congress Information Center. This resource has a very nice menu-driven interface that is easy to navigate. You will be able to find the entry on non-U.S. locations and explore its contents.

Other interesting telnet sites

- Cd*now*! (Telnet **cdnow.com**). This site offers more than 100,000 different video and record titles and an All Music Guide database.

- Cetys-BBS (Telnet **infux.mxl.cetys.mx**). This is a Mexican bulletin board system (BBS) with a variety of Spanish discussion groups. Log in as "bbs."

- ISCA BBS (Telnet **bbs.isca.uiowa.edu**). Reportedly the largest BBS on the Internet, this site includes a variety of discussion groups. It attracts users from around the world. Log in as "guest."

- Vienna Stock Exchange (Telnet **fiiv01.tu-graz.ac.at**). For those who can read German, this site offers investors interesting insights.

- The MarketBase Online Catalog of Goods and Services (Telnet **mb.com**). This site provides a forum for buyers and sellers to exchange information on their goods and services. Log in as "mb."

Netnews, Usenet, and Newsgroups

Within the Internet, there is a phenomenon called Netnews (also known as Usenet or newsgroups). Essentially, these are both moderated and unmoderated electronic discussions on virtually every topic you can imagine—and some you probably cannot imagine.

OnLine Access magazine (April 1994) referred to Usenet groups as "the ultimate post-it note." Usenet consists of discussion forums called newsgroups that focus on topics including opinions, philosophies, questions, jokes, recipes, and trivia. Each newsgroup contains messages, also called articles. For example, **alt.entrepreneuers** has some articles on new business opportunities. The newsgroup **comp.ai.fuzzy** has answers to questions about artificial intelligence. Currently, there are more than 10,000 newsgroups, with new ones springing up and others folding regularly.

To read Usenet, Netnews, or newsgroups, your service provider needs to offer you software called a newsreader. This can be done selectively. For example, AOL originally offered only certain newsgroups rather than making access to everything available. This helps AOL address concerns about content as well as regulate traffic flow on its network. Other providers will offer a newsreader with no restrictions, or you can use new software being developed by organizations like Netscape Communications Corporation (formerly Mosaic Communications).

Newsgroups are identified as a series of topics, with subcategories identified and separated by a dot. Thus, in the newsgroup **comp.ai.fuzzy**, "comp" stands for computers, "ai" is the artificial intelligence subcategory, and "fuzzy" is the subsubcategory. Other high-level categories that are of frequent interest include bionet (biology), bit (BITNET mailing lists from universities and colleges), biz (business, marketing, and advertising), clari (live feeds from the United Press International news wire), gnu (Free Software Foundation), ieee (Institute of Electrical and Electronics Engineers), k12 (kindergarten through high school education issues), rec (recreation, hobbies, and the arts), sci (science), soc (social issues), talk (debating or sharing), vmsnet (Digital Equipment Corporation computing issues), and the infamous alt (alternatives) newsgroups.

Samples from the biz Usenet groups include **biz.technical.books** (technical books, advertising), **biz.comp.telebit** (telebit modem support), **biz.oreilly.announce** (O'Reilly Publishing products), and **biz.zeos.**

announce (Zeos products). Anyone can create a newsgroup as a discussion place or as a public user group for his or her own products and services.

The most popular newsgroups today are **news.announce.newusers**, **misc.forsale**, **misc.jobs.offered**, and **alt.sex**. The first three are fairly self-explanatory. The last one you need to either make a point to avoid or see for yourself.

Search Tools

When using the Internet, it quickly becomes apparent that you need to search the information quickly and easily. Otherwise, the vast storehouse of information becomes frustratingly useless.

A variety of tools can assist you, and no doubt many more are under development or available by the time you read this.

Some of these tools include Gopher, archie, wide area information server (WAIS), and a variety used to search World Wide Web (WWW) servers. The following sections describe these tools and their benefits. More information about these tools can be found in many of the references included in the bibliography.

Gopher

Gopher is a menu-driven client/server application for browsing the Internet. It was developed at the University of Minnesota, home of the Golden Gophers. An estimated 10,000 Gopher servers are available, and they are growing at 10 percent to 15 percent each month. Most Gophers include pointers to other Gopher servers, allowing the browser to use multiple systems in a single search. Gopher lets you browse through Internet resources, wandering through the Internet looking for information. Gopher essentially serves the purpose of Internet "librarian," helping to provide some sense of order to the vastness of the Internet.

Gopher only searches those resources that it "knows" about. This means the information must be shared across the Internet via a Gopher "server" or computing machine specifically dedicated to this purpose. A Gopher search may not yield information that is held in a WWW server or on a listserv machine. Today, the Internet remains a multifaceted community of information rather than one seamless repository. For this reason, you must understand the composition of the Internet before you can successfully search for desired resources.

To use Gopher, you need Gopher access from your service provider. Normally, you would select "Gopher" from your service provider's menu of options by clicking on the Gopher icon or, in some cases, simply type "Gopher" at the prompt line. This will permit you to "Gopher" to a general Gopher server at the University of Minnesota, enter the address of a Gopher server that you wish to reach, or page through a series of Gopher menus before zeroing in on the ones you wish to visit. For example, to see Greyden Press's online information, you would Gopher to **gopher.zip.com**.

Understandably, attempting to navigate among 10,000 Gopher servers—which are growing by leaps and bounds every week—is a formidable job. To assist in this task, the Texas Department of Commerce has developed Gopher Jewels, a catalog of Gopher sites organized by category. Gopher Jewels includes a subject tree with more than 1,800 pointers to information on Internet Gopher servers. It also includes two list servers (information sources) to help users stay current with the latest Gopher developments. EINet (a secure Internet service offered by the Microelectronics and Computer Technology Corporation, Austin, Texas) includes Gopher Jewels in its Galaxy WWW service.

To subscribe to the Gopher Jewels list services send e-mail to **listproc@einet.net**. Leave the subject blank and send the following message on the first line: **Subscribe Gopherjewels** (your first name) (your last name).

Gopher is a valuable service on the Internet and is certainly worth a try during your "netsurfing."

Archie

Archie is a system that lets you the search indexes of files that are available on public servers on the Internet. This is a good place to start if you are seeking information on a particular topic. There are several thousand servers available offering millions of different files.

Archie helps you find files; ftp helps you move them to your machine.

As with the other tools described here, you can gain a much more detailed understanding of how they work by consulting other references. In short, though, archie works because once a month, people at McGill University in Montreal run a program that contacts every server it knows via ftp. It then copies a directory listing of all the files contained in that server and stores it in a composite file. Archie then can scan that merged file—using a set of keywords that you have identified—and provide a list of all matches, along with the location of the server where each file is available.

To use archie, you should first ask your service provider if it offers the service directly. More and more providers are doing so, making the task much easier for users. If your service provider does not offer the service, it should be able to suggest a convenient archie server. When all else fails, you can find many archie sites listed in other reference documents.

Wide Area Information Server (WAIS)

WAIS (pronounced "wayz") is a distributed text-searching system, based on the ANSI Z39.50 standard, which describes methods for one computer to ask another computer to conduct searches for it.

With WAIS, you need to identify a specific library from a list provided by the WAIS server and then search it for topics matching the keywords that you provide. For businesses, WAIS tends to be hit and miss because of the volunteer nature of most of the libraries. WAIS servers are for the most part maintained by donated time and effort, and coverage is mixed at best.

A few commercial information services, like the Dow Jones Information Service, use a WAIS interface. There is a fee for use of the service. Once you are a subscriber, the functionality is essentially the same as in general Internet use. WAIS access is normally provided by your Internet access service provider. Check with the various alternative providers before you subscribe to one of their services to see which search tools each offers.

World Wide Web (WWW)

The World Wide Web, or WWW, is an information tool based on the hypertext technology. Hypertext presents information by linking words within a document to other documents, and even to those stored in completely different servers at remote locations. For example, a discussion on the implications of Melville's *Moby Dick* might reference the current *In the Company of Whales*. By clicking on this underlined topic, you are transferred to an electronic version of the book.

To use WWW services, you or your target marketplaces must have a graphical interface capable of connecting effectively to WWW servers. Mosaic and Netscape are the two most prominent today. Several vendors have promised Mosaic-like capability in the next versions of their operating systems. IBM's OS/2 Warp already offers this functionality, and is providing it in Microsoft Windows 95. In addition, most Internet service providers will offer you these capabilities when you use a SLIP or PPP account.

Web servers are becoming increasingly common as a marketing tool. More and more businesses are either establishing their own Web servers or "leasing space" on someone else's electronic storefront. This phenomenon is discussed in later chapters of this book.

For a sample of a WWW server, if you have a Mosaic or Mosaic-like service, you can visit the Maloff Company by opening the Universal Resource Location (URL) to: **http://branch.com/maloff**. This is one way to peruse the most current postings of the Maloff Company, including newsletters, schedules of appearances, and extracts from upcoming books and articles.

Figure 2-2:
The Maloff Company's web page markets its services.

WWW was started as a project at the CERN particle physics research facility in Switzerland in 1989. In 1992, total worldwide WWW usage consisted of 500MB of data—the equivalent of 500,000 pages of text or 1,000 average-sized images. Between January and March 1993, total WWW use was 5GB—ten times that of all of 1992. In February 1994, WWW traffic was 347GB. Today, it is not unusual for 10GB of data to move in a single day.

Another interesting point of comparison is the number of requests rather than the amount of data that is flowing. A snapshot of requests to WWW servers for a full week in 1994 is shown in Table 2-1.

Table 2-1:
Requests to WWW Servers

Week	Requests
January 7	12,019
March 11	50,304
May 13	199,292
July 15	195,160

Another fact helps shed light on the recent growth of the WWW. Between 1989 at the beginning of the WWW project and the end of 1992, traffic was relatively insignificant. In February 1993, however, Marc Andreesen at the National Center for Supercomputer Applications released the first version of Mosaic for X. Shortly thereafter, WWW use began to skyrocket.

Usage of WWW servers throughout the world increased by more than sixteen times from January 1994 to July 1994. A variety of factors are driving this increase.

Given the continuing growth rate of Internet-connected individuals and companies (estimated at 12 percent per month) and the growing number of organizations seeking to market themselves across the Internet, WWW usage will continue to expand. It is difficult to forecast a continuing growth rate of 2.6 times per month (based on the most recent growth experiences). That would put the number of WWW requests at nearly three million per week by mid-1995. While this may be possible, a more conservative estimate is that the rate of growth will slow as the market matures.

In May 1995, CMP Media released an electronic version of its picks of the best one hundred WWW sites in the world. By their estimate, there were over 30,000 WWW sites, of which about one-third were for commercial purposes. Of these, few exhibited creativity or attempted to use the technology to its fullest in creative and innovative ways.

To visit CMP's top one hundred sites, check out **http://techweb.cmp.com/ia/13issue/13hot100.html**. The address may not be easy to use, but the sites you will see are certainly "pushing the envelope." The information presented when you enter this site is provided in Figure 2-3.

Figure 2-3:
TechWeb lists the most popular Web sites.

Special Report:
100 Best Business Web Sites

Of the 30,000-plus sites residing on the World Wide Web, the best estimates are that about 10,000 are commercial. Of these, many are simply electronic billboards with limited content, hypertext links, and ambition. They stake their claim on the cyberspace frontier and offer little else. But then there are others. They seek to take advantage of the Web's unique capabilities in pursuit of their business goals. Easy to access and navigate, some offer unusual or timely content, bristling with hot-links to other resources; others offer eye-catching design and interactivity. A few manage to combine these elements to create a site that illustrates the future of electronic commerce.

How they won

The editors at *Interactive Age* have selected the one hundred best business sites based on these key criteria: richness of content, ease of use, use of hot-links, and quality of design.

Each category had equal weight. *Interactive Age*, its sister publications, and its competitors were not eligible for consideration. Reviews were written by David Joachim and Stuart Gibbel. Congratulations are in order for all one hundred of *Interactive Age*'s winners. But they get this warning as well: Nothing changes so fast in modern American business as online technology. The only way to stay a winner on the Web is to keep evolving and innovating. We look forward to seeing how many of these springtime winners are still on the list the next time around.

Table 2-2:
Top 100 Listing

Business Site	Address
Afro-American Newspapers	http://www.afroam.org/afroam
Ameritech Corp.	http://www.ameritech.com
ANS CO+RE Systems	http://www.ans.net
Apple Computer Inc.	http://www.apple.com
AT&T	http://www.att.com
BankAmerica Corp.	http://www.bankamerica.com
BBN Planet Corp.	http://www.bbnplanet.com
Booklink Technologies	http://www.booklink.com
Cablevision Systems	http://moon.cablevision.com
CBS Inc.	http://www.cbs.com
CommerceNet	http://www.commerce.net
Compaq Computer	http://www.compaq.com
CyberCash Inc.	http://www.cybercash.com
CyberSource Corp.	http://www.software.net
Cyberwalk	http://www.mca.com/index.html

Table 2-2:
Top 100 Listing *Continued*

Business Site	Address
Dell Computer Corp.	http://www.dell.com
Digital Equipment Corp.	http://www.digital.com
Dun & Bradstreet	http://www.dbisna.com
Eastman Kodak Co.	http://www.kodak.com
Electronic Data Systems	http://www.eds.com
Ernst & Young L.P.	http://www.webcom.com/~ey/ cons.htm
Federal Express Corp.	http://www.fedex.com
Fidelity Investments	http://www.fid-inv.com
First Chicago Cap. Mkt.	http://fccm.com
First Virtual Holdings	http://fv.com
Folio Corp.	http://www.folio.com
fX Networks Inc.	http://www.delphi.com/fx/fxtop.html
The Gate	http://sfgate.com
General Electric Co.	http://www.ge.com
Goodyear Tire & Rubber	http://www.goodyear.com
Hewlett-Packard Co.	http://www.hp.com
Hitachi America Ltd.	http://www.hii.hitachi.com/hal2.html
Hollywood Online Inc.	http://www.hollywood.com
HotWired	http://www.hotwired.com
IBM	http://www.ibm.com
InfoSeek Corp.	http://www.infoseek.com
Intel Corp.	http://www.intel.com
Interleaf Inc.	http://www.ileaf.com

Table 2-2:
Top 100 Listing *Continued*

Business Site	Address
internetMCI	http://www.internetmci.com
Internet Shopping Net	http://www.internet.net
Jones Interactive Inc.	http://www.meu.edu
J.P. Morgan & Co. Inc.	http://www.jpmorgan.com
Kaplan Educational Careers	http://www.kaplan.com
Lockheed Martin Corp.	http://www.lockheed.com
Lotus Development Corp.	http://www.lotus.com
Macmillan Pub. USA	http://www.mcp.com
Maloff Co.	http://www.trinet.com/maloff
MasterCard Int'l Inc.	http://www.mastercard.com
MCA/Universal	http://www.mca.com
Mercury Center	http://www.sjmercury.com
MGM/UA	http://www.mgmua.com
Microsoft Corp.	http://www.microsoft.com
Motorola Inc.	http://www.motorola.com
NationsBank Corp.	http://www.nationsbank.comm
Netcom	http://www.netcom.com
NetManage Inc.	http://www.netmanage.com
Netscape Comm. Corp.	http://www.netscape.com
NewsPage	http://www.newspage.com
Northern Telecom Ltd.	http://www.nt.com
Novell Inc.	http://www.novell.com
Oracle Corp.	http://www.oracle.com

Table 2-2:
Top 100 Listing *Continued*

Business Site	Address
Pacific Bell	http://www.pacbell.com
PacifiCorp	http://www.upl.com
Pathfinder	http://pathfinder.com
Performance Sys. Int'l	http://www.psi.net
Personal Library Software	http://www.pls.com
Planet Reebok	http://planetreebok.com
Prodigy Services Co.	http://www.astranet.com
Quarterdeck Off. Sys.	http://www.qdeck.com
RAD Technologies Inc.	http://www.rad.com
RSA Data Security Inc.	http://www.rsa.com
Saturn Corp.	http://www.saturncars.com
SBC Comm. Inc.	http://www.sbc.com
Sci-Fi Channel	http://www.scifi.com
Seagate Technology Inc.	http://www.seagate.com
Shiva Corp.	http://www.shiva.com
Signet Bank	http://www.infi.net/collegemoney
Silicon Graphics Inc.	http://www.sgi.com
SoftQuad Inc.	http://www.sq.com
Sony Online	http://www.sony.com
Southwest Airlines Co.	http://www.iflyswa.com
Spry Inc.	http://www.spry.com
Spyglass Inc.	http://www.spyglass.com
Starwave Corp.	http://www.starwave.com

Table 2-2:
Top 100 Listing *Continued*

Business Site	Address
Sun Microsystems Inc.	http://www.sun.com
Sybase Inc.	http://www.sybase.com
Tele-Comm. Inc.	http://www.tcinc.com
Terisa Systems Inc.	http://www.terisa.com
3Com Corp.	http://www.3com.com
Toronto-Dominion Bank	http://www.tdbank.ca/tdbank
Toshiba America Inc.	http://www.tais.com
US West Inc.	http://www.uswest.com
UUNet Technologies Inc.	http://www.uu.net
Ventana Press	http://www.vmedia.com
Visa International Inc.	http://www.visa.com/visa
VocalTec Inc.	http://www.vocaltec.com
Walt Disney Co.	http://www.disney.com
Wells Fargo & Co.	http://www.wellsfargo.com
WilTel Network Services	http://www.wiltel.com
Windham Hill Records	http://www.windham.com
Xerox Corp.	http://www.xerox.com

Reprinted by permission, *Interactive Age*, Copyright 1995, CMP Publications.

Other Internet Tools

The Internet works exceptionally well for the transport of data—both in real time as well as stored—but it does not handle voice particularly well. Later chapters of this book discuss using the Internet as a supplement or replacement for corporate private leased line networks. I still contend that it works best when used for data transmission rather than primarily for voice.

In April 1995, however, VocalTec introduced Windows-based software called Internet Phone (US$99). Combined with a standard sound card, speakers, and a microphone, Internet Phone allows CB radio-like voice communication between two people connected to the Internet anywhere in the world. The company has developed technology to ensure clear and unbroken communication regardless of the user's location.

For the software to work, you and your destination partner need a minimum of a 14.4Kbps modem, a SLIP connection to the Internet, and an Intel 486 PC operating at 33MHz. Because the communication is in one direction at a time, each person must finish speaking before the other can begin. This can make the normal flow of a conversation a bit difficult.

In a test with people in Connecticut, Florida, Israel, Norway, and Washington state, *Internet World* magazine's staff found the transmissions to be, for the most part, reasonably clear and similar to that of CB radio.

Internet Phone is not likely to be used by businesses to negotiate a strategic deal. On the other hand, spending $99 one time to make unlimited international voice calls to family or friends seems like an interesting bargain. A free demo of the software—allowing a maximum 90-second transmission—is available on the Internet by ftp at **alpha.cso.uiuc.edu/pub/users/vocaltec**. Additional information is available at **info@vocaltec.com** or (201) 768-9400.

Another area where the Internet works well is in helping people with certain disabilities. Several organizations have been working on solutions for the visually impaired by developing products that "read out" Internet information like e-mail and Usenet postings. Berkeley Systems' Macintosh-based outSpoken, for example, employs a text-to-speech converter that automatically describes whatever passes under the on-screen cursor, including fonts, styles, and icons. A speech synthesizer "talks" to blind users, allowing them to "see" what is happening on the screen. The speech quality depends on the synthesizer in use at the time. A copy of the demonstration program can be downloaded at **http://access.berksys.com**. For more information, send e-mail to **access@berksys.com**.

Internet Phone and outSpoken are certainly not the last innovations for use of the Internet. As you read this, entrepreneurs are busily finding new problems to address and new ways to use the technologies available. Some will be useful; others not so.

Conclusion

In summary, the Internet works as well as it does because of a clearly defined set of tools. These tools continue to be supplemented, upgraded, and modified. As the population of the Internet grows, so too will the pace at which new and better tools are made available.

Rely on your provider of Internet access to stay up to date with new features and capabilities. Your provider should offer training and insight into how to use Gopher, WAIS, archie, WWW, and any number of new approaches that are being developed at this moment.

Internet access providers are likely to become plentiful over the next several years. Thus, it is to your advantage as a consumer to demand the best and, when you are not satisfied, look for better alternatives. After all, this is *your* business tool.

The remaining chapters of this book explore specifically how these tools can be useful to you and how to go about acquiring them as quickly and efficiently as possible.

Chapter Three

THE INTERNET AND

THE BOTTOM LINE

FOR BUSINESS

The terms "Information Superhighway," "Information Highway," and "Internet" have been heard repeatedly over the past few years. What exactly do these terms mean to you? How might these new technologies be of benefit to you, your employees, your coworkers, or others in your organization? Do these business tools contribute to the efforts of your organization or are they extraneous and too expensive? Many organizations have begun to grapple with these questions, each arriving at its own set of conclusions derived from its particular perspective.

One set of answers comes from the Society of Information Management (SIM) 1993 membership survey on the perceived benefits of the "Information Highway." The group found that electronic interchange was the most attractive area for potential use among members. Some of the topics covered under electronic interchange were electronic data interchange (EDI), electronic databases, electronic mail (e-mail), and electronic imaging and document exchange.

The second highest scoring category on the SIM survey was business coordination. Subcategories included here were better responsiveness to customers; better coordination with suppliers and regulators; and better coordination among business units, divisions, and sites of the firm.

The third highest rated grouping was business strategy. Topics included new strategic applications/uses in business, new information for decision making, access/exploitation of niche markets, and reduction of business costs.

Other categories included business opportunities (increased market opportunities, creation of "barriers to entry" for potential competitors, increased business profits, and increased business sales) and consumer benefits (providing consumer information, understanding consumer needs and demands, expanding consumer product variety, and providing consumer protection).

In still another survey by SIM, more than half of the 320 corporate information systems managers that responded indicated their companies were already implementing aspects of the Information Highway. The most common applications were EDI and electronic marketing to consumers. This survey also concluded it will take seven to twelve years for the Information Highway to be completely implemented; the potential benefits to business are greater than to education and consumers; information exchange will be the principal use rather than business strategy, opportunities, or coordination; and internetworking is essential for national competitiveness.

In a survey by the American Electronics Association (AEA), 400 high-tech companies expressed their views of the most important reasons to build the Information Highway. Asked to evaluate the importance of the concept to sixteen broad industry segments, education was thought to be the most important, followed by media/publishing and banking/finance. More than half the respondents felt electronic communications would enable them to be more responsive to customers, and more than a third said it would help their employees "telecommute."

As you can see, we are still dealing with the old "blind men and the elephant" syndrome. The Internet and the Information Highway each look a bit different depending on who you are and your particular perspective. Despite the fact that there are so many differing views of *how* the Internet and the Information Highway will be of value, one point is surely not lost. Business people worldwide believe that there *will* be benefits—they just aren't sure yet what they will be. Most importantly, though, a large number of businesses and related professional organizations are busily trying to figure out how this will be of direct benefit to them and their constituents.

Impact on Specific Industries

Through the identification of specific areas of use, we can begin to explore how these new approaches and techniques might be of direct tangible value. Much of this book focuses on finding examples of the areas mentioned in the above studies and demonstrating how the Internet and the Information Superhighway can be used to gain these benefits.

The following sections provide a glimpse of a few specific industries and how internetworking has affected them in an effort to help you start thinking about the impact it could have on your organization.

Health care

Health care is one area where the use of internetworking may hold a great deal of promise. Medical facilities will need considerable bandwidth to send images (X-rays, CAT scans, NMRIs) so that doctors in remote locations can consult with specialists across the country or around the world. In addition, the ability of physicians, nurses, medical researchers, and other medical professionals to exchange vital information throughout the world will enhance as it is increasingly conducted via the Internet. This remote practice of medicine is called "telemedicine."

Many demonstrations involving health-care applications have been conducted recently, especially in the United States. At Syracuse University, for example, pediatric cardiologist Dr. Frank Smith used facilities provided by NYNEX to consult with another doctor fifty miles away as they simultaneously viewed an ultrasound of a child's heart.

Kaiser Permanente in Rockville, Maryland, is working with Bell Atlantic and Oracle Corporation to deliver telemedicine services as well as multimedia to the examining room and even the patient's home. Their efforts are designed to assist in educating consumers about their treatments and illnesses and also in ensuring that the prescribed therapy is followed. In many areas, clusters of hospitals, insurance companies, and regulators are establishing "community health information networks" to exchange insurance claims and medical records.

Prudential Health Care Systems recently indicated plans to use AT&T's Global Information Solutions and InterSpan services to connect its southern service locations and allow them to exchange medical images and patient records, in an effort to improve primary health services and cut costs. The network now covers forty-five cities. This application uses a proprietary network—AT&T's—rather than the public Internet, yet it is still a good example of internetworking.

Prudential's chief information officer, Andrew Garling, said his organization is enlisting telecommunications to make health care more efficient and less expensive, and to cater to a patient who is likely to live in several locations during his or her life. Prudential is attempting to move patient care to the patient, avoiding redundancy, increasing quality, and keeping costs down.

Garling further described Prudential's use of high-speed data technologies to create new healthcare services. "In the future, doctors will be discussing a patient's chart online. It will provide new capabilities for document management," Garling said. Additionally, specialists could be brought into the initial examination to avoid redundant services. For example, if a patient develops a rash, its first manifestation usually provides the clearest symptoms and the best information for treatment. Instead of taking weeks to get an appointment with a specialist, the physician could conduct a joint consultation online more quickly.

These are part of an emerging applications set known as "outcome analysis." These tools could search a patient's medical history to give physicians a guideline for treatment; but to accomplish this, a network infrastructure is needed, as well as electronically accessible databases and access technology.

MCI and United Medical Network Corporation (Minneapolis, Minnesota), a provider of telemedicine services, have joined to offer a purportedly complete suite of voice and data communications capabilities for health-care services.

At a 1994 news conference at George Washington University, doctors and students were instructed in new surgical techniques from other doctors, using diagrams, X-rays, and live video transmitted via MCI services.

United Medical prices the data transmission at 15 cents per minute for each 56 to 64Kbps of bandwidth. The estimated cost for customer premises equipment ranges from $30,000 to $70,000 per system. The network operates on a switched virtual circuit basis, with a hospital on the network able to contact any other hospital on the network by dialing a seven-digit number. This effort seems to be a cost-effective approach to the problem of remote medicine, once past the initial start-up costs. It is quite likely that a dedicated Internet connection may be able to drive the cost per communication down even further. This is due to the flat-rate pricing structure available from most Internet access providers for dedicated connection services.

Gene Theslof, CEO of United Medical, said the company now serves more than 300 customers worldwide. Theslof noted that the company is perfecting surgical gloves that will transmit the sense of touch electronically, as well as endoscopic surgical equipment controlled by a doctor's eye movements.

Cablevision Systems Corporation (Woodbury, New York), using Grumman Data Systems as the systems integrator, has created FISHnet (Fiber optic, Islandwide, Super high-speed Network), an ATM (Asynchronous Transfer Mode)-based high-speed information system connecting physicians and researchers at the Brookhaven National Laboratory, State University of New York (SUNY) at Stony Brook, and Grumman. This may be the first time that a traditional cable TV company has built a test bed for businesses. Cablevision Systems is the fourth largest cable TV operator in the United States. FISHnet will emphasize three applications: transvenous angiography (sharing of cardiology images online between Stony Brook's cardiology department and Brookhaven); a groundwater prediction model, tracking the movement of pollutants in potable groundwater supplies using ATM to link into the Paragon supercomputer at Stony Brook; and a radiology/oncology examination, permitting doctors at Brookhaven and Stony Brook to conduct medical image manipulation and real-time conferencing with Grumman imaging software.

GTE has begun a telemedicine trial in Hawaii, sending medical images in real time between Queens Medical Center in Honolulu and the University of Hawaii. With equipment provided by Newbridge Networks, one of the primary goals of the trial is to establish real-time communication between the islands to improve emergency health care in rural areas and allow a remote user to consult with a primary physician without having to travel around the islands.

Telemedicine offers tremendous potential for reducing costs and increasing the quality of health care. It also could have an impact on health and life insurance costs by enabling more timely and accurate diagnoses. A major concern raised by these new announcements, however, is the creation of "islands of connectivity."

In the Prudential example, only facilities connected to AT&T can interact with one another, and it is unlikely that all physicians are connected to the same "virtual network." This one doesn't talk to non-AT&T networks.

The MCI network is still a proprietary network—not an open one. By creating an "internet," proprietary networks can interconnect with one another. Also, we are not alone in the United States. These networks need to be interconnected throughout North America, and to as many other continents and countries as are financially feasible.

As the number of high-quality service providers offering Internet access grows, the Internet will increasingly offer an alternative open transit highway for telemedicine, and at potentially lower costs than a closed system environment such as those offered by AT&T or MCI.

Later chapters of this book discuss the use of World Wide Web (WWW) servers as a way of communicating information. As a telemedicine example, the New York University Medical Center has established such a system as part of the GASnet (don't laugh, I didn't make this up!) Anesthesiological Server. This tool provides multimedia manuals, videos of procedures, and other information important to anesthesiology.

Relatively few real-life telemedicine consultations have occurred in the United States, compared with widespread use in Canada, Australia, and Norway, because of questions about insurance reimbursement, malpractice liability, and licensing. According to *Computerworld* (September 26, 1994), most private medical insurers, Medicare, and Medicaid require a personal consultation between the patient and doctor for insurance reimbursements, thus offering a financial disincentive for creative alternatives.

Additionally, there is a significant question of where the doctor is licensed. Can a physician in North Dakota provide a valid second opinion on a patient in Louisiana if he or she has not practiced in Louisiana? Furthermore, it is unclear which of the doctors involved in a telemedicine effort has legal liability for the case. "Telemalpractice" may be an issue for the not-too-distant future. Lastly, will the advent of telemedicine require physicians to be licensed in every state in which they "virtually" appear?

Despite these concerns, learning how to incorporate these new technologies into medical practices while still retaining the best parts of today's approaches will be the challenge for medical practitioners over the next decade.

The Internet as a marketplace for retail and services

Direct mail, consumer services, and retail companies are discovering the Internet and the Information Superhighway in a big way. Some are using the Internet and online services like America OnLine and CompuServe; some are hosting their catalogs and other information in computing facilities that are reachable through the Internet; and still another approach is the use of electronic shopping malls. Later chapters of this book discuss how florists, art dealers, and other seemingly nontechnical businesses are using the Internet for profitable electronic commerce.

There are many examples of companies that have begun to explore the Internet for retail sales. Here are a few to whet your appetite.

Denny Chittick, vice president of Information Systems at Insight Direct, Inc., a $200 million computer products mail-order company in Tempe, Arizona, views online links to customers as a huge competitive opportunity. Insight Direct expects the Internet to allow customers to check on everything from prices to availability and invoice history. In short, the Internet gives them a competitive edge not otherwise available. Chittick's organization can now sell its services to the millions of computer systems buyers anywhere the Internet reaches (more than 150 countries at last count).

The Electronic Newsstand demonstrates another approach to retailing and offers free access to all Internet users for reading selected articles and subscribing online to publications like *The New Republic*, *The Economist*, *Communications Week*, *Internet World*, *Sloan Management Review*, *The Washington Quarterly* and many more. You can log in via Gopher at **enews.com** or by telnetting to **enews.com** and logging in as **enews** (no password required).

The Electronic Newsstand is a new way to retail magazine subscriptions. You can scan materials and decide whether you want to become a regular (and sometimes paying) customer.

A variety of other sellers of printed material are beginning to use the Internet as a supplement to their retail activities. SoftPro Books, a small computer bookstore in Boston and Denver, has an online catalog of more than 1,000 titles. You can contact SoftPro by sending e-mail to **softpro@world.std.com**. In Canada, Roswell Computer Bookstore in Halifax, Nova Scotia, offers more than 7,000 books online. Gopher to **nstn.ns.ca** and select items four and eight to review their offerings.

The world of retail sales is beginning to change quite rapidly. You can order pizza online, view the menu of restaurants before you decide where to have dinner, or buy that book you have been looking for—all without leaving the comfort of your home. . . Now, if we could just make the pizza arrive while it's still hot and not stuck to the top of the box, *that* will be an accomplishment!

Financial services

Finance and banking is another area seeing tremendous growth in use of the Internet. Companies already connected include Fannie Mae, Fitch Investors Service, Inc., Kidder, Peabody & Co., Inc., MBIA Corporation, NationWide Finance, Bank of America, Paine Webber Group, Inc., Fidelity Investments, and the Vanguard Group of Investment Companies.

Some of the applications for financial services companies include the "price blasting" of daily mortgage rates to hundreds of branches, exchanging individual account information between branches and headquarters, and using the Internet to track industry changes for the commodities markets.

Venture capitalists also are quite interested in the Internet. Among those connected are General Atlantic Partners, Charles River Associates, Masters Associates, and the Paul Allen Group.

Among the uses found by investment capitalists are the capability to research market information before investing in a particular industry, exchange investment proposal drafts, and maintain close management relationships with investment companies.

For example, BankAmerica Corporation expects the Internet to produce spontaneous EDI on a multilateral basis across industries and regions. This is likely to speed communications between the bank and its customers and afford BankAmerica a competitive advantage over other banking institutions.

Financial Economics Network, a new Internet-accessible resource, is working in cooperation with the FinanceNet portion of Vice President Al Gore's reinvention of government group. This group is attempting to find ways in which technology—including the Internet—can make government more efficient, less costly, and more valuable to its citizens. The ultimate aim of FinanceNet is to connect local, state, and federal financial officials in an electronic network.

Some of the areas covered by FinanceNet include actuarial finance, job postings, auditing, banking and finance in less developed countries, electronic commerce, job resumes, financial engineering, and financial theory.

Financial Economics Network was formed in January 1994. By early February 1994, it had more than 2,900 subscribers, with nearly 250 being added each week. In less than a month, the network had become the largest electronic network in the world, linking people with scholarly and practical interests in business and economics. Its distribution points include the United States, Canada, the United Kingdom, France, Germany, the Netherlands, Italy, Norway, Sweden, Australia, Finland, the former Soviet Union, Estonia, Israel, South Africa, Zambia, New Zealand, Japan, Singapore, Malaysia, and Thailand.

The goal of the Financial Economics Network is to become the best, largest, and most truly global network on the Internet—equivalent to the Financial News Network on television (but interactive and worldwide).

Access to the network is free, but you must request a subscription. For further information contact Wayne Marr at Clemson University, e-mail: **marrm@clemson.clemson.edu**; phone (803) 656-0796; fax: (803) 653-5516; or John Trimble at Washington State University, e-mail: **trimble@vancouver.wsu.edu**; phone: (360) 737-2039.

Fidelity Investments is one of the more aggressive financial companies in the use of the WWW. When Fidelity first appeared on the Internet in February 1995, it was clear that the company had thought this through carefully. Its Web site (**http://www.fid-inv.com**) is designed for information only. Fidelity customers cannot complete transactions such as trades via this site. According to Neal Litvack, Fidelity executive vice president of retail marketing, "secured transaction" technology is not yet mature enough.

In preparing for its foray into the Internet, Fidelity conducted a survey in October 1994. The survey found these facts:

- Two-thirds of Fidelity households in the United States have PCs (compared with the U.S. national average of one-third of households).

- Fifty-five percent of Fidelity households have modems.

- Thirty-five percent of Fidelity households use online services on average eight hours a week.

- Twenty percent of Fidelity households have "surfed" the Net.

Fidelity has 8 million customers. Managing personal finances was one of the top PC applications for Fidelity customers. Fidelity also maintains an investment center on Prodigy and will continue to run the Web site in parallel with Prodigy. Eighty percent of queries received via Prodigy are from non-Fidelity customers. Fidelity's electronic marketing objective is to be ubiquitous. This may include The Microsoft Network and other major online service providers in the future.

Fidelity has clearly done the homework needed to become successful using the Internet as a tool. Its site has been selected by CMP Media as one of the one hundred best sites in the world.

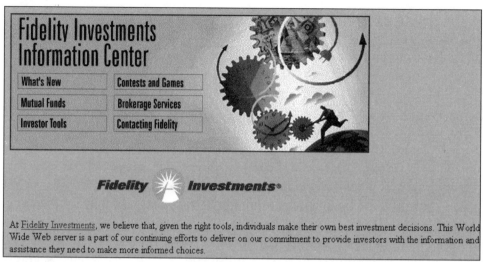

Figure 3-1:
Fidelity Investments offers information on its Web Site.

The Charles Schwab Corporation began offering financial services over the Internet in July 1995. Each shareholder attending Schwab's May 1995 annual meeting received a copy of Fundmap, software designed to help customers shop for mutual funds. The company had earlier established Telebroker, an interactive telephone service that now accounts for more than 55 percent of Schwab's discount services. Clearly, Schwab views technology as an important part of its business strategy.

In an interesting side note to the May 1995 shareholder meeting, Schwab also indicated a desire to expand internationally, particularly in Germany. The Internet may play a large role in the success of these and other expansion efforts.

Other Internet-related services focused specifically on the finance and banking industry are expected to emerge in the near future. The applications are just now being fully explored. It also is quite likely that we will see customized software packages for this and other industries that include Internet "navigation tools." As an example, I believe companies that introduce a combination Internet access service, Internet connection software (including versions of TCP/IP, SLIP, and Netscape, Mosaic-like navigation tools), and point-and-click capabilities offering access to services like FinanceNet, a Fannie Mae Web server, Charles Schwab, or similar resources, will be highly successful. Business people will be increasingly open to using the Internet when it appeals directly to them and when access to desired services becomes easy and essentially intuitive.

Law firms

The legal community has quickly adapted to the Internet. This is probably due to the broad availability of legal information from companies such as West Publishing's WestLaw and Mead Data's Lexis service. It also has much to do with the ease of access and communication with clients and partners. Rather than having legal assistants spend hours searching through canyons of journals or reference documents, they can use keywords to search online databases and arrive at the proper conclusions in minutes rather than hours or days.

Communicating with clients who keep busy schedules has been a long-time problem. Law firms can send drafts of legal responses, contracts, or summaries of meetings across the network in a secure fashion, and clients can read and respond the next time they are able to log in and read their e-mail. Maintaining clear and concise communications with clients or other associates is critical.

Personally, I would much rather have my legal counsel send me an e-mail document rather than have it faxed or sent via postal mail. I can get it wherever I may be traveling, and I can review and respond with comments immediately. This technique has the potential to shorten the business process cycle by at least days and perhaps weeks.

Many law firms are active on the Internet. For example, Pepper & Corazzini, L.L.P., announced on several Internet discussion groups the launch of reportedly the first Internet site devoted to communications law and the emerging field of information law. Their information is reachable by WWW, ftp, or Gopher. The access sites are **http://www.iis.com/p-and-c** and **gopher://gopher.iis.com/11/p-and-c**.

Figure 3-2:
Pepper & Corazzini launched a Web page devoted to information law.

This is an attempt by the firm to present itself as proficient in this particular industry and as a leader in the employment of new technological approaches. For instance, they indicate that their organization has more than thirty years of experience in radio, television, and cable matters, including satellite and radio common carrier issues. They even have a pointer to "Links to Other Legal Resources on the Web." Those include the FCC Gopher, a variety of university law school resources, and FedWorld. For those of you in the legal profession, it would be worth a trip to the P&C server.

By June 1994, Mike Walsh of InterNet Info had uncovered more than fifty legal firms with Internet addresses. His list of law firms online appeared originally in the Information Law Alert Internet discussion group. It is likely that these organizations will add to the growing bounty of information provided by servers on the Internet. Walsh can be reached at **mwalsh@internetinfo.com**. Information Law Alert's address is **markvoor@phantom.com**.

Table 3.1 provides a sampling of law firms currently reachable through the Internet.

Table 3-1:
Law Firms Reachable Through the Internet

Firm	Address
Arnold and Porter (DC)	aporter.com
Baker & McKenzie (SF)	bakermck.com
Hinman & Carmichael (SF)	beveragelaw.com
Bailey, Harring and Peters (Denver)	bhplaw.com
Boulder Law (Boulder)	bldrlaw.com
Brobeck Phleger & Harrison (LA)	brobeck.com
Rajiv. S. K. (DC)	businesslaw.com
Cadwalader Wickersham et al. (NY)	cadwalader.com
Cadwalader Wickersham et al. (NY)	cwt.com
Dow, Lohnes & Albertson (DC)	dla.com
Davis, Polk & Wardwell (NY)	dpw.com
Kelley Judd & Associates (Ft. Laud.)	estatelaw.com
Fried, Frank, Harris, Shriver & Jacobson (NY)	ffhsj.com
Gray Cary Ware & Freidenrich (San Diego)	gcwf.com
Giancarlo & Gnazzo (SF)	gglaw.com
George H. Lowrey (Tulsa)	glowlaw.com
Hale and Dorr (Boston)	haledorr.com
Law Offices of I. W. Halperin (LA)	halperin.com

Table 3-1:
Law Firms Reachable Through the Internet *Continued*

Firm	Address
Heller, Ehrman, White et al. (Palo Alto)	hewm.com
Hogan & Hartson (DC)	hhlaw.com
Holme, Roberts & Owen (Denver)	hro.com
Law Offices of Rajiv. S. K. (DC)	immigration.com
Beckman Hirsch & Ell (Burlington)	iowalaw.com
Jones, Day, Reavis, & Pogue (Cleveland)	jdrp.com
Miller & Folse Attorneys (LA)	juris.com
Justlaw, Inc. (NY)	justlaw.com
Jones - Zurawik (Tulsa)	jzlaw.com
Morrison & Foerster (Denver)	mfdenver.com
Milbank, Tweed, Hadley & McCloy (NY)	milbank.com
Miller & Folse (LA)	miller-folse.com
Morrison and Foerster (SF)	mofo.com
Canter & Siegel (Scottsdale)	pericles.com
Robinson & Cole (Hartford)	rc.com
Rosen, Dainow & Jacobs (NY)	rdjlaw.com
Schnader Harrison Segal & Lewis (Philadelphia)	shsl.com
Squire, Sanders & Dempsey (Cleveland)	ssd.com
Marger Johnson McCollom (Portland)	techlaw.com
Robert J. Keller, P.C. (DC)	telcomlaw.com
Venable, Baetjer, Howard (DC)	venable.com
Venture Law Group (Menlo Park)	venlaw.com
West Services, Inc. (St. Paul)	westlaw.com
Dennis White & Associates (Naples)	whitelaw.com
Wilmer, Cutler, and Pickering (DC)	wilmer.com
Winston & Strawn (Chicago)	winston.com
Wiley, Rein & Fielding (DC)	wrf.com

West Publishing, well known for its WestLaw services, is now advertising West's Legal Directory—the self-described legal directory for the Information Age. This complimentary directory of lawyers allows you to find a lawyer or law firm that meets your specific needs. It currently includes more than 700,000 listings of both U.S. and Canadian lawyers and their firms. To access West's Legal Directory, either Gopher to **wld.westlaw.com** or telnet to **163.231.231.3**.

Conclusion

It is virtually impossible to think of an industry—large or small—where the sharing and exchange of information is not crucial. From the smallest deli to the largest corporation, the Internet affords the possibility of reduced expenses or expanded market reach.

The Internet is not just for the big, multibillion-dollar corporations. Country Fare Restaurant certainly isn't in the Fortune 1000. You need not spend thousands of dollars to make the Internet work for you. Part Two explores a variety of ways that the Internet and the use of internetworking can bring immediate benefits to you and your organization.

Part Two

What Internetworking
Can Do for Your
Organization

*C*hapter *Four*

T H E

H U M A N

E Q U A T I O N

People use networking to collaborate, sell, plan, research, and share knowledge while remote from one another. Networking—in all its forms—is with us every day. This includes interpersonal networking, such as sharing business leads, or making new acquaintances at the local Chamber of Commerce. It includes sharing thoughts or ideas with coworkers or other colleagues. And we haven't even mentioned wire networks yet!

The Internet, local area networks, wide area networks, and computers are nothing more than the vehicles that we use to accomplish our interpersonal networking in a more efficient manner. In fact, computer networking is likely to change the way in which we live, just as the telephone, automobile, and Interstate highway have.

Think about how your day would be without the telephone, automobile, and Interstate highway systems. These are "invisible tools"—invisible because we never think about them. We just take them for granted.

In the last century, people would craft carefully written, well-structured letters, covering everything from affairs of the heart to business propositions. (Some might argue that, at times, there is little difference between the two!) Time was spent organizing thoughts and then committing them to paper. We still have examples today of letters from the great and not-so-great: diaries, anecdotes, propositions, and capitulations. Much of what we know about how people formulated their thoughts or the rationale behind their actions comes from these personal communications.

During the latter part of the twentieth century, however, many people have become too busy and too pressed for time to sit and draft letters. Even if the postal service could deliver a letter in a day or two or three, it still doesn't have the immediacy or the intimacy of a telephone call. In a way, we have lost the art of writing articulate expressions of feelings and viewpoints because of our obsession with the here and now.

Electronic messaging has the potential to bring us full circle while still accommodating our need for immediacy. In fact, by participating in the electronic cyberspace world, we can be heard by dozens, hundreds, or even thousands of our peers simply by creating a written message and pressing a "send" command.

We can correspond with electronic pen pals, develop business relationships, or conduct long-distance love affairs—just like the letters of the nineteenth century. Today, however, the messages can arrive in milliseconds instead of weeks.

There was a time when most people lived in cities, not because they liked congestion, noise, apartments, and crime, but because they needed the benefits of walking to work or taking public transit to a business meeting or the park for a weekend picnic. Even with a horse or wagon, you certainly did not want to live more than a few miles from your place of business.

With the advent of motorized transportation, people began to spread out. Suddenly, farmers were not the only ones living in the country. Those city slickers could now work in the city but come home to a quiet new bedroom community. New forms of transportation gave rise to suburbs.

Then came the Interstate highway system. Originally intended to move troops and missiles, our opportunistic natures saw a new way to travel. Now we could avoid traffic lights, small town speed traps, and endless delays by whizzing by at the maximum allowable speed.

A century ago, the thought of living sixty miles from your work and commuting every day would have been laughable. Today, an hour commute is considered acceptable by many.

Conclusion

History has shown that technology has changed the way we interact socially and professionally. Today's electronic networking is already beginning to reveal its impact on us. For example, the term "telecommuting" was coined a few years ago. We now see people regularly "logging in" to some sort of computer network system from home as well as in their offices, or even on a train or plane. Electronic information services, such as America OnLine, CompuServe, Delphi, GEnie, and Prodigy, purport to have more than 5 million subscribers combined—and most of these are people using the services from their homes or small businesses. Combined with the more than 30 million now estimated to be accessible through the Internet, that community demonstrates the potential for significant business and social impact. The numbers of new users are growing at a rate of 15 percent to 18 percent *per month* and are expected to maintain that pace for at least the next two years. At that rate, there will be more than 100 million users on the Internet worldwide during 1996. If the pace of growth escalates—which is quite possible—we could see several times that number of users.

So how are people intercommunicating using these networks? How are organizations exchanging vital information? The chapters in this section examine some of the many ways that internetworking and the Internet are helping to facilitate the flow of useful information. As a suite of tools, Internet has the ability to make us a more literate society, more productive in our businesses, and more able to interact globally—whether for business or personal reasons—than ever before. Read on to find out how!

*C*hapter Five

THE INTERNET AS A SALES AND MARKETING TOOL

The Internet has tremendous potential as a tool for both marketing and sales. Yet, as with any tool, it must be properly understood and used in order to be effective. This chapter examines ways in which the Internet can be successfully used as a sales and marketing tool.

Because I have served in a variety of marketing and sales roles, including vice president of Advanced Network & Services (ANS), this is an area near to me, and one that I find often fraught with misunderstandings. Perhaps it would be helpful to start this discussion with a few basic definitions: What is the Internet as it applies to sales and marketing, and how are we distinguishing sales from marketing? The answers to these questions will make it easier to determine how the Internet can benefit your organization.

Let's start with the Internet. First, despite what you may have heard, the Internet is not a marketplace of thirty-five million or more users worldwide. Rather, it is hundreds or perhaps thousands of micromarkets! This is an important distinction. To be an effective "marketeer," you must understand your targets, be able to quantify the size of your opportunities, and zero in on them so that you can maximize your success with a minimum of required investment.

Within an Internet environment, you will find a fertile field for some sales opportunities, whereas others may not have yet reached a proper level of maturity. Some may never be quite suitable for electronic commerce. The only way to properly determine the appropriateness to your products or services is the old-fashioned way: analysis, design, testing, and if warranted, deployment.

Clearly, you do not want to distribute your information intrusively to thousands of newsgroups and millions of unqualified users. Other books and authors may sing the praises of such an approach, but I am not a believer in creating inordinate amounts of bad publicity and hard feelings. Rather, I believe a systematic approach will save you a great deal of time and effort and ultimately, deliver the best results.

What is marketing? *Webster's New World Dictionary* defines marketing as: "All business activity involved in moving goods and services from producers to consumers, including selling, advertising, packaging, etc." In fact, sales is considered a part of marketing.

As we can see, however, marketing encompasses a much broader scope. It includes collecting information about potential target markets, reviewing information about products or services, and establishing proper pricing methods. It also includes gathering intelligence on competitors and creating strategies to succeed in the overall marketplace. You might quickly see roles in which the Internet might play a part in your marketing efforts.

Webster's defines selling as the act of gaining agreement for the exchange of property or services for an agreed-upon sum of money or other considerations. To accomplish this task, you must be able to show your products to potential buyers and give them the opportunity to agree to the purchase. The Internet is also increasingly helping business do just that.

To successfully market in an Internet environment, it is important to remember that the Internet is a community—not a service—and that the many citizens of cyberspace are not always connected in a common fashion. This means that they each have varying levels of functionality and capability.

For example, some are connected to services that offer e-mail only. In these cases, Gopher and Web services may not be of much use, especially if these are your target customers; listservs may be more appropriate.

Other people are connected through "shell accounts" or "terminal emulation" accounts using dial-up modems. In this case, graphics may not be effective because of the type of account and speed of the modem.

Last, businesses, universities, and other large organizations may have dedicated or leased-line connection services, offering substantial speeds for communication ("bandwidth"). These corporate services may not be available for use on a personal level, however, further impacting your efforts. The key is to know your target markets and to identify how well each Internet tool will work with that population.

Marketing in an Internet Environment

The Internet can help an organization's marketing efforts in a variety of ways. One of the most critical is setting expectations of potential sales. This can be properly accomplished by answering the following questions: Who are you targeting? How large is the likely market? Where is the target market (domestic, North America, Europe, global, etc.)? How technically sophisticated is the market? What response rate does your marketing generate today?

You will need to answer many of these questions yourself before you even begin to consider the vehicles to implement your plan. Who knows better than you to whom your products or services might appeal? Once you have an approximation of your targets, it is appropriate to determine whether the Internet may be able to play a positive role.

For example, if you plan to introduce new software, you might consider making it available—in a test fashion—over the Internet. In this way, the most sophisticated users in the world will put your product through its paces and give you their candid (at times, even brutal) feedback. The result will be a tested product ready for the general marketplace. The best resources for this approach include appropriate listservs, newsgroups, and mail reflectors. A mail reflector uses a company's e-mail system to set up a common interest group. For example, **sales@xyz.com** might "reflect" to the e-mail addresses of twenty salespeople. Through these resources, you can tell people about your product, with directions on where to find more details if they are interested. As long as the topic is appropriate to the group and is relatively unobtrusive, you will likely receive many beneficial replies.

This approach will also provide a sample of the magnitude of interest for your product or service. Although you may be convinced this is a product that we cannot do without, the real measure of success is what the consuming public thinks. The Internet can give you the opportunity to fine-tune your approach, packaging, and deliverables before you spend enormous sums of money on an ill-conceived roll-out strategy.

Remember, too, that the Internet is truly international, and for no additional cost you will receive feedback from people worldwide. This kind of feedback is invaluable in the market planning process.

There are many examples of how the Internet can be used successfully as an immediate "sounding board" for your concepts and product plans. One of the most interesting is the Internet's impact on current entertainment and programming. For instance, the Fox Broadcasting series "X-Files" has gained a cult-like following on the Internet, including many discussion groups and newsgroups. In fact, the writers and producers follow these discussions carefully and build public thinking into new plot themes. Also, the script for the recent movie *Star Trek: Generations* was circulated on the Internet; the feedback resulted in some last-minute rethinking prior to shooting the film.

Consider the potential power of this tool—the Internet—for your marketing efforts. Compared to traditional advertising and focus groups, the investment is minimal. This does not preclude these other methods at all—and, as you will see later in this chapter, a comprehensive plan that uses all appropriate resources is strongly encouraged. The Internet alone is not the answer to any organization's business challenges. In conjunction with other tools, however, it may be exceptionally effective.

Gathering marketing information

One of the most important uses of the Internet is gathering information. At minimum, organizations require information on targeting customers or clients, competitors, and environmental constraints.

By using some of the search tools on the Internet (e.g., Gopher, WAIS, or the various Web search engines), you can identify similar products or services or even keep track of your competition's activities.

The Internet also offers the opportunity to identify potential intellectual resources. By participating in various discussion groups or through focused searches, you will be able to identify individuals or organizations that can be of direct benefit to you. In many cases, this can result in days or weeks of saved personnel efforts. Quite frequently, there are postings asking if others have a certain set of information.

For example, someone was trying to find a listing for all of the alternative access providers in the United States. These are organizations that construct fiber-optic or other physical telecommunications facilities in major metropolitan areas and compete with local telephone companies. I happened to have such a list and provided it free of charge across the network. Several others saw my response to the original requestor and asked to be included as well. For me, it was good publicity; for the recipients, it was days of work saved.

A good rule of thumb is to ask in an appropriate forum. Do not be timid. If the group feels it is inappropriate, it will say so. For the most part, however, there is little harm in posting the question.

Analyzing and evaluating marketing information

Once you have gathered information—whether you used the Net to do so—you need to analyze and evaluate the information. One of the best ways to do this with remote branches, partners, or consultants and other colleagues is through the Internet.

The Internet provides a channel for you to exchange concepts and ideas quickly and easily across great distances and time zones, thus taking advantage of talent that is physically remote yet intellectually attuned to your project. E-mail, access to shared servers, or use of groupware products such as Lotus Notes all can be facilitated using Internet as a communications method.

Selling in an Internet Environment

Sales is the act of presenting a product or service for others to purchase. This section examines some critical issues of selling in an Internet environment.

It is important to keep in mind that the Internet is an extension of your existing marketing and sales plans. It is not a stand-alone technique that will work without influence and support from a broader business plan.

Because of the nature of the Internet community, the Internet offers a means to expand market presence in a user-initiated fashion. This is important. As long as you do not flood the various discussion groups with unsolicited advertising, you will be well within the acceptable norms of conduct. In fact, by asking people to visit your Web site or ftp server or to send you e-mail for more information, you have assisted in the creation of a self-defining marketplace. Those that respond to your postings *want* to hear about what you are doing and what you have to offer. Take advantage of that interest by providing high-quality responses to their inquiries. How you do this depends on your unique requirements.

Is selling permissible on the Internet?

The short answer is yes, and it always has been. There has simply been a code of conduct that has constrained those efforts and kept them in a passive mode. Nevertheless, people have been "selling" their products or services across the Internet for more than twenty years.

The long answer is a bit more complicated. Selling over the Internet is appropriate as part of a well-constructed plan that considers the composition of your target markets, the positioning of your products or services, and their capability to be of value to each other.

What business could expect much success if it simply decided on the spur of the moment to sell swimsuits in Antarctica? Business planning is important and takes time. The Internet is no different. You need to understand why you want to use the Internet, experiment with it, and then test your plans. In this way, you will quickly learn whether you are on the right path, and you will be able to make the needed course corrections.

What can successfully be sold using the Internet?

For starters, anything that is easily digitized can be sold via the Internet. This includes software, books, magazines, and music.

All of these are likely created today on a PC, Mac, or other computing device. As such, they can be transported digitally across the Internet. Ensuring that your intellectual property is safeguarded and that you get paid are separate issues.

Anything that can be delivered better due to interactivity or shortened time cycles is also a candidate for sale across the Internet. This includes, but is certainly not limited to, printing services, products, legal services, and financial services. In fact, see if you can find one that doesn't fit! By sending the product electronically or by taking an order for it over the Net, you can shorten delivery cycles and speed payment.

Methods of selling using the Internet

Two methods can be used to sell across the Internet: passive and active. Passive methods are designed to have potential users identify themselves as interested parties. Active methods seek to attract potential buyers in a more overt fashion.

Passive methods

As mentioned earlier, an excellent way to promote yourself across the Internet is through participation in discussions. You can observe what others are saying on a particular topic and, when appropriate, enter the fray. Simply expressing an opinion or intimating that you have more information on a topic will likely lead to responses—both privately (direct to your e-mail address) or publicly (on the forum). In either case, you have begun to establish an image for both yourself and your organization. It is wise to consider that image and ensure that it is the one you want to propagate!

Another passive method is the posting of your news releases and other press announcements to appropriate news or discussion groups. If nothing else, the Internet is a source of constant information flow, and this is normally a quite acceptable practice.

Listservs and mail reflectors can become "self-defining infomercials." By announcing on a newsgroup that you have created a listserv for your company or area of interest, anyone who subscribes has indicated at least a tentative interest in your topics. They can always choose to unsubscribe, but at least in the beginning a level of compatibility appears to exist.

Listserv is a specific program that runs on IBM mainframes with VM/CMS/MVS software. This means you must have one of these systems if you plan to run the program yourself. If you are new to the field, that may not be a great idea. In addition, listserv is e-mail-based. It uses e-mail as its method of communicating with those "subscribed" to the service. For more information on many of the listserv systems currently available, see *Internet: Mailing Lists* by Edwin Hardie and Vivian Neou, PTR Prentice Hall.

A similar program, called listproc, runs under Unix rather than on IBM mainframes. Listproc is a bit easier to administrate, especially if you or your staff are familiar with a Unix environment. Nevertheless, there are many reasons you may not wish to run this yourself.

Mail reflectors can be set up under any e-mail environment. They are simply an alias for a group of names. For example, **market@abc.com** could include the names of all thirty people in the ABC Company marketing department. When someone sends a message to **market@abc.com**, all of those registered receive the message in their electronic mailbox. They can reply to the entire reflector or only to the originator.

Mail reflectors can be a very effective tool for reducing the number of times you must send a common message.

Potential uses for passive marketing over the Internet include product catalogs, description of services, solution sets, automated user groups, and FAQs (frequently asked questions).

You can implement listservs and mail reflectors in a variety of ways. If you are certain that a listserv meets your requirements, you might consider contracting with a university or corporation running a listserv to provide the service for you. This reduces your management requirements and may shrink the amount of Internet access and bandwidth that you require.

Remember, when you provide information via an Internet server, that server must be reachable twenty-four hours a day, seven days a week. Having an unreachable server is a sure way to create an undesirable image. An outside organization, such as a university, that hosts your listserv, must have dedicated connectivity, but you can connect through a dial-up service whenever required. This helps in a variety of areas, including personnel, hardware, Internet access, and security.

Another alternative is to set up listproc on a Unix machine. This would still require management, dedicated bandwidth, and hardware on your part. Explore all of the implications carefully before you take on this task yourself. Several years ago, there were few alternatives. Now, many organizations can host this service—probably at a substantial cost benefit to you.

Perhaps the easiest method is to establish an appropriate mail reflector. Any e-mail postmaster should be able to help you set up the process and assist with maintenance. Mail reflectors tend to be more private and, from a sales perspective, more under your control. You can establish criteria for participation as well as any usage policies. A customer user group or comment "line" are uses that could be quite beneficial.

The last alternative is to outsource to an electronic marketplace. This is described in more detail in the Active Methods section in this chapter.

In summary, passive methods are those by which you make the information available, tell consumers where to reach the information, yet force them to exert some degree of effort to retrieve it. These vehicles are great for image enhancement but do little for direct sales.

Active methods

Active methods of sales are those by which your organization aggressively seeks new customers or participants in your services. Electronic marketplaces are an excellent example of an active approach.

You can implement an electronic marketplace in many ways. By establishing an anonymous ftp server, you can make available a variety of information to anyone who wants to retrieve it. These include text documents (e.g., white papers) and program announcements (workshops, training sessions). Through the use of a Gopher server, you can offer various text-based documents; via a World Wide Web server, your organization can make available sound, video, and graphic images. All of these tools can provide an appropriate environment for sales activities.

Electronic newsletters are another active method of marketing that requires nothing more than e-mail capability. By sending out notification electronically that you have a newsletter available, potential customers can access your newsletter through any of the various available server techniques. In this way, they come to you for information and have responded to your invitation.

Implementation alternatives

You can implement these sales tools in a variety of ways. The first is to do it yourself. If you do not already have a mainframe, minicomputer, or local area network (LAN) environment, you need to know a few things. A server is essential. It can be a mainframe computer or a Unix workstation. It can even be a 486 machine or an Apple Macintosh. In any case, it must be a computing machine with sufficient memory and functionality to meet the needs of your application.

To house a server, you must be connected all of the time. This requires dedicated Internet bandwidth. The lowest denomination is 56Kbps (64Kbps in Europe and elsewhere). The next step up is called T-1 or DS-1, which carries 1.5Mbps in the United States (in Europe, the same service is called E-1 and carries 2.04Mbps).

Staffing is another important consideration when planning server services. Servers must be maintained, information must be changed regularly, and reports must be issued. Personnel resources are required to address these issues.

Once a facility is permanently "up" on the Internet, it becomes crucial to identify and address areas of vulnerability and security risk. Securing your network will certainly cause you to incur additional expenses that must be factored into your "make versus buy" decision. Security is discussed in Chapter Eleven.

Another alternative is to subscribe to one of the many emerging cybermalls or electronic marketplaces and acquire an "electronic storefront." These services range in price from $30 to thousands of dollars per month. Each offers different functionality and capabilities. Both pricing and performance will certainly improve as the market matures. Today, quality varies widely. Examples of cybermalls include The Internet Company, The Internet ShopKeeper, CyberSpace Development, and The Branch Mall. Cybermalls are discussed in Chapter Eight.

Benefits and disadvantages of each approach

Each of these methods has benefits and disadvantages. Doing it yourself offers greater control, instant access to statistics, in-house production, and perceived cost reduction. Because it comes from a personnel budget or capital expenditures, the costs may be spread across the budget and not as visible as if they were a single procurement. The do-it-yourself approach also requires greater bandwidth, more personnel attention, and an awareness of potentially expensive security measures.

Cybermalls or electronic marketplaces offer instant (or nearly instant) productivity, leverage from other storefronts, reduced requirements for bandwidth, and someone else to maintain the systems for you. They also require regular payments to someone else and loss of some degree of control, and they put you at the mercy of the proficiency of your "landlord."

Security and financial transactions

Once you have successfully created an image and begun to market on the Internet, you will quickly realize that a good means of conducting financial transactions is required. Unfortunately, we are only beginning to see proper effort devoted to addressing this problem. A variety of techniques are emerging, and it is possible to conduct business today over the network using a combination of these approaches. Better solutions are under development. It is important, though, to understand what works and the limitations of each existing method.

Understanding security implications

Within the Internet, you have essentially two ways to connect to the outside world: dial-up accounts using a modem to reach an Internet access provider (IAP) or dedicated access services that connect your facility to an IAP's facilities.

From a security exposure perspective, you have little to worry about if you dial in, check your mail, and wander about on the Net now and then. If you are connected for hours at a time or if your organization has dedicated access, it is possible for unwanted adventurers to enter your computing systems. This can be especially dangerous if they can reach your critical intellectual property— research, business plans, financial documentation, accounts receivables, personnel records, and the like.

Chapter Eleven reviews security issues on a broad scale and discusses how they impact your ability to cost-justify Internet access. This section focuses on the need to address security up front and the importance of having an acceptably secure manner in which to conduct financial transactions across the Internet.

Security planning implications

Before we discuss security and its impact on sales and marketing in more detail, these questions need to be addressed:

1. Do you have a LAN environment today, an existing dedicated Internet connection, or the need for either one?

2. Do you have existing modem services that permit employees or others to dial into your organization's computing facilities?

3. Does your organization have any level of security or usage policies concerning external network use, such as how often pass codes on modem access must be changed, whether they include both alpha and numeric characters (and possibly non-alpha or non-numeric characters), who can use these services, and when they are permitted to use them?

4. Is this policy written and distributed to all personnel who may be using these services?

5. Are you comfortable that the policy is adequate today? Do you know who is responsible for maintaining the policies? Who is responsible for enforcing the policies?

If you are typical of the respondents to informal surveys that I have done at conferences over the past year, two or three people out of an audience of three hundred will answer affirmatively to all questions. There is a tremendous need to better understand and plan your approach to ensuring corporate information and network security.

The Internet can be made acceptably secure. The trick is to understand precisely what that means to you and your organization. Only solid planning can provide that answer.

Security planning and tools to implement the plans are discussed in Chapter Eleven.

Methods of handling financial transactions

This section reviews some of the approaches available today to handle purchases on the Internet. More are under development. It is important for you—both as a consumer and as a seller—to understand the implications of each.

Consider each option carefully. Understand how it may impact your ability to successfully sell across the Net, and select the tools that best suit your needs. Remember, you do not need to pick just one. How many shops carry VISA, MasterCard, American Express, Discovery, and also take cash or checks?

Using "in the clear" credit card numbers is the easiest method today, but it has some obvious problems. By providing your credit card in writing on a form or in an e-mail message, you run the risk of a "pirate" capturing that information and using your credit card anywhere in the world.

To put this in perspective, using a credit card number over the telephone or in a restaurant also has its risks. Neither are especially secure, and fraud occurs on a daily basis. Most credit card companies are prepared to minimize your exposure when fraud can be demonstrated. Normally, this involves products shipped to an unusual address. This may be a lot more difficult in an Internet environment, but it's not impossible. I seriously doubt, however, that the credit card companies are set up to do "trace routes" across the Internet, although they may be in the future.

In short, some companies use this approach today, and some consumers are willing to take the risk. I do not know of any examples of a credit card number being stolen because of Internet use, but it will certainly happen. The question for buyers and sellers is how much risk and exposure is there? Your answer to this question will be important to your use of this technique across the Internet.

Call-back confirmation is another approach used today. This involves combining Internet product or service ordering with a telephone call for the exchange of confidential information such as a credit card number. You place an e-mail, Web server, or other similar order for a product or service with an Internet provider and include your telephone number. The vendor calls you to confirm the order and takes your credit card number over the telephone. The vendor can then assign to you, for future use, a discrete account number not related to your credit card number. You need only set up the account with one call, and then you can do follow-up business with minimal inconvenience. If the discrete account number is stolen, it cannot be used anywhere but on this service.

Encrypted credit cards are also beginning to emerge. If your vendor accepts Pretty Good Privacy (PGP), you can obtain this software free on the Internet and use it to ensure some degree of confidentiality across the Net. This is not a particularly elegant solution because it takes both time and technical acumen to make it work. This will certainly have a limiting effect on the number of buyers who can reach you. Nevertheless, it is an important option for those who are more technically savvy and are concerned about confidentiality.

Third-party banking is the latest concept to address financial transactions across the Internet. Essentially three different approaches are in place or in testing now:

- A token-passing arrangement whereby a string of numbers is assigned a value and ownership. You then can use this string as legal tender across the Internet. A central "bank" acts as a clearinghouse, ensuring that a string can be "spent" only once.

- A mathematical model that identifies ownership and the ability to spend a "token" without the need for central intervention or clearing services.

- A third-party agent that lets you use a credit card to set up an account with them and then use that account with any Internet vendors that accept payment in that form.

In the January 1994 issue of *Boardwatch*, an editorial identified seven requirements for an electronic monetary transaction environment:

- It must be incremental.

- It must be finite.

- It should be anonymous.

- It must be portable.

- It must be unrestricted in use.

- It should be non-directional.

- It must be immune to fraud.

A concept first made public by Bob Houston of Software Agents, Inc. (Germantown, Maryland) involves Netcash and a Netbank.

Netcash meets all of the *Boardwatch* requirements, except immunity to fraud. Yet, to be honest, people steal real cash and credit card numbers all the time. Is this any reason to reject an interesting concept?

Netcash is negotiable currency that looks like a string of characters, such as: **Netcash $1.00 F23678ZX 8797**. You obtain Netcash just as you obtain money—someone gives it to you. This can be payment for something, a loan, an advance, or any other normal financial transaction. Once it's yours, you can send an e-mail message to **netbank@agents.com** with the following in the body of the message: **Netcash $1.00 F23678ZX 8797**.

Once the Netbank has established the validity of your transaction, it replies to you with a new code number different from the original one so that now the "money" belongs to you and can be spent as you wish.

Netcash is an interesting alternative to credit cards. For more information, see the January and July issues of *Boardwatch*, or send mail to **netbankinfo@ agents.com**.

In addition, a variety of other organizations are looking to cash in on handling digital transactions. Some of the emerging leaders are described below.

Cisco Systems, the leading manufacturer of Internet routers, and Premenos Corporation, one of the leading Electronic Data Interchange (EDI) companies in the United States, began a secure electronic commerce experiment in early 1995.

DigiCash has created E-Cash, a software product that permits digital cash transfer across the Internet. The software for end users will be provided free of charge and will encrypt transactions to ensure anonymity. E-Cash uses a mathematical modeling formula to ensure this confidentiality rather than a third-party intermediary. For more information, contact DigiCash at **info@digicash.nl**, or on the WWW at **http://www.digicash.com**.

First Virtual Holdings combines the talents of well-known Internet technical people like Marshall Rose, Nathaniel Borenstein, and Einar Stefferud with those of music and entertainment luminary Lee Stein. Together, they have created an organization that attempts to bridge traditional banking with the new world of the Internet.

The First Virtual approach lets any Internet user initiate a purchase via e-mail. The user sets up his or her account offline using a telephone call. That account can then be used with any vendors that accept First Virtual for payment. Registration fees are US$2 for consumers and US$10 for sellers. In addition,

Figure 5-1:
DigiCash enables encrypted cash transactions.

sellers pay a US$0.29 fee plus 2 percent of the transaction and a US$1 processing fee each time a payment is made to their account. First Virtual also lets the buyer indicate—after up to one day to review the downloaded information—whether the purchase is valid, fraudulent, or something he or she does

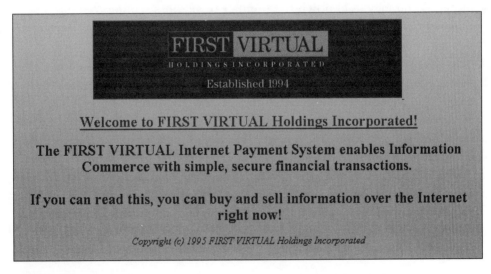

Figure 5-2:
First Virtual handles online money transfers for a fee.

not want to pay for, regardless of reason. For more information, contact First Virtual at **info@fv.com**, or on the Web at **http://www.fv.com**.

Microsoft recently announced an arrangement with VISA International that will let users make secure credit card purchases over the Internet. RSA Data Security's encryption techniques and VISA's VisaNet will be used to authenticate payments.

Netscape will support secure credit card transactions through First Data Corporation. Using RSA's encryption technology, Netscape will scramble sensitive data. Vendors can purchase the Netsite server software for US$5,000, and buyers can access the systems through freely available client software. Netscape has also introduced its Secure Socket Layer (SSL) functionality to support electronic transactions, via its Netscape Web browser.

NetCash (as opposed to Netcash, mentioned above) is under development at the Information Sciences Institute of the University of Southern California. The service will allow service providers and users to select payment mechanisms with varying degrees of confidentiality.

Clearly, areas of concern are represented by each of these models. The capture of credit card information ("in the clear") and potential fraudulent use certainly are major issues. Vendors need to assess just how difficult the alternatives are for potential buyers and estimate the overall impact on commerce.

Assurance of payment is an issue with First Virtual's approach. The company contends that vendors have no inventory or exorbitant advertising costs and should therefore be willing to accept some degree of nonpayment. This is presumptuous and may hold down the number of vendors willing to jump on the bandwagon. I expect this position to be modified and for First Virtual to become a major player.

The clumsiness of current encryption methods will be an inhibiting factor for new and novice users. Once the security methods become transparent to the end user, we will see a surge of buying across the Internet.

A combination of methods can work today. By offering some or all of these approaches, you can appeal to a wide market and identify the site of your best success. Much attention and competition are being focused on new methods, and we will certainly see significant improvements. Try not to lock yourself into any one approach. The verdict is still out on which will succeed.

Conclusion

The Internet cannot be used as a sales tool in a vacuum. It must be incorporated into existing marketing and sales plans and campaigns. Use traditional market targeting in assessing the Internet's role. Know whether this method will reach those targets. For example, do your target markets use e-mail-only accounts, VT100 emulation, SLIP/PPP, Mosaic, or leased-line high bandwidth services? Your answer will make a great deal of difference in whether they can reach your services.

Having a wonderful "home page" on a World Wide Web server may be useless if the majority of your targeted market has e-mail-only capability. I have heard many people complain that they did not get the traffic they had hoped for across the network or that they were getting many more browsers than buyers. Go back to basic marketing and sales techniques. Make sure that your e-mail address or server addresses are on your business cards, advertisements, and stationery.

When potential buyers call your organization asking for information, ask if they are Internet-connected. If so, direct them to your online resources. This can save you time and effort, and also help spread the word about your new Internet marketing efforts. No new technique succeeds by itself. You need to build into it.

The Internet and the electronic marketplaces are not the "Field of Dreams," magic, instant cures to your marketing problems, nor are they going to be successful without a great deal of thought and planning. But the Internet does offer tremendous opportunities to the calculating adventurer!

C hapter Six

Electronic mail (e-mail) is a method for computer systems to communicate information to other computer systems serving people or resources that you would like to reach.

Most large corporations have already implemented e-mail within their local area network (LAN) or office environments. Today, many of these companies, such as IBM, MCI, Tandem Computers, Digital Equipment Corporation, Amoco, and Merck Pharmaceuticals, could not conduct business without the capability to communicate in writing electronically. Think of the tons of paper that are no longer needed.

This is not to say that we have eliminated the memo or the letter. We have not. We certainly have reduced the volumes that are required and enhanced the certainty that the message will arrive where we want.

E-mail offers many advantages over paper correspondence. One of these is its "store-and-forward" nature. Because your machine communicates with the destination party's machine, messages are deposited in a "mailbox" and retrieved at the convenience of your recipient. For this reason, e-mail is essentially time-zone insensitive. You can send messages from anywhere in the world, and the recipients will receive them the next time they check their mail.

This helps eliminate telephone tag, even more so than voice mail. With voice mail, there is the possibility of not quite hearing the message clearly and losing the response telephone number, failing to get the proper spelling of someone's name, or missing key information (like your caller forgetting to leave his or her number!). With e-mail, you always have a "from" header including the sender's e-mail address. If something in the message is omitted or unclear, you simply respond by asking for further clarification.

This chapter explores some actual uses for e-mail in an internetworked environment. There are certainly many more. These examples will give you a place to start in your quest to understand the value that the Internet can bring to you. The numbers that are affected in your organization will be unique. The key is to start looking for them.

Reduce Your Phone Bill

Our world of communication has expanded dramatically during the last several years. Very few individuals or organizations haven't had to communicate out of state, around the country, or internationally. Business has grown beyond local or domestic political borders. We manufacture, sell, and ship to locations throughout the world.

When I was vice president of sales and marketing for a large Internet services provider, it was not unusual for me to receive telephone calls from the United Arab Emirates, Mexico, Canada, or the Netherlands. When considered against the needs of our business, the costs of long-distance phone calls to other parts of the world seemed reasonable.

Yet, we have grown so accustomed to picking up the phone and calling anywhere we like that we fail to see the hidden costs. How many of us have played telephone tag? What percentage of the time do you get voice mail or automated attendants when calling someone? How many times do you get through to your party on the first try? All of these experiences have an impact on our business day and introduce various levels of unseen costs.

We call people when we are prepared to speak to them, but they are not available. When they call back—if they call back—we may be on the phone, unavailable ourselves, or involved in something else. The message we wanted to communicate fails to get through in an efficient or timely fashion. There must be a better way to deal with these situations.

In most cultures, it would be considered impolite and rude to place a phone call to someone, say precisely why you called, and end the conversation. Our conventions dictate some level of chit-chat and pleasantries before we "get down to business." There is certainly an important place for pleasantries and getting to know one another better. There are also times when we need to communicate a simple and direct message and would rather not be constrained by social codes. We just want to inform someone that the meeting time has been changed from 3 p.m. to 4:30 p.m.

An e-mail message can do that quite nicely.

A key advantage to this form of communication is its time-zone insensitivity. I can reply to a message from Dubai and not be concerned about what time it is on the Arabian Peninsula. The response will be there when I choose to check my mail.

Given that we actually do check our messages in a regular and timely fashion, it is quite conceivable that an organization can see a reduction in long-distance bills of 20 to 25 percent per year. That could add up to "real money" very quickly.

Think about the savings in time and money. What is 20 to 25 percent of your long-distance telephone bill? Who are you calling? Where are they located? Are they available on any form of e-mail, including MCIMail, AT&TMail, CompuServe, or others? If reducing your annual long-distance telephone bill by 20 percent is of interest to you, the Internet is a place to explore. Your costs are likely to be much lower, resulting in significant savings and improved efficiency.

So, just how satisfied are you with the effectiveness of your long-distance telephone service? Don't forget to include your point-to-point leased lines. Is reducing or better controlling those costs important? How about reducing telephone tag frustration? The Internet is an excellent supplement to your long-distance telephone "diet."

Establish More Frequent and Meaningful Communications with Customers

It is actually more important to keep existing customers or clients than to garner new ones. If you are signing up ten customers a week, but losing two, the impact is obvious. You are working twice as hard on the front end as you should.

Keeping customers, or minimizing "churn," is difficult, particularly if you are in a highly competitive, commodity market. Some customers are fickle and can be enticed away from their existing suppliers with the promise of lower fees.

How do you keep competitors from stealing your customers? One proven answer is for you to remain visible to your customers, in reasonably frequent contact, and deliver sensitive, responsive service. In other words, you need to professionally and politely "keep in their faces"!

In lieu of hiring an army of sales and service professionals, many companies use newsletters and customer communiqués to help enhance their visibility. It's amazing how much new business you can get from existing customers just by being visible. I refer to this as the "oh, yeah" syndrome. They had been too busy to remember that they wanted to call you and order that extra widget, but when they received your newsletter, suddenly you get new business from an old customer. It does work.

Now, how much does it cost to produce these client communiqués—printing costs . . . staff . . . mailing expenses . . . time? It can quickly become a big project, and one that often gets pushed to the back burner. When that happens, how much business have you lost? You may never know.

Consider using electronic distribution for your customer communications. Many customers are probably reachable today through direct Internet access or proprietary services (America OnLine, CompuServe, Delphi, GEnie, Prodigy, MCIMail, AT&TMail, SprintMail, etc.). You may find that you can increase the exposure of your message (sending the communication to several people in the customer's organization), reduce costs of production, and send out more frequent messages. How about: "Come see us at Booth 341 at Comdex. We are demonstrating our new Holographic Video Conferencing System."

In sales and marketing, it is critical that your message reach the consumer earlier and speak more clearly than that of your competitors. This is especially true for those customers in which you have already successfully invested considerable time, money, and effort.

Explore the many ways in which the use of internetworking will bring you closer more frequently to those who want to buy from you. I can assure you that your competitors will be trying to get closer to your customers! Beat them to the punch by enhancing your scope and breadth of market interaction. Make the Internet "tool" work for you.

Begin including your e-mail address or Web location on your letterhead or in other written materials. Tell your customers about the new Internet-based information you are publishing. You may be surprised at how many of them are already on the Internet and welcome the input from you.

"Publicize" Your E-Mail Address

Have your e-mail address printed on your business card to show that you are "with it."

This may sound like an appeal to vanity, but it is not. As more and more organizations become indoctrinated in the ways of electronic communications, businesspeople worldwide will begin to ask for your e-mail address.

Consider these scenarios:

- *That phone number of an important contact* . . . I can e-mail it to you when I get back to my office.

- *That posting I saw on Sprint's new announcement* . . . I can forward that to you electronically.

- *Let me confirm that date for our next meeting* . . . I'll have my secretary message your assistant to make certain.

Communicating electronically is easy and efficient. You cannot have an e-mail address on your business card if you do not have an e-mail account. It also does not work very well unless you or someone you authorize checks the mailbox regularly. I check my mail several times a day. You never know when it might contain a new multimillion dollar opportunity.

Flatten Your Organization

Use of networks, and particularly the Internet because of its international scope, will change the way companies are managed and operated. A less structured and more informal style begins to pervade the organization. As reported in *Fortune,* "Fundamental management jobs, such as planning, budgeting, and supervising must be done differently. Tools like e-mail, teleconferencing, and groupware let people work together despite distance and time, almost regardless of departmental or corporate boundaries." Learning how to take advantage of these tools and how to use them properly takes a considerable amount of thought and planning, yet the benefits are becoming readily apparent to organizations worldwide.

One area to consider is that the Internet and the new world of internet-working is highly egalitarian. Without the physical facade that we use so frequently to assess people, we are at a bit of a loss. While on the Net, you might be talking with a high school sophomore or the CEO of a reasonably sized company, yet never know. Sometimes, even when you ask tactfully, people will choose not to respond. It is important to understand the sources of this new-found fountain of wisdom.

Within your own organization, the network creates greater accessibility and flow of information among various people and departments. Andy Ludwick, CEO of SynOptics Communications, said, "It takes hours or days for information to go from an out-box through the mailroom to an in-box while the project is idle. E-mail is instant." And that's if your personnel are in the same location. Expand this concept to organizations that are distributed throughout the country or around the world! The benefits in time and productivity will be rapidly apparent with e-mail.

In addition, networks help ameliorate functional boundaries. Sales and marketing organizations can make their activity reports and customer interaction records available to senior management in finance, legal, engineering, general administration, or any other group that needs access.

This may help in small ways, such as sharing insight into how customers perceive your pricing policies, service methods, or contracts. How many sales have you lost because the language in your contract was undesirable or even offensive to some customer prospects? If you do not know the answer, perhaps you have a problem yet to be recognized and addressed. The best way to stay on top of what is going on within your organization is to create easy-to-use, convenient, and hospitable channels of communications. E-mail affords those opportunities.

Flattening the organization—breaking down traditional organizational barriers—can also help develop better products and services. According to Jim Manzo, vice president of engineering at Pitney Bowes, "To develop complex products, you need lots of people with specialized knowledge, working together in little virtual departments."

An employee of Sun states, "In a networked organization, people with knowledge almost always get into the discussion, because somebody somewhere draws them in."

You may be surprised where the insight comes from within your organization. A company is a living thing, and the more it is able to draw from its internal resources, the better.

In many companies, technical and sales personnel collect information that will eventually be filtered to other departments in summaries and reports. This information is then used in filtered form as input for new products, service enhancements, or indications of potential customer problems. In fact, it may go only to senior managers and never be seen by those charged with identifying and addressing these issues.

Internetworking can help address this challenge. Groupware software, a relatively new application category, helps people share information, databases, updates, files, and records across traditional organizational boundaries. Information obtainable via groupware is available to any authorized personnel with access to the server. Anyone with access to the data can search according to his or her needs, rather than accept someone else's idea of what numbers to crunch. Interdepartmental problem-solving teams form spontaneously. Best of all (in the case of Notes developer Lotus, for example), about 500 companies can enter the database directly and share solutions. Net result: Many more employees watch the market from front-row seats.

The benefits of an interconnected workforce, and even customer base, can be substantial.

Reduce Fax Costs Annually by 15 Percent

In a Gallup Poll released in April 1994, it was disclosed that the average Fortune 500 company spent 36 percent of its annual phone bill for fax transmissions alone. This equates to $3.75 to $5 million annually. Typical user organizations fax 207 pages daily (forty-one documents averaging five pages each). The 1995 update of this report noted that businesses are now spending 40 percent of their annual long-distance phone bill on fax. With the typical Fortune 500 company spending $34 million for annual long-distance telephone service, 40 percent equals $13.6 million spent on fax alone. If we can assume that these ratios extend to smaller organizations, and assume that half of their faxes can be reduced through the use of electronic messaging to other connected organization sites, customer locations, or supplier facilities, what would this alternative be worth? What's 20 percent of your company's annual long-distance phone charges? For a small company with only $100 per month in long-distance toll costs, that's a potential $240 savings per year, or better than two months of billings.

At $1,000 per month in long-distance toll charges, you may need to provide a dedicated leased-line connection to your facility for sufficient throughput and performance. This can cost as much as $500 to $1,000 per month, diminishing the potential for cost savings. One of the benefits of leased-line connectivity, however, is that the fixed cost structure permits you to add other applications (e.g., file transfers or interoffice memos) at relatively low incremental additional costs. These additional "applications" may prove to offer significant cost displacement and justification of internetworking access.

At the $5,000 per month level, you could save as much as $7,000 or more per year after factoring in the cost of network access. As you can see, the value in costs alone may be significant, and other benefits, such as shortened turn-around time or reusable digital file formats, may provide additional "soft savings" that are more difficult to quantify but no less significant.

Another area of potential savings easily overlooked in the "fax versus Internet" cost displacement discussion is the reduction in personnel time. How much clerical or managerial time is spent administering a fax machine, ensuring that the documents go through properly, resending when needed, or simply adding paper when the machine runs out? How often does an incoming fax need to be copied so the paper does not turn yellow with age, or need to be scanned into a computer-usable format for further manipulation? Can you identify the number of hours that your employees are investing in these areas? How much can they be reduced? The number may be hidden, but it could be quite substantial.

If we speculate that the average Fortune 500 company's personnel are spending five minutes each for the forty-one documents sent daily from each site, that equals 3.4 hours a day—or nearly half of one full-time employee. If we can find ways to reinvest some portion of that time, especially when we consider the number of employees engaged in this practice, additional cost displacements are realized.

These changes in the way we conduct business will not come about suddenly. They will evolve. I can promise, however, that you will be asked more and more frequently, "What's your e-mail address? Can I e-mail it to you?" When you can answer positively, you may well see your fax costs come down substantially.

Another advantage of e-mail over fax is the potential for confidentiality. Even without any additional tools, an e-mail message will come directly to your mailbox—not sit on a public fax machine that can be viewed by anyone walking by. With the further addition of Privacy Enhanced Mail (PEM) and other tools under development, you can send or receive urgent correspondence with a relatively high level of confidence in its confidentiality.

Reduce Courier Costs by 25 Percent

Most companies today do not think twice about sending important documents via courier services (Federal Express, DHL, UPS, etc.). In fact, if the documents being sent are more than ten to twenty pages, most companies would rather ship than fax them.

Does your company have any written policies about when a package can be shipped overnight, or who must authorize such a shipment? How about unwritten policies? Does it use a single courier service? Do you have one corporate account, or do departments or business units have their own accounts?

The point here is that you need to get a handle on how much your company spends on couriers, and to identify how often the documents or other contents could only have been transferred by hand delivery.

I suspect that many packages include documents that were created digitally on a word processor, printed out, copied, enclosed in an overnight package, sent to a distant receiver, scanned or rekeyed into a new document, and printed out again for final use. Is that process familiar?

Not to belabor the personnel side of communication, but how much time does it take your staff, perhaps already overburdened, to prepare documents for shipping? Could that time be invested in more productive efforts? Could this also help promote employee morale?

Why not simply transfer the file in its original form electronically? Given that one overnight package can range in cost from $9.95 to $30 or more, the savings could add up very quickly.

There certainly are times when the need for hard copy is real. Electronic communication will not entirely eliminate the need for couriered documents. But it makes good business sense to review why you work this way in light of the alternatives presented by the Internet and other networking solutions.

In these times of economic consolidation, outsourcing, and downsizing, a hard look at what you send by courier, why you send it that way, and any feasible electronic alternatives certainly make sense. Take a critical look at how you communicate with others and ask yourself why you do it that way. If the answer is "because that's how we have always done it" or "I hadn't thought about it," perhaps you should reconsider. It may make a difference in your corporate bottom line. One courier package a day at $20 each results in more than $5,000 per year in cash outlay. International packages are more expensive. These relatively small expenses can add up quickly. Consider the Internet one of your new alternatives.

Route Faxes over the Internet

Now that you have discovered you can cut your annual long-distance telephone bill by as much as 20 percent or more by sending e-mail or using ftp, what do you do about the faxes to those not connected to the Internet?

Well, you're still in luck. Many service providers (America OnLine, FaxLinq [**info@antigone.com**, **faslinq-faq@antigone.com**], and FAXNET [**info@awa.com**]) will let you send a single electronic message addressed not only to people with an Internet address but to a telephone fax number as well. In this way, by sending a single "broadcast" message, you can accomplish the entire communications task without having to use different media (Internet, telephone, fax, etc.) and investing extra time and effort.

To do this, you can set up a predefined list of addresses—both e-mail and fax—associated with a particular group or interest. For example, to distribute my bimonthly newsletter, I set up a list (a mail reflector) called **newsletter@maloff.com**. Every time I send a message to that address, everyone I have identified as part of this group receives the distribution—some through e-mail and others through fax. I do not need to have clerical support to distribute my newsletter in traditional ways; I just write the articles and electronically send them out.

Replace Faxes and Courier Services with Remote Printing

Another alternative to faxes and expensive courier services is the capability to print remotely at a distant site.

For example, let's say that you are working on a draft of your business plan and want to share it with the CFO at your company. Perhaps you have included some graphics that are available only with the software on your machine and not at corporate headquarters.

By using telnet (remote log-in capability), you can establish a connection with the headquarters LAN and use a printer there.

Another use for this capability is remote printing of custom contracts. Most legal organizations do not want the full text of a contract available to the field sales organization in a word processor file format. No offense to salespeople, but the temptation to modify language just a tad to make the sale is perceived as too great a risk. On the other hand, by using remote printing, a revised, custom, and authorized contract can be in the salesperson's hands within moments. Instead of intense negotiations followed by days of drafting and distribution via fax or courier, the salesperson can wait for the revised original to go directly to the customer's site (assuming the customer has an Internet connection). This permits closure on the deal and minimizes the chances of losing the sale because of the introduction of new information or the customer getting "cold feet."

Consider how effective remote printing might be with your branches or legal or accounting support services, or as a way of maintaining better contact and quality of information distribution to your customers. After all, a freshly printed document always looks better and is more legible than a fax—even a plain paper fax.

Deliver Electronically Encoded Resources Immediately to Locations Worldwide

How many offices, branches, or facilities does your organization have? How many customers, clients, or prospects? How many different suppliers do you rely on, and where are they located?

It is possible to deliver electronically encoded resources to all of these locations in a matter of moments with one electronic transmission. Using Multipurpose Internet Mail Extensions (MIME), all of these resources can be appended to an e-mail message.

Imagine sending the draft of a new brochure from your PR department to the heads of marketing in six different regions simply by sending one e-mail message. Imagine posting the corporate president's speech to shareholders in his or her actual voice, retrievable electronically from your server.

In this way, you can make the same information that is available at corporate headquarters accessible to all employees worldwide, reducing the "Foreign Legion" syndrome. Often, people in offices other than the corporate headquarters feel left out and as if they are not considered or consulted in corporate decision making. Use of e-mail, particularly MIME, can assist in minimizing this situation.

Improve Morale Through Regular Electronic Employee Communications Channels

How many employees feel they are truly being heard by management? The problem becomes more acute the larger and more decentralized an organization becomes. It is very easy to become distanced and disillusioned.

How much does retraining cost your organization every year because of employee turnover? Is the turnover rate too high, compared to similar organizations in your industry?

Several internetworking techniques can be used to help prevent barriers between employees and management. One is the use of simple internal electronic "mail reflectors." These can be used on a continuing basis or for a predetermined period of time on a specific issue. For example, all of those interested in helping plan the company picnic should indicate their interest to **picnic@ourcompany.com**. This is an e-mail address, but it does not go to the mailbox of just one person. It is "reflected" to everyone who indicated an interest.

Likewise, any responses to comments on a reflector are sent to everyone. This is important. You do not want to respond to the entire list when your comments were meant only for the eyes of the author. The result can be rather embarrassing. Nevertheless, this is a very effective tool for fostering group discussions electronically.

Another, more serious, issue might revolve around a discussion of social or political importance. For example, if your company was considering a self-imposed embargo of Antarctica due to the treatment of penguins, you might want your employees to know about the plans and give them the opportunity to express their support or concerns before the policy was enacted.

Another technique involves "moderated distributed decision systems." In this case, an organization chooses people to participate in important business discussions and decisions. They may be in the same room or located across the country or the world. Each is online with a moderator. The moderator poses questions and lets everyone respond freely, with the knowledge that the source of the responses will be kept confidential.

In one case, ten people from the same company attempted to chart a strategic course for the next several years. Included were the president, several vice presidents, and a variety of department heads. Answers appeared on all monitors as a composite of the participants' responses. When asked the one single thing that the company could do to improve its chances of success, several people entered, "get rid of the president."

Needless to say, some messages are heeded more than others. The process does work and permits a more open discussion of views and alternatives. Using the Internet, these sessions can be conducted with participants in many remote locations.

Corporations spend millions of dollars to improve employee morale. Investments range from cute posters and group meetings to expensive cruises or incentive travel awards. These activities are certainly important and useful, yet sometimes employees simply want to know that management does not take them for granted and recognizes them as important contributing factors to the organization. By creating enhanced bidirectional electronic communications channels, you can show them exactly that!

Reduce Turn-Around Time for Proposals

How long does it take your organization to respond to a Request for Proposals (RFP)? Do you have a proposal response team? Are members located in the same facility? How do you incorporate subcontractors or other partners in the response to the proposal request? If you are a buyer, do you use RFP, Request for Quotes (RFQ), or Request for Information (RFI)? Have you considered incorporating the Internet and electronic submissions of both questions and proposals?

More and more buying organizations are finding that a formal request permits them to conduct apples-to-apples comparisons from prospective vendors. This, in turn, creates more work for those bidding. It is not unusual for an organization to devote several people for more than a week to respond to even modest proposal requests. This might include engineers for technical responses, finance people for the "pencil-sharpening" exercises, marketing people for the industry customization, and salespeople for putting together the final package for the prospect.

Normally, when responding to an RFP, RFQ, or RFI, companies require you to submit a predesignated number of neatly bound copies by a specified time and date. More and more frequently, companies are issuing their requests electronically and asking for responses to be submitted in the same fashion. This has several consequences: faster responses, easier redistribution to prospective evaluators, and reduced mailing costs to the bidders.

Additionally, many companies are putting their standard offerings "up" on the network electronically. In early 1994, I issued an RFP for one of my clients for Internet access. The request went out electronically on a Sunday to eighteen prospective bidders. Within an hour, I had eight responses from vendors—seven using an automated response system that had most of what I required and one (Dennis Fazio of MRNet in Minnesota) who happened to be working and responded immediately.

Within a few hours, I was actually able to begin evaluations and consider recommendations for my client. The alternative would have been a time-consuming postal mail and telephone solicitation and response process.

To a consultant or purchasing agent or any other organization involved in procurements, the electronic RFP/RFI/RFQ offers many advantages.

Imagine—as a buyer or a vendor—you could do all of this without bringing everyone together face to face for days or weeks at a time. I have been involved in this process whereby we turned out a very sophisticated, complete one-hundred-page proposal in less than four days. And, as you might expect, we won the business.

Sometimes you may be the best qualified to meet a customer's needs, yet you cannot get a satisfactory proposal on the table in the requested time frame, and therefore do not get the business. Hustle and smart use of technological tools still pay off today.

The Internet gives you a vehicle to connect with your own personnel in distant offices, talk with potential partners from other organizations, and submit questions and/or proposals electronically. The benefits in cooperation, time, and results can be substantial.

Let's put this in perspective. If, as a vendor, you win one more contract a year by using the Internet, what is the potential value? $1,000 . . . $10,000 . . . $10 million? It may not take many such wins to make exploring the Internet pay off handsomely. As a buyer of services, you may reach a large number of prospective providers of the service you desire without expensive advertising or mass mailing costs.

I recently completed issuing an RFP for a client where we announced the procurement on several Internet newsgroups and mail reflectors only. We received more than 115 indications of interest.

The process works well for both buyers and bidders. Can you afford not to be prepared to respond electronically?

Supplement Employee Training Through Electronic Updates and Bulletins

Consider the following questions:

- What kinds of internal training programs do you have for your personnel?

- Are the programs job-specific only?

- Do you include training programs on such matters as corporate policies, diversity, safety, etc.?

- Does your organization have a full-time training staff and center?

- Are others required to take on training as an adjunct to their full-time jobs? (For example, the installation manager may also be responsible for safety checks on the crew.)

- How much money does your organization spend per person per year on training?

- Is the level of training you are delivering sufficient or is it less effective than desired?

Training is an extensive and complex issue, and it certainly cannot be treated fairly in this short discussion. Some methods of communication can supplement your existing training efforts, so you both enhance the level and frequency of information exchanged with your trainees and reduce some training costs.

Having been intimately involved with the Marketing Learning Center for Chesapeake and Potomac Telephone Company many years ago, I found that a major problem occurred after the students left the intense six-week New

Salesperson Basic Training Program. They remembered a fraction of what they had learned after only a few weeks "out in the field." Their managers were responsible for assisting them, but all managers had six to twelve account executives in their groups and were often unable to provide the level of reinforcement needed by a new representative.

At the same time, it was difficult to contact the student's former instructor via telephone because the instructors were often in class and could not possibly handle regular calls from hundreds of students.

The result was that questions went unasked, and some students, who already represented a significant investment on the part of the company (estimated at more than $100,000 per person in 1982), perhaps unnecessarily "washed out." This is not only a loss in terms of the company and its investment, but also in human terms for the individual.

The Internet offers ways to supplement traditional forms of training with extended, remote learning and discussion techniques.

Within the postgraduate environment, "distance learning" has been used for quite some time. Essentially, it involves an instructor who is remote to some or all of the students and who uses some form of telecommunications to maintain contact with the class. This may include real-time, full-motion video and voice, or it may be electronic, non-real-time communications. In any case, it permits greater utilization of scarce instructional resources.

The University of Michigan has offered for some time extended degree programs in conjunction with major automobile manufacturers, such as General Motors and Chrysler. Company employees take two to four hours a week to study design or other appropriate fields at an on-site classroom remote from the instructor. The employers pay for the programs.

One difficulty with this approach for smaller companies is the need for expensive telecommunications bandwidth. This normally means establishing direct microwave links or leasing costly "private lines" from local or long-distance telephone companies.

As our capability to exchange data improves, we are quickly seeing a move toward interactive "desktop" video. This will permit the exchange of video images with others remote from us, while still having our work in another "window." This could permit the transport of an instructor's image directly to a desktop workstation rather than requiring students to go to a predesignated classroom.

At this time, the quality of the video is not likely to be the same as that of your home TV or a video conferencing room. On the other hand, you can now purchase and establish desktop video for as little as $3,000 per station. By using existing telecommunications facilities, such as the Internet or your corporate private networks, usage costs may prove relatively minimal compared to the benefits.

Internetworking will also help training by the availability of constantly updated frequently asked questions (FAQs). Students are unlikely to be alone on a given topic. Why not create a repository that includes all questions with the proper answers, and keep it electronically accessible online, any time, from anywhere the employee or trainee might be? To be of most value, these FAQs also need to be "keyword searchable." This permits employees to identify a specific term and see all of the areas where that term or set of terms is covered.

Another use is the actual delivery of written and graphical instructional materials. Dr. Steve Eskow at the Electronic University Network (EUN) has pioneered the use of the network as a delivery vehicle. EUN has been available over America OnLine for several years. In conjunction with accredited universities, you can actually earn a degree through the EUN.

Consider how you might be able to employ internetworking within your organization to create new training programs, deliver courses worldwide with a reduced need for instructors, evaluate courses online, and provide continuing support and follow-up services to your students.

Incorporate the Internet and internetworking into your training efforts, and you will quickly realize enhanced efficiency and lower costs per employee trained. The potential benefits to your organization, including better performance from employees and lower per-employee training costs, could be substantial.

Broadcast Press Releases Immediately

How often does your organization issue press releases? This is normally part of a well-structured public relations campaign. How frequently are your stories picked up by magazines, newspapers, or radio and television reporters? Would you like your success rate to be higher?

One of the difficulties these days is that so many press releases are issued that busy editors and reporters do not have time to evaluate or use them all. If your press release is received electronically, however, the media has the ability to reuse the information without having to rekey or scan it into another document. They can simply cut whatever they would like to use into their story, increasing the likelihood that you get the exposure you want.

How many press releases do you send out each year? One per month to fifty different publications? That's a small amount, and yet this adds up to more than $90 per year in first-class postage alone, plus the additional costs from your PR agency or internal marketing people for assembling the packages and sending them out. This may not be a huge expenditure, but imagine getting the same degree of distribution with one transmission per month rather than fifty!

You can easily accomplish this task by creating a distribution list for the media organization that you want to notify regularly of your activities. Establish a mail reflector (like **media@maloff.com**) that includes all of your destination reporters and editors. Every time you send a notice to **media@maloff.com**, everyone you want to reach will get a copy of your release. This permits them to use it easily and conveniently.

Your e-mail systems operator can easily set up a mail reflector. If you do not have a systems administrator, create a word processor or spreadsheet file that contains the addresses, and simply copy that into the "To:" section of an e-mail message whenever you need to distribute a press release. Although some e-mail systems may limit the number of destinations on each message, you can still accomplish your task with substantially less effort and expense.

Experience has demonstrated that editors and reporters find this method attractive as well, and that appeal certainly enhances your potential for coverage. Check with your target media to see if they accept e-mail press releases and find out their addresses.

Provide Daily, Variable Information to a Number of Sites with a Single Transmission

In certain industries, such as mortgage banking or commodities brokerage, information changes daily and must be communicated to a large number of locations around the country or throughout the world almost simultaneously.

Particularly when you serve smaller sites, it is impractical to have costly dedicated leased lines everywhere. Leased lines (also known as point-to-point private lines) are provided by both local and long-distance telephone companies and can be quite expensive. Rates are determined by each service provider and by the mileage between the connected locations. In some instances, such as the home loan business, a new office may need to be established in a few days or a week.

How do you ensure that accurate and timely information is getting everywhere it should?

A major home loan mortgage company had exactly this problem. With more than 500 locations, solving this issue was critical. When analyzed, it became clear that the amount of information was small—perhaps one page or a few thousand bytes of data. The problem was distribution. Try calling or faxing 500 sites every morning with the new interest rates!

By setting up a mail reflector, one message goes to all 500 sites with a single transmission. Implementation is easy, and the results are significant in terms of increased efficiency, reduced manual labor efforts, and reduced fax costs.

Communicate with Anyone While He or She Is at School or Traveling

This may or may not be suitable as a business application—unless you consider that at least one phone call home per night is considered an acceptable business expense by most companies while you are out of town on business!

Human interaction is important. Our ability to communicate clearly over great distances is one of the characteristics that distinguishes us from all other forms of life. Having the capability to either compose a note offline and send it to an important acquaintance or to receive one and respond accordingly can be important in our daily lives.

The impact of a kind note on the rest of our business day can be significant. On the other hand, Dear John/Jane notes on the Internet may not be far behind.

Submit Invoices or Expenses More Quickly

Most organizations pay invoices on net 30 days after the bill is received. If we could find a way to submit these invoices electronically, our accounting could be cleaner and payments made in less time than today. How important is a shortened "invoice to payment cycle" to you? If you received your payments three days sooner on the average, what would be the tangible benefits?

How many of us, when traveling on business, have found that company reimbursement checks are issued somewhat later than when the bill is received from Visa, MasterCard, or American Express?

It would be much easier to submit expenses electronically—retaining the required approvals and chain of events. The Internet offers a better way to submit expense reports than normal "snail mail" procedures. Accounts payable departments should consider the Internet a possible enhancement in this area. Turn-around time and employee satisfaction may improve markedly.

Finding ways to use the Internet in traditional business transactions may provide direct return on investment (ROI) benefits, improved employee morale, and greater accuracy in reporting due to the immediacy of submissions. How often have you not been reimbursed for a legitimate company expense because you forgot it or lost the receipt and failed to report it?

The Internet won't solve all of these problems, but it can make life a bit easier for both those on the road as well as the accounts payable people.

Establish Function-Specific Discussion Groups Within Your Organization

For organizations that are widespread (whether that means in one large building, a multiple-building campus, or sites across the world), it is important that people with common interests be able to exchange information in an easy, yet clear manner.

For example, how many purchasing agents does your company have? Are they all in the same facility, or does each branch or business unit have its own purchasing organization? These questions apply to almost all disciplines: legal, administrative, sales and marketing, and engineering.

The benefit of establishing small, intimate, discipline-specific discussion groups is greater communication resulting in enhanced efficiency and productivity.

Such groups can be easily created by developing a common interest mail reflector and using it as an internal discussion vehicle separate from broader company discussions. In this way, people may feel more open to explore their thoughts than if the entire company were watching.

Another method is to establish an internal server (World Wide Web server, Gopher, or simple remote access server) designated exclusively for this group. For example, the legal department server may have recent articles from the *Congressional Register* or *Commerce Business Daily*. Opinions from senior counsel on how new regulations may affect the organization can be filed in another area.

Do not limit use of servers to the outside world. They can be quite powerful for internal purposes as well.

You will need the assistance of a competent systems administrator to set up servers, but except for hardware (you may be able to "partition" part of an existing workstation or server), your costs will be primarily in administration and maintenance. The benefits should more than offset the costs.

Receive an E-Mail Message on Your Pager

Within the business world, use of those annoying pagers is becoming more and more common. It seems we simply cannot go anywhere without our "electronic tether." Formerly the tool primarily of doctors and other emergency service personnel, the pager is now used by almost everyone.

One of the problems, however, is the inability to clearly communicate the message rather than relying on the person calling back. Sometimes, the person paged is in an airplane, car, train, or other form of transportation and cannot get to a telephone in a timely fashion. He or she may be in the midst of a key client presentation or a board of directors meeting. How critical is the page? Is immediate action required? A short but specific message could be quite useful.

Using e-mail, it is now possible to send a short written-language message directly to the pager. "Your meeting has been canceled. Don't board the plane!" might be a timely message to receive. Or, "Million $$ deal needs your OK now!"

Sometimes, a few words are all we need. This method helps get them to us quickly and clearly. In many cases, you can also send a copy to your electronic mailbox so you have a written record when you require it.

Many companies, including RadioMail, Ardis Company (United States), and Bell Ardis (Canada), have introduced these services. Ask whether your pager provider accommodates e-mail and how many characters can be sent. Normal restrictions are up to eighty characters. This makes a difference in how lengthy the message can be.

Negotiate the Framework of Business Relationships Electronically

In today's fast-moving business world, many crucial business discussions can be slowed down or even derailed because we cannot get the right people in the same place at the same time. Bringing entrepreneurs together with venture capitalists, getting the right experts to help put together that business plan, or negotiating an international partnership all fall into this category.

Internetworking can help smooth the difficulties of busy schedules, time zones, and distributed talent.

The Internet can be used to attract potential interested parties. I am not suggesting that you be so tactless as to post a message to a newsgroup saying, "Midwestern pharmaceutical firm looking for capital investment." However, in a newsgroup focusing on topics of interest to your corporation, you might say: "Our company—a Midwestern pharmaceutical manufacturer—has been working on the inability of golf balls to go where we direct them. One of our approaches has been a new drug that appears to work quite well, although at the present time, it is an unfunded project. Should this change, we might be able to bring it to the market within six months."

By taking this subtle approach, you will reach a great many participants worldwide and will likely receive quite a few private e-mail messages asking for more information. Some of them may even lead to potential partners or funding sources.

By using the Internet, you can spread the word that you are seeking alliances, without being obtrusive or counterproductive.

Once you have established interest from prospective partners, you'll experience a significant flow of information—nondisclosure agreements, preliminary plans, financial reports, and attempts at valuation of your company or the portion for which you seek investment. All of these documents and data files can easily be sent using file transfer protocol (ftp) for the larger files or simple e-mail messages for the smaller ones. Chapter Eleven addresses the issues of confidentiality and security affecting this area.

Once all preliminary information is exchanged, it is likely that some degree of face-to-face meeting will be required. After these meetings, however, many details must be finalized.

Much of this can be done with short, direct, electronic message exchanges. For example, "In your first plan five months ago, you indicated that the rate of growth in your swizzle stick line of business was 20 percent per month. Has that changed?" Small details can be handled quickly and efficiently, and with a written record. This can be quite a bit more efficient than a telephone conversation, assuming you can even catch up with your counterpart. With e-mail—if you both check it regularly—you will often have an answer later the same day.

In addition, by conducting portions of your negotiations electronically, information is in computer-usable form. This means you can cut portions of a response into a report going to other investors or key personnel, without having to scan, photocopy, or rekey the information. By itself, this can be a tremendous time-saver.

The use of internetworking may cut days off negotiation cycles, and it may help position you to beat competitors for the same alliance. After all, if you can respect your counterpart's time and arrive at a high-quality "everybody wins" agreement quickly, your competitors may never get a chance!

Visit a Coffeehouse and Send E-Mail to Your Friends

Now, you might ask, how does this particular use of the Internet qualify as a business function? What if you happen to own a coffeehouse or another public establishment?

In San Francisco, more than a dozen coffeehouses will make Internet access available to you for a nominal fee. Just bring your laptop, plug into one of the access ports, and off you go!

Just think, bars might make more money from people using the Internet than from all of those quarters thrust into pinball machines and video games. The entrepreneurs out there will find other new and exciting ways to make Internet access available to the next generation of Internauts.

Reduce International Communications Costs and Improve Response Time

Communications costs to international locations can be substantial. Regular, dial-direct costs add up quickly. Costs for dedicated-access leased-line services can be exorbitant. Leased lines, also known as "private lines," can cost several hundred thousand dollars or more per year when connecting international sites.

Given the rapid rate of expansion of Internet access worldwide (more than 150 countries are now online in some manner), it is possible to establish a 56Kbps dedicated connection to the Internet for as little as $10,000 per year, including all services and equipment, and to establish a similar connection in Europe for perhaps $15,000 to $30,000 per year.

Essentially, you can have the same transmission capability for less than half of the cost offered by traditional methods. Additionally, those dedicated Internet access facilities let you reach other Internet-connected sites for no incremental costs. In short, it is a very effective way to do business internationally.

The major difficulty today is the dearth of Internet access providers outside of North America. This is changing rapidly, and by the time you read this there will be many more commercially available Internet services in Europe, the Far East, the Middle East, and South America. Africa appears to be moving forward now, but it got started on the Internet bandwagon later than others. South Africa has a moderate level of connectivity already, as do some North African countries. This is covered in greater detail in Chapter Thirteen.

Given existing Internet access, use your IAP as a source for connectivity options in other countries. Your IAP should have the most current listings of service providers and can help you contact them. After all, your service provider benefits from the greater number of desired destinations because you are likely to need more bandwidth or connections in other sites it serves. There is nothing wrong about asking your IAP to invest a little time in you. The successful IAPs know this and offer it gladly.

Conclusion

E-mail is a great deal more useful as a business tool when we consider all of the functions it can serve. You will find a variety of ways to make e-mail work for you. Consider your options. Announce availability of your e-mail address to your customers. You will not be disappointed in the results.

Chapter Seven

INTERNET NEWS,

LISTSERVS, AND

DISCUSSION GROUPS

Internet newsgroups, also known as Netnews or Usenet, have proven exceptionally valuable to business. News is easily accessed from traditional Internet service providers, as well as America OnLine, CompuServe, and Prodigy. In addition to these public discussion groups, there are several other similar resources, including listservs and mail reflectors.

Internet news is more like a series of discussions than the reporting of current news events. It is important to identify which newsgroups are of value to your organization. Watch them to determine whether they are what you expect, and then begin to participate.

I have heard many stories of people who have purchased computer equipment, selected vacation destinations, found business partners or customers, or even met their "spouse to be" through Internet discussion groups. The value of newsgroups lies in their sense of "community."

As a consultant, I have used various newsgroups to announce procurements of my clients and have received hundreds of responses worldwide. In this way, I can cast as large a net as possible for my clients and provide them with the best solutions available. This would not be possible without the Internet and newsgroups.

In addition to Netnews, the Internet offers other discussion vehicles, including listservs and mail reflectors. (We discussed some uses of these two Internet features in Chapter 5). Listservs are similar to Netnews in that they are generally public and you must subscribe to them. You communicate with a listserv through e-mail rather than a specifically designed Netnews reader.

Mail reflectors are normally set up by specific organizations for a distinct purpose and are usually not intended for wide public use, although there are certainly exceptions. Other resources can provide the detail required to set up, manage, or participate in each of these techniques.

This chapter provides specific examples of how Netnews, listservs, and mail reflectors can fit into your business activities.

Identification and Collaboration with Colleagues

Do you know everyone working in your mutual area of interest? How do you identify colleagues worldwide working on the same issues that you face?

You can follow trade publications, publish papers, or attend conferences. But it sometimes takes time and money to travel, prepare formal documentation, or attend conferences.

By using Internet news, you can participate in existing discussions that pertain to your business with people from around the world. For example, if you conduct business in Canada, you may wish to follow **clari.canada.biz**. If you use equipment from Digital Equipment Corporation, you may wish to subscribe to **biz.dec.decnews**.

Many thousands of newsgroups exist, and more emerge every day. The key is to find ones that are of value to you. Do this by brief exploration and by references from colleagues who have found a particular discussion group useful.

In addition to Usenet, there are a variety of other ways to stay electronically connected with your colleagues. Mailing lists are another form of public discussion groups, but unlike Usenet (where you need to enter Netnews to participate) these messages come directly to your electronic mailbox. If you have e-mail, you can get to a listing of these groups by sending an e-mail message to **listserv@kentvm.kent.edu**. Include the following in the body of your message: GET ACADLIST READ ME. Soon you will receive an e-mail message with information on the Directory of Scholarly Electronic Conferences, a listing of hundreds of mailing lists on all topics.

Infomagnet, a search tool designed to work particularly on listserv, was developed by John Buckman at the Walter Shelby Group. I know of no others like it. Buckman can be reached by phone at (301) 718-7840 or by e-mail at **jbuckman@shelby.com**.

Mail reflectors are generally private discussion groups, established for a specific purpose or defined period of time, and open only to invited or interested parties. They vary widely and can be used as an internal communications channel. For example, I established a mail reflector to keep my entire sales and marketing department aware of events and to announce conference calls or meetings.

A well-known discussion group on the commercialization and privatization of the Internet is **com-priv@psi.com**. The Internet Engineering Task Force (IETF), the technical group concerned with the Internet, has several mail reflectors.

Mail reflectors can easily be set up by people who are familiar with e-mail and the Internet. Mail reflectors can be quite useful but require commitment from your organization to administer and manage them properly.

Now, how do you take advantage of these interest groups?

In a demonstration to the Trane Company, one of the world's largest manufacturers of air-conditioning systems, I was asked to use the network to see what I could find on chlorofluorocarbons and R11 refrigerants. To be honest, I had no idea what an R11 was. I conducted a search using a wide-area information server (WAIS) with "chlorofluorocarbons and R11" as keywords. I received more than fifty "hits" or locations where these words were found, including articles from a Department of Energy mailing list and an environmental newsgroup. One of these contained a posting (message) from a professor at a British university who was working on precisely the issue that Trane wanted to address. Trane could contact the professor directly through his e-mail address and, if appropriate, begin a collaborative effort.

Consider how this might work in your organization. Are you looking for experts in your particular areas of research and development? Do you want to find those active on the Internet?

Once you have identified newsgroups, mailing lists, or mail reflectors of interest to you, it is relatively easy to search for people of interest to you. In addition, by participating in these forums, you and your organization become more visible to others, and you never know who might contact you! When I post a message to a discussion group, it is not at all unusual for me to get ten to twelve private messages from others who want to discuss a specific area of interest, and possibly to contract for my consulting services. Exposure works!

Establish Contact with Potential "Strategic Partners" Worldwide

Most organizations know they cannot succeed worldwide without partners. These relationships may be as diverse as venture capital, sales and marketing agreements, foreign commerce agents, printers and publishers, and government agencies.

A growing number of these organizations are accessible using e-mail, as well as by monitoring appropriate discussion groups on the Internet.

The 1994 and 1995 Mecklermedia Internet World conferences in San Jose, California, brought significant participation from the venture capital community. Investors are now becoming connected to the Internet as well as funding ventures involving the technology.

If you are in the business of providing capital, an established business seeking funding, or an entrepreneur with an idea, you may want to explore Internet discussion groups that appeal to your interests. Try subscribing to **clari.biz.mergers** or **misc.entrepreneurs**, as well as groups that meet your specific needs.

The Internet is an enormous community, and newsgroups are the town squares where people gather to see and be seen. How do you identify potential partners in Europe or Asia? It is not possible to travel everywhere you might like while still controlling costs. Smart businesses use the Internet as a means of identifying professional assistance, partners, and suppliers.

I regularly receive inquiries for my consulting services and Internet research reports from distant places such as Guayaquil, Ecuador, and Israel.

By targeting areas of interest, you can subscribe to discussion groups and watch who participates in a way that is appealing to you and your organization. Exchange e-mail privately and see if there is any reason to pursue the topics further. You may have found a valuable business ally.

Post an announcement or thought-provoking comment to a newsgroup or bulletin board that deals with topics of interest to you, then evaluate the nature of responses. This is a good way to determine how useful are the other participants in the discussion. Remember, there are many "lurkers" out there—people who monitor a list but rarely post comments. They may be too busy or simply not interested in investing the time in a lengthy "back and forth" discussion. Nevertheless, they are there and might be interested in what you have to say.

You can also do a keyword search on the network to gather background information on your partner prospects.

No matter how you use Netnews and other discussion groups to identify business prospects, you will quickly see the extent to which your competitors are active on the Internet. By itself, that could be excellent strategic information!

Identify and Solicit Prospective Employees

Just as you might use the various newsgroups, mail reflectors, and bulletin boards to identify potential partners, so can you identify and solicit prospective employees.

Never before in the business world has there been the opportunity to make known available positions to so wide an audience.

In conjunction with several online career posting servers, just knowing who is seeking or offering new jobs can be valuable knowledge. I wouldn't be at all surprised to see a posting like this:

"Despite all this talk about Network Access Points (NAPs), we still need to deal with the human issues. I've had enough of twenty-below-zero cold here in Chicago. Anybody need a good systems administrator in Phoenix?"

The number of private responses will certainly be greater than zero and might even result in a job offer.

The Internet is rapidly becoming the most important new tool for human interaction that has come along in some time. If you are looking to solicit contract services, try **misc.jobs.contract**. General discussion on job searches can be found at **misc.jobs.misc**. To post general position announcements, try **biz.jobs.offered** or **misc.jobs.offered**. Two newsgroups are devoted exclusively to women: **bionet.women-in-bio** and **info.wisenet**. Both are oriented toward women in the sciences; WISENET stands for the Women in Science and Engineering Network.

Enhance Your Career Through Expanded Exposure to Various Opportunities

Many anecdotes have reported people reading newsgroups, mail reflectors and Internet discussion groups, and so becoming known to potential employers. Corporate "headhunters" are increasingly lurking on Internet discussion groups looking for potential "heads" to recruit.

The good news: You have an opportunity to participate in these various "communities of interest" and make points to a very diverse and distributed peer group. This can lead to an enhanced image and other opportunities.

MSEN, an Internet access provider in Michigan, has pioneered the OnLine Career Center, a job posting and employment opportunities server. You simply access MSEN's system to check for jobs that interest you. You can search by keywords, such as position titles, geography, industry, and so on.

To reach the MSEN system, gopher to **garnet.msen.com 9062**. A menu of areas to explore (career assistance, employment events, posted positions, etc.) appears.

Subscribe to a List for the Public Discussion of Bugs, Systems Problems, and Viruses

Most of us who work with computers have learned one lesson all too well—they break! We have learned the hard way that the time to back up disks is *now*—not after the hard drive crashes or the floppy disk is compromised.

It is helpful to hear about potential problems as they become known to others. The Internet is a fabulous source of alert information, suggestions for corrective action, and the transport of bug fixes from software vendors. The Net can also be a vehicle for vendors to examine your systems remotely to diagnose problems, saving costly field visits.

On the Internet are many newsgroups focused solely on the support of specific hardware or software platforms. By participating in these groups or monitoring their content, you can learn about issues that have affected others. Similarly, vendor companies often host private discussion groups on their own servers, inviting their customers to express opinions, ask for help, or make suggestions.

Another source of assistance is the Computer Emergency Response Team (CERT), an organization at Carnegie-Mellon University in Pittsburgh that is devoted to identifying, tracking, and resolving Internet security breaches worldwide.

CERT issues alerts about any identified software bugs that are exploitable by hackers, verified intrusions, or other efforts to compromise the network. CERT works closely with a variety of law enforcement agencies, as well as with equipment and software vendors.

Conclusion

Netnews, listservs, and mail reflectors all offer you a singular advantage—the ability to meet people that frequent "neighborhoods" of interest to you in CyberSpace. The tools represent the public square of the Internet. They afford you the opportunity to meet, converse, exchange ideas or points of view, and learn. Understanding how to use them effectively will significantly enhance your Internet experience. Use search tools to identify those of interest to you and then experiment. Remember to review the "Frequently Asked Questions" (FAQ), and remember to "lurk" (observe) before you begin to post messages. By understanding and becoming part of the culture, you will meet new friends and business associates worldwide.

*C*hapter Eight

Servers are computer systems that are intentionally made available to authorized users on the Internet. In some cases, these servers are open to the public. In other cases, they are restricted to authorized employees, customers, or others to whom access is granted. Some offer services for a fee and are usable only by those with account authorization.

There are several different kinds of servers, including anonymous ftp, Gopher, and World Wide Web (WWW) servers. Each has its own strengths and weaknesses.

Anonymous ftp is the oldest type of server and can be a bit more difficult to use. Gopher and WWW incorporate telnet and ftp capability, but their interfaces are easier to use. Most of these servers have been passive sources of information (documents, statistics, white papers, technical drafts, etc.).

A recent interesting use of servers is in sales and marketing. Historically, the Internet community has been biased against using the Internet as a medium for commerce. This has now changed. As the true dollar value and market potential of the Net grows from an amusing anachronism into a fully fledged marketing vehicle, more and more well-funded professional, business operations are beginning to explore its potential.

This offers both a wider range of buying options to the purchasing public and a new way to market products and services.

The Electronic Marketplace

One of the new approaches is the "electronic marketplace" or "cybermall." Cybermalls provide your company with an "electronic storefront," eliminating the need for you to establish a server yourself.

The number of cybermalls mushroomed during 1994 and 1995 and will certainly continue to grow. Several of the more interesting organizations in this field deserve particular attention:

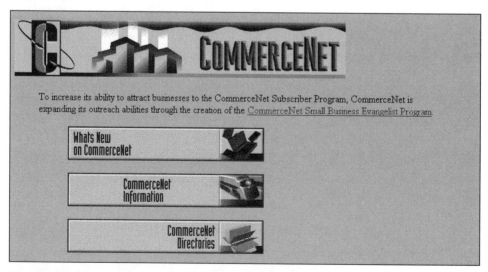

Figure 8-1:
Commercenet hosts one of the first cybermalls.

- CommerceNet (**http://www.commerce.net**) was formally launched on April 12, 1994, by Bay Area Regional Research Network (BARRNet), Enterprise Integration Technologies (EIT), and Stanford University's Center for Information Technology (CIT). BARRNet was subsequently acquired by Bolt, Beranek and Newman (owners of New England Academic Research Network [NEARnet] and Southeastern University Research Association Network [SURAnet]).

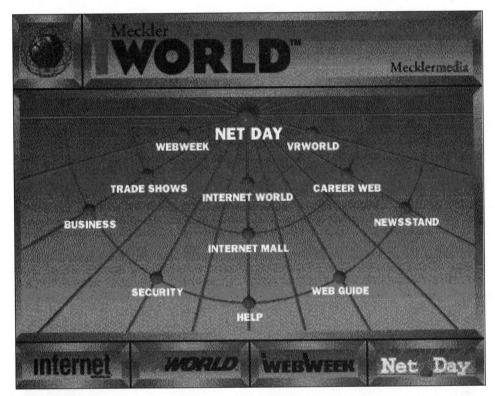

Figure 8-2:
MecklerWeb offers shopping for many goods and services.

- MecklerWeb iWORLD (**http://www.mecklerweb.com**), the web site of Mecklermedia Corporation, hosts the Internet Mall, a venue for close to 2,000 vendors of products and services in all conceivable areas, from accounting, tax, and legal services to automotive equipment, software, food products, and gifts.

Figure 8-3:
Branch Information Services provides an electronic marketplace.

- Branch Information Services of Ann Arbor, Mich (**http://www.branch.com**) is another electronic storefront business, offering Internet sales and marketing opportunities to organizations with backgrounds or desires to be technically competent in the Internet.

- The Internet Shopping Network (**http://www.internet.net**) was acquired by the Home Shopping Network in late 1994. Internet Shopping Network distributes more than 20,000 computer software and hardware products as well as *InfoWorld*, a computer news weekly magazine. There is no charge for membership, and prospective "members" need to preregister with an approved MasterCard or Visa.

- Global Network Navigator (**http://www.gnn.com**), recently purchased by America OnLine from O'Reilly and Associates, is a hybrid between an

Figure 8-5:
Global Network Navigator provides magazine-style resources.

online information service and an electronic magazine, with many web-based information resources linked from it.

Figure 8-6:
MCI is one of many big-name businesses online.

- Many California and New York advertising agencies, such as start-up On-Line Ad Agency, Messner, Vetere, Berger, McNamee, Schmetterer, and Euro RSCG, have signed on clients like apparel manufacturer Esprit, 1-800-Flowers, video-production company Radical Media, Volvo USA, and MCI (**http://internetmci.com**). These organizations, and other similar ones around the world, will merge the traditional worlds of advertising and promotion with the new world of the Internet.

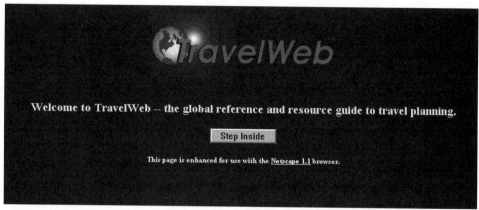

Figure 8-7:
TravelWeb lets you go online to plan offline expeditions.

- You can access TravelWeb on the WWW at **http://www.TravelWeb.com** and, as a business traveler, see a broad catalog of hotel information. This includes

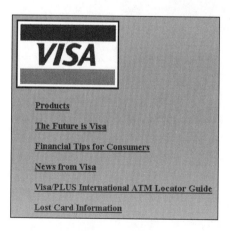

Figure 8-8:
VISA also provides customer services online.

pictures of guest rooms, restaurants, meeting rooms, golf courses, and other amenities. More than 15,000 properties will be covered by the end of 1995.

- By visiting **http://www.visa.com/visa/** you can see more than 232,000 automatic teller machine locations in more than 87 countries.

Southwest Airlines Home Gate

Figure 8-9:
Southwest Airlines promotes specialists at its WWW "home gate."

- Southwest Airlines is promoting its services at **http://www.flyswa.com**. Information on fares and Fun Packs are available.

A closer look at three of these cybermalls—Branch Information Services, the Internet Mall, and Global Network Navigator—shows how some of these resources are being used by small- and medium-sized businesses today.

Branch Information Services

Jon Zeeff, founder of Branch Information Services (**http://www.branch. com**), describes the company's Branch Mall service as a way for organizations that are "technically challenged" to take advantage of the new markets offered by the Internet.

As an example, Farmer Grant's Market Florist and Greenhouse in Ann Arbor, Michigan, sells flowers to customers as far away as Japan. Larry Grant, general manager of the family-owned business, began selling flowers online in early February 1994 and had forty orders for Valentine's Day. By Mother's Day, the company was taking more than forty orders a day because of its Internet visibility. Farmer Grant's has benefited from the Internet with minimal cost and minimal technical knowledge about computers or the Internet.

As of April 1995, Branch Information Services had more than one hundred "storefronts." It reads like an on-screen catalog. The menus include descriptions of services and full-color images of the displaying company's logo and products. Customers place orders online with a few keystrokes or clicks of a computer mouse.

Branch Mall rents a one-page storefront for $480 per year; five pages cost $900 per year. In comparison, large companies like Land's End spend more than $20 million to print and distribute catalogs. Print advertising in major newspapers or magazines can cost several thousand dollars each time an ad is placed, yet the longevity is quite short. Online, customers can continue to reach your message, and modification is as easy as upgrading any software.

Some of the "stores" in the Branch Mall include the following:

- Bonsai Boy of New York, selling Bonsai trees

- Forest Hill Vineyard, selling premium California Chardonnay

- Muscovy Imports, providing contemporary Russian fine art

- Sweeps Vacuum and Repair Center

- Werger Comfortable Clothing

- Nova Videos from WGBH

- Colonel Kernals Gourmet Popcorn

Other Branch Mall merchandise are 1950s' burp guns, international flags, exercise equipment, prepaid telephone calling cards, books, videos, and tuxedos. It's fun just to look at the graphics.

Now, how much are they selling? That's another question, and it's probably too early to answer. One vendor recently reported a single sale of more than $40,000 to a European customer. The success of each individual storefront depends on the degree of planning and preparation that took place prior to opening the store, and on modifications that have taken place since the initiation of services.

The Internet Mall

The Internet Mall (**http://www.mecklerweb.com/imall**), at nearly 2,000 storefronts, claims to be the largest central spot for shopping in cyberspace. (It is more than twice the size of the physical Mall of America in the Minneapolis area!) With dozens of stores in the same department in the mall, it can be difficult for stores to differentiate themselves from their competitors. For this reason, the Internet Mall introduced new advertising and sponsorship approaches. These include two primary options:

- *Internet World* magazine (circulation 175,000+ monthly) offers a special advertising section available only to Internet Mall vendors. Advertising in this popular magazine is a cost-effective way to reach a large audience and attract them to your cyberspace site.

- Sponsor a department, floor, or even the whole mall. The featured sponsor in the Web Mall for March/April 1995 was the Internet Shopping Network. For a fee the Internet Shopping Network got its own business graphic (a hot button) at the top of the Internet Mall home page. Paying companies get their own graphic hot buttons as shortcuts to accessing their storefronts in the standard manner.

Dave Taylor, the proprietor of the Internet Mall, can be reached at **taylor@netcom.com**; the Mall is administered and hosted by MecklerWeb's iWORLD.

Global Network Navigator (GNN)

Established in October 1993 by O'Reilly & Associates and sold in June 1995 to America OnLine, GNN (**http://www.gnn.com**) organizes information accessed through the Internet so that it is more approachable. You might call GNN and its clones an effort to make the Internet less hostile and more "user friendly."

Since its establishment, GNN has captured more than 30,000 registered users, and the numbers continue to grow at a substantial rate.

GNN is offered free of charge to anyone with access to the Internet *and* with WWW capability using Mosaic or Lynx. The service consists of three distinct areas: a travel resource center, personal finance center, and an Internet information center. The travel resource center is an exploration area for those interested in travel. The personal finance center offers resources on such topics as mutual funds, mortgages, and credit card interest rates. The Internet information center contains a wealth of Internet-related resources.

The beauty of these electronic magazines is that you can find increasing levels of detail on topics of interest to you. For example, if you are reading a general article on the Internet and you come across a reference to the NSFnet (the National Science Foundation's network program), you simply click on that underlined phrase to be instantly transported to a file on the NSFnet. It may actually be provided from another server located thousands of miles away, yet it matters little where the information comes from as long as it is timely and useful.

GNN currently has a staff of twenty people who search the Internet for interesting information sources and then create "articles" that are, in essence, guided tours of existing Internet-reachable databases on specific topics of interest.

Dale Dougherty, the creator and driving force behind GNN, expects the service will be profitable through the sale of advertising and possibly by charging subscriptions to users. Already, advertisers like The Lonely Planet, a tour guide publisher, use GNN as part of a comprehensive marketing program. Visitors to the GNN travel resource center see an image of The Lonely Planet's logo. Clicking on the logo gives the user more details on the company's specific guidebooks.

Heller Ehrman White & McAuliffe, another GNN participant, characterizes itself as one of the "nations' fifty largest law firms with a diverse group of clients involved in such industries as biotechnology, medical and health care, computers, software, telecommunications, consumer products, investment banking, international business, and venture capital. The firm has offices in seven major West Coast commercial centers."

By summer 1994, GNN had nearly forty advertisers, including NordicTrack and DEC.

AOL's purchase occurred as this book went to press; it remains to be seen what new enhancements will be added to GNN's many-faceted services.

Transporting Software

Organizations like CommerceNet, MecklerWeb, Branch Information Services, the Internet Shopping Network, and America OnLine's GNN are only the beginning of many entrepreneurial opportunities offered by the information access and services side of the Internet.

Another interesting function is using the Internet to transport software. Many companies, such as Microsoft, IBM, and DEC, have routinely used the Internet to upload revised versions of code for many years.

In fact, one software company had, as a practice, provided software updates to its 4,000-some users by "shrinkwrapping" the updates and shipping them by ground carrier to the customer at a total cost of about $50 each. In essence, every time the company did an update or bug fix, it cost them $200,000!

Now, assuming that the developer accurately estimated its cost of goods sold and established a fair price that covered cost plus margin, there shouldn't be a problem. Two points, however, jumped out: The marketplace was significantly more competitive than when the company started business, and about one-quarter of its customers never unwrapped the software. Perhaps they had discontinued using the original package or were satisfied with the earlier version, but in any case, it was a waste of money for the software firm.

The company subsequently found that at least another quarter of its customers were already connected to the Internet. This led to the decision to establish a server containing the latest software release. Anyone connected to the Internet could access the server and, once authenticated as a paying customer, download the "fix."

Let's look at the economics of this example. The cost to set up the server was about $7,000—mostly for equipment. As a software company, its personnel were already well acquainted with computing environments and servers, so that was no incremental expense. The company already had a 56Kbps connection to the Internet (costing approximately $10,000 per year). By reducing the distribution to those interested, and using the Internet for those that were connected, the company saved an estimated $83,000 ($100,000 minus $7,000 minus $10,000) *every time it issued an update*! If an update is issued three times a year, that equates to more than a quarter of a million dollars!

Furthermore, as the remaining customer base of 2,000 becomes connected to the Internet, this company's savings will continue to grow. The Internet will be directly responsible for a substantial increase in profit margin and, at the same time, a substantial improvement in the quality and immediacy of service to customers.

Specific Business Uses for Servers

Let's look at some other examples of how server technology can benefit your organization.

Ten Business Uses for Servers

- Provide immediate access to your catalog
- Permit customers to place orders electronically
- Reduce costs of goods sold through reduced personnel
- Enhance your sales force's performance at a customer's site
- Use multinational sites to create "around the clock" productivity
- Establish open access servers to provide answers to repetitive inquiries
- Establish an electronic "help desk" for nonemergency requests
- Order books from online publishing sources
- Reap benefits from the Trade Point Programme
- Package "Internet" access into your service offerings

Provide immediate access to your catalog

Do you have a catalog of your products or services? Can customers order by part number or product name? Do they frequently need answers to the same questions?

You can establish on the Internet an electronically accessible catalog that is available to any of the more than 30 million (and growing) users of the network. This can be accomplished in several different ways.

You can provide access to a server (normally a Unix machine, although a Mac or PC works as well). This server can be set up for Gopher, WWW, anonymous ftp, and a variety of other techniques. To put it simply, you create a public access machine that provides a menu-driven, user-friendly method of browsing your catalog and a description of services available wherever the potential customer is—Des Moines, Amsterdam, or even McMurdo Station, Antarctica.

This takes a bit of work to set up. If your staff does not have the required technical background, a variety of consultants can provide assistance on a project basis.

One advantage of this approach, beyond the immediacy of access, is that your customers can place orders on the same connection. They simply move down the menu to a section invites them to place orders and enter the required information. This can be done twenty-four hours a day, seven days a week. You simply fill the order and collect the payment.

That brings us to a possible disadvantage for this method. Unless you are already set up to take credit cards, you can only issue an invoice to or accept a purchase order number from your new customer. You can apply to accept plastic, but this may be too burdensome for a small business. See Chapter Five for information of emerging new ways (First Virtual and DigiCash) to address this challenge.

An alternative to doing the "server thing" yourself is to use someone else's server. An increasing number of Internet access providers and electronic marketplaces will essentially rent you an "electronic storefront." (For specific examples, see The Electronic Marketplace section in this chapter.) The best way to find them is to "surf" the net. Compare their fees and check references from customers.

These organizations generally accept plastic from your customers or have established other methods of payment and will collect the fees for you. At the end of each month (or some other agreed-upon accounting period), they issue you a check for the difference between what you owed for the space rental and the income received. They set up your storefront and maintain the system. You simply provide the information in a usable electronic format.

You can advertise the availability of your services using the electronic marketplace. Browsers to other storefronts will see yours. You can use traditional advertising methods (e.g., magazine or newspapers ads, coverage in news features, or word of mouth). When I produce reports for general availability, I give potential buyers the option of hard copy (including shipping costs) or electronic across the Net. Often people order both. (Now there's a novel way to increase sales!)

In a hotly competitive environment, potential customers—when faced with a tough buying decision—may select the one that is easiest to obtain. Why not make that yours?

Permit customers to place orders electronically

How many people are at your customer order desk? What are your order entry department's business hours?

By establishing an Internet server with an electronic order-entry function, you can have twenty-four-hour-a-day, seven-day-a-week ordering capability. Customers can enter orders through a simple question-and-answer menu.

As a supplement to your existing operation, this is an area worth exploring by companies of all sizes. Consider how you currently take orders today, and evaluate other alternatives that could be more efficient, available whenever your buyers need them, and less personnel-intensive.

Reduce costs of goods
sold through reduced personnel

As with all of the examples in this book, internetworking and the Internet are not solutions or replacements for all forms of business communications. They are, however, viable business alternatives to consider.

Reducing the costs of goods sold through reduced personnel requirements can be a very viable strategy. For the small entrepreneurial company that does not have the luxury of a robust inside sales organization, this technique can be very important. For the large firm that employs hundreds of inside salespeople, this could have a significant impact by either reducing the number of people needed to take orders or increasing the volume of orders without a commensurate expansion of sales personnel.

Remember, reducing costs of goods sold can have a more immediate and significant impact than increasing sales. Reducing expenses by $100,000 directly enhances the bottom line. Increasing sales by $100,000 with a 10 percent profit margin only accrues a $10,000 advantage. Networking technology can address both cost reduction and revenue enhancement.

Enhance your sales force's
performance at a customer's site

The Trane Company, a subsidiary of American Standard Corporation, is one of the world's leading manufacturers of large-scale air-conditioning systems. Trane has found that internetworking and use of the Internet is likely to have a substantial impact on its sales force's performance.

The two driving "applications" for Trane when the company considered replacing its large distributed synchronous network architecture (SNA, the IBM standard for data communications) network were product configuration and order entry. Both are critically important in the sales cycle and directly impact the company's capability to accrue revenues.

Product configuration is the process whereby a sales engineer evaluates different equipment that might satisfy a potential customer's needs and then develops a proposal for that customer. Having this information readily available on a server lets the sales engineer use a remote connection across the Internet, potentially from the client's premises (perhaps using wireless to connect into an Internet dial-access point), and deliver a firm quotation in a matter of moments.

The impact on the sales process can be substantial. Potential buyers have everything that they need to make a decision, including shipment dates, delivery and installation dates, and final pricing. This enables Trane's representatives to more effectively close the sale.

Order entry permits the sales engineer to pass the order directly into the business unit for immediate processing. This, in turn, shortens the delivery cycle and speeds the accounts payable timeframe. The sooner the product is ordered, the sooner it is delivered, and the faster the payment is received. Consider the impact on your business if your accounts receivable were deposited in 50 percent less time. The incentives can be substantial.

Why would a company like Trane, a subsidiary of a Fortune 200 company, submit to this Herculean effort without a clearly defined revenue or expense payback? Why put employees through the turmoil of a major overhaul without any apparent crisis? Why use the Internet as a communications vehicle, rather than the proven services of a major provider?

"The fundamental reason," according to John Severson, vice president of business transformation, "is to get out ahead. We know that our competitors are not sitting on their hands." As business changes from regional to national and now to a global environment, taking every advantage offered by enhanced communications techniques becomes a survival issue. A company the size of Trane cannot afford to wait until its competitors have implemented new information flow systems.

Why do we need this network today? We don't know for sure. We do know that we are building a highway—an interstate—for graphics and business documents.

If Trane can identify a customer's requirements, complete all of the needed internal processes, and deliver a finished $100,000-to-$1 million system to the customer's site within one to six days, and its competition takes three times as long or longer, how much impact will that have on the corporate bottom line? Whatever the answer, it will be well worth the investment made thus far. As a leader in business transformation, Trane's competitors have two choices: Watch to see whether Trane falls on its face, or be two to three *years* behind and play catch-up if Trane's programs succeed.

Consider the effectiveness of you or your sales organization if you had access to critical information, presentation materials, or PC-based videos of your technical experts while you make your "big pitch" to an important prospect. This is one more tool in the sales and marketing battlefield.

Use multinational sites to create "around-the-clock" productivity

An attorney in Toronto is quite proud of how his organization uses its offices in London to operate almost around the clock.

On an important project, the U.K. office will begin work at 9 a.m. They might work on the project until closing time—approximately 5 p.m. At that point, the Toronto office will pick up the efforts early in the afternoon Toronto time. At the end of the day, they return their work to the corporate server so that the London staff can pick up the task again when they return.

The attorney's competition has not yet figured out how his company is working eighteen hour days. Imagine adding a Far East office (such as Hong Kong or Tokyo) and now you truly could keep an important project going twenty-four hours a day.

Establish open access servers to provide answers to repetitive inquiries

In addition to answering employees' questions about training, companies must answer frequent and repetitive inquiries from potential customers, existing customers, suppliers, and service providers.

By establishing an online server with a graphical or menu-driven interface, frequently asked questions (FAQs) can be addressed without costly human intervention. A "real person" can be contacted subsequent to the inquiry. In many ways, this permits you to get needed information into the proper hands quickly, efficiently, and without the modern nuisances of telephone tag, automated telephone attendants, or less-than-knowledgeable personnel. You can determine the degree of technical depth required, then let the inquirer navigate through your database using Gopher, WWW, or other emerging tools.

In short, people get what they need. You can economize on personnel requirements. And the server never gets frustrated, surly, or takes a vacation!

Establish an electronic "help desk" for nonemergency requests

As the business world becomes increasingly competitive and international, high-quality, responsive customer service is more and more critical.

Personnel assigned to help customers through those small but annoying steps are your company's image to your entire customer base. Yet, except for larger organizations, it isn't likely that staff is available twenty-four hours per day. If an inquiry is not an emergency, how do you provide the best possible support in the timeliest fashion?

One way is to establish an e-mail "help" center (i.e., **help@maloff.com**). Anytime, day or night, your customers can send an inquiry to the help desk, knowing they will receive a helpful response within twelve to twenty-four hours, depending on the complexity of the question.

If you have an existing help desk that normally takes inquiries over the telephone or through letters, this step is an easy one. Your systems administrator can set up an appropriate "help" e-mail address and ensure that the proper staff receive its messages. This should include not only those responsible for responding but also management, so you can keep in tune with your customer's concerns.

Last, you need to ensure that your personnel are trained in how to respond to these inquiries, and that they have a clear understanding of how frequently they need to log into the help line and how quickly they must respond. Training and clear policies are critical to the success of this function.

Order books from online publishing sources

One of the advantages of the Internet is the readiness of written material. Many organizations offer online textbooks, magazines, and other material traditionally available only in print. For example, Mecklermedia offers full text of *Internet World* back issues and teasers of current and forthcoming issues on its MecklerWeb's iWORLD site.

Laura Fillmore is the driving force behind the On-Line Bookstore. With a background in traditional print publishing, Fillmore recognized the opportunities afforded by the Internet, and now actively seeks authors to publish electronically.

As consumers of materials, we now can traverse the network electronically, browse information, and pay for what we want to use.

Many issues are still being resolved. For example, what happens to copyrights? How does an author and/or publisher protect against unauthorized use? These issues are receiving a great deal of attention, and I have full confidence that they will be addressed satisfactorily to all concerned. I also believe that the ability to publish electronically is important both to producers of the intellectual property and to consumers.

Few small businesses and even fewer schoolchildren can purchase scanners to digitize documents. This means important data must be rekeyed into research reports or term papers. If the documents, magazines, or book chapters were available electronically—for a fee—data could be reused with ease.

Reap benefits from the Trade Point Programme

Business is no longer confined to a single city, state or province, country, or even continent. Most businesses today are beginning to function on a global level.

An interesting program has emerged from the United Nations, whereby the Internet will be used to link more than fifty countries for the purpose of accelerating international trade. These servers will provide information specific to the country, such as customs regulations, and perhaps more detailed information, including the names of prospective freight forwarding agents or legal counselors.

By identifying target areas of importance, your organization can use the network as a way to evaluate opportunities, open contacts, negotiate agreements, and conduct business.

Package Internet access into your service offerings

What is the nature of your core business? Does it involve or rely on the communication of information? If so, you might be able to incorporate internetworking into your product and service lines as a new benefit for your customers and a new source of revenue for you.

A computer-aided design (CAD) and computer-aided manufacturing (CAM) software developer explored offering Internet access as part of its software. Customers purchase the software for many different facilities, yet find that these locations are "islands." By establishing an easy-to-use Internet link, each site can interact with others, thus enhancing efficiency. The customer wins, and so does the software company.

Another example of incorporating Internet access as an adjunct offering comes from the information providers industry. Traditional information providers like Delphi, America OnLine, Prodigy, and CompuServe offer full Internet access for dial-up connectivity.

Any organization with a reasonably large existing customer base and a business driven by intercommunication may do well to become an IAP—but in their specific industry niche and area of expertise.

Your organization can become a niche-oriented IAP in one of two ways: by establishing your own Internet nodes, management capabilities, and engineering teams; or by establishing an original equipment manufacturer (OEM) relationship with another provider whereby you use their service under your private label and leverage their existing infrastructure.

The first option is costly and, in all likelihood puts you into an entirely different line of business. The second option permits you to establish an arrangement with Sprint, Alternet, PSI, MCI, or any other existing provider that serves the areas you require. You could call the new service "Joe's CAD/CAM with Internet Service," despite the fact that Sprint takes the order from your team to implement the Internet access services.

If this is of interest to you, explore the possibilities with several potential Internet providers and see if you can establish a positive, forward-thinking business relationship.

Host live discussions in your own private meeting hall

Prospero Systems, a San Francisco-based company, developed Global Stage, the world's first commercial chat system that lets organizations host live discussions within their own private virtual meeting hall on the Internet. With Global Stage software, organizations can invite guests to chat with a virtual Internet audience of up to 1,000 people worldwide, bypassing current commercial online services.

Previously, organizations wanting to hold real-time discussions have gone through providers like America OnLine, Prodigy, and CompuServe. Using Global Stage, organizations can produce their own forums and chats on the Internet. Information and directions for online registration are available by e-mail to **jcarey@prospero.com** and on the WWW at **http://www.prospero.com/ globalstage/**.

Figure 8-10:
Globle Stage enables private online conferences via the Internet.

Global Stage could be used for large, open online events—including virtual town hall meetings, press conferences with international newsmakers, and discussions with entertainers and creative artists. Early users of the service include book, newspaper, and magazine publishers who selected the Global Stage to communicate directly with their readers. Hosting live interactions between writers, subscribers, and special guests is one of the best ways to promote publications and build a loyal online community.

To provide the option of selling tickets for access to high-demand Internet events and community fundraisers, Global Stage has a built-in event box office fully integrated with the First Virtual Internet Payment System. This system was created specifically to enable buying and selling of Internet information without encryption or requiring additional software or hardware. With Global Stage's enabled password authentication, event producers can control access or participation to live "members-only" special events.

During Prospero's beta period, event producers paid an hourly fee of $195 for access to the Prospero server operated jointly with GeoNet Communications of Palo Alto, California. Fully licensed turnkey systems became available in June 1995.

Another similar offering, Co-motion Lite, comes from Bittco Solutions. This software, designed for Macintosh users, allows participation on the Internet in real-time, multiuser group discussions. Users connect through the Internet to a host where, in a session window, they can immediately add, react, or respond to comments.

Co-Motion Lite requires a Serial Link Internetworking Protocol or Point to Point Protocol Internet connection. A Windows version is under development. Additional information can be obtained at **bittco@ccinet.ab.ca** or (403) 922-5514.

Conclusion

As you can see, servers offer tremendous opportunities. From cybermalls to global private meetings, the potential for entrepreneurs and businesses abounds. Explore and evaluate them carefully! This includes exploring all of the roles that a server might play for you and your organization. Regardless of what you do in cyberspace, any actions that can be attributed to you or your organization are part of your online image-creation process. This means that it is essential for you to carefully plan before implementation begins! Think of your cyber presence as a trade show exhibit. Are you interested in simply building or enhancing your image, generating leads, or actually closing business on the spot? Set your expectations clearly. We will discuss the various methods of obtaining these services—either by bringing them in-house or by outsourcing them—later in this book. For now, consider the different ways that your business might benefit from the use of server resources.

*C*hapter *Nine*

DATA, DATA EVERYWHERE, AND NOT A BYTE TO EAT!

Information resources come in all shapes and sizes: free, fee-based, company-provided, government-provided, open discussion groups, news forums, and many more. Figuring out what out there can directly benefit your organization is another issue.

This chapter looks at a variety of information sources, with specific examples of how these have been applied in a business context.

Outsourcing Internet Information Searches

Many companies are overwhelmed when presented with the vast amount of information available through the Internet. And many companies would rather not invest the time in learning how to conduct in-depth searches.

In this case, many companies can do the work for you. These organizations offer private intelligence-gathering services to governments, organizations, companies, and individuals.

- Open Source Solutions, Inc., based in Oakton, Virginia, collects and analyzes open source data as an effort to boost national security efforts and economic performance.

- Mary-Ellen Bates is a Washington, D.C.-based information broker, charging between $500 and $1,500 for an online search, seeking information on issues as diverse as Bosnia or the paper products industry.

- Psytep Corporation (Corpus Christi, Texas) offers both open source and customized investigations.

- Larger companies include specialized consulting services from FIND/SVP in New York and BDM Federal. FIND/SVP claims to have more than one hundred subject experts who have access to more than 3,000 online publications, 12,000 subject files, and 17 affiliated companies worldwide, enabling them to offer rapid-response intelligence to decision makers.

On today's Internet, however, offers a variety of tools are at your disposal. Users with a graphical interface, such as Mosaic, Netscape, Cello, or one of the new WWW capable browsers like those in IBM's OS/2 Warp or Windows 95, should try tools like the WebCrawler, EINet Galaxy, or the CUI W3 Catalog.

My current favorite is Yahoo. Each of these tools has different capabilities based on the resources they "know." For example, I conducted a search for the word "insurance" and found six hits on one tool and 216 on another. Try the different tools and see which work best for you.

You can access these tools through the WWW as follows:

- CUI W3 Catalog: **http://cui_www.unige.ch/w3catalog**

- WebCrawler: **http://www.biotech.washington.edu/webcrawler/ webquery.html**

- EINet Galaxy: **http://www.einet.net/galaxy.html**
- Yahoo: **http://www.yahoo.com**

Access to Rare Manuscripts

In 1994, Xerox and Ernst & Young began a project to scan, image, and electronically store priceless manuscripts that have been locked away from the public in the Gregorian University and its Pontifical Library in Rome. The nine-million-volume library had no previous automation. Online access to the library image database via the Internet is expected to be available in the near future.

Xerox's Documents on Demand equipment and software will allow books to be "reprinted" as they are requested from the library, with bound reprints costing approximately $14.

Similarly, scholars have been using the Internet for more than a year to examine portions of the Dead Sea scrolls.

For writers, publishers, or others interested in conducting research in these areas, the Internet offers an easier way to explore ancient information and use machine-readable versions of the information than scanning or rekeying the data manually. It may not be as enjoyable as a trip to Rome or Jerusalem, but it is considerably more convenient and cost-effective.

Developing Internal Network Use Policies

A major challenge to many large businesses considering implementing wide-scale internal networks as well as internetworking is how to set up and distribute meaningful guidelines for employee use. A national computer ethics and responsibilities campaign was launched. The program, initially chaired by Peter Tippett, director of security products at Symantec Corporation (Cupertino, California), is designed to foster communications about the issues and to effect changes over the next decade. The group plans to create an electronic repository of information resources, training materials, and samples of ethics codes. It will also tackle such sticky issues as what constitutes plagiarism on the Internet.

These resources, to be accessible via servers on the Internet, should assist managers attempting to devise internal policies on subjects ranging from customer privacy to the confidentiality of corporate electronic mail (e-mail). The information is intended to help managers make responsible use of information technology, but is not intended to endorse legislation or to judge right or wrong.

The campaign's principal sponsor is the Computer Ethics Institute (Washington, D.C.). Other sponsors include the Software Publishers Association, CompuServe, and the National Computer Security Association. Corporate sponsors include Merrill Lynch and Monsanto Corporation.

Use the Network to Gather Information for Strategic Analysis and Planning

Are you considering offering a new product, entering a new market, trying a new strategy or tactic? If so, you will need to gather information for your analysis and planning. How are you going to do that? Are you going to spend days at the library scanning lots of magazines and books? The Internet provides a wealth of resources that might be of assistance.

By using a Wide Area Information Server (WAIS), you can do a keyword search to narrow down your search to a few sets of resources. You can use Gopher and the WWW search tools described in Chapter Two to find other resources on the network. You'll be amazed at what you find! Many new Internet browsers, like Netscape, build these search tools directly into the interface, making it easier for you to be successful in your searches immediately.

Prepare Materials for Meetings with Input from Many Distributed Sites

Every organization has its share of important meetings (the board of directors, annual shareholder's meetings, key sales meetings, financial audits, etc.). How do you currently prepare for these?

If your organization is like most others, you scramble around at the last minute putting together a final agenda, identifying who will speak, and preparing pre-meeting mailings and handouts for the meeting. Often, the people and resources you need for these preparations are remote. These last-minute efforts often entail costly overnight shipping or even travel to finalize the arrangements.

The ability to transfer information electronically can cut down on much of the last-minute panic. Establishing a server as the central repository of information can be very useful. Everyone who has a commitment to completing a task must upload their contributions to the server so the presentation can be viewed as a whole by anyone—especially those responsible for coordinating the events. In this way, everyone involved—and authorized—can see the entire project and feel more a part of a team effort.

Additionally, there may be a need to prepare supportive documentation for your meeting. For example, how have your competitors positioned themselves in the marketplace? Or, if you're meeting with potential investors, how are your services viewed by your customers or clients?

You can use the Internet to gather these types of information. Using information tools, such as Gopher, WAIS, or WWW, you can conduct a keyword search for areas of interest to you and the important participants at your meeting. Such a search can turn up information from news releases, comments in discussion groups, or articles published on topics that concern your group.

Another way to gather information in a more passive manner is establishing a public server providing your information (press releases, brochures, white papers, maps, technical drawings) to other people. You could also establish an electronic user group so your customers can interact using e-mail, exchange thoughts, and swap suggestions pertaining to your products and services. By monitoring the traffic on these servers, you can quickly gauge how well or poorly your customers think of you. You could also identify the number of inquiries and determine what percentage of them you can convert into sales.

All of this information is invaluable as you prepare to meet with managers, owners, shareholders, or potential investors. The information may already be at your fingertips!

Gather Information for Repackaging and Sale

Many organizations are using information found on the Internet as a saleable product.

For example, Walnut Creek CDROM, founded by Bob Bruce in late 1991, was built on the concept that the Internet offers a large amount of valuable information, but is difficult for most people to reach. The company took that wealth of software and made it accessible by placing it on CD-ROM. Today, Walnut Creek CDROM operates out of Concord, California. It employs sixteen people and has produced more than thirty-five CD-ROMs.

A typical Walnut Creek disc might contain several thousand small programs (freeware) that others created and made available through various servers across the Internet. Walnut Creek does the legwork; its customers pay about $35 for the CD-ROM. What they are buying is convenience.

Walnut Creek then uses the Internet as part of its publicity campaign, posting announcements of new CD-ROMs on appropriate newsgroups and mail reflectors. In this way, it can sell CDs anywhere in the world.

Obtain Access to Security and Exchange Commission Filings

Arguably the most valuable collection of financial data in the world, the electronic filings of the U.S. Security and Exchange Commission (SEC) are now available across the Internet.

The SEC's Electronic Data Gathering and Retrieval program (EDGAR) currently contains information on several thousand companies. By 1996, it should include all SEC-regulated organizations (15,000 companies as of mid-1994).

EDGAR contains annual reports, proxy statements, and other important documents. A document downloaded using the Internet may cost a few dollars at most, while a paper copy could cost more than $50.

EDGAR information is available for a fee through Mead Data Central, Disclosure, and Dow Jones. As of February 1994, it became accessible free of charge to Internet users (although fees are charged for downloading documents).

Conclusion

The Internet has the ability to provide you with access to billions of bytes of data. Unless that data comes in the form of usable information, however, it is not of much value to you. Whether it is stock market information from EDGAR, items that you have repackaged for sale on CD-ROM, strategic planning information for a new product, or components for a presentation to your Board of Directors, the Internet may have information that could be invaluable to you. Take your time to explore the alleyways, nooks, and crannies that this wonderful shared information utility offers. Only then can you determine if there are "bytes" for you to consume!

*C*hapter Ten

HORSEPOWER!

HORSEPOWER!

HORSEPOWER!

Information has become so prevalent today that we can drown in a sea of data or go out of business because we could not easily access the information we needed in a timely fashion. Office computing power has grown dramatically over the past ten years. The power that was once available only on large mainframe computing systems now resides in notebook PCs; supercomputers, which were once measured in MIPS (millions of instructions per second) are now viewed in terms of teraFLOPS (trillions of floating operations points per second).

How do you obtain the computing power that you need at every location, yet maintain control of costs? It isn't practical to have Unix workstations on every employee's desk, nor is it appropriate to have Thinking Machines or Cray super-computers at every production facility.

Rural medical facilities, for instance, will not necessarily have the latest medical imaging, and perhaps they need not have them in all cases. Through the use of internetworking, these resources can be accessed remotely.

These expensive resources are referred to as "rare, remote devices." By the use of internetworking, equipment can be shared and leveraged over great distances. This by no means eliminates the need to invest in these devices. Rather, it gives you the capability to use them more efficiently and have access to them in locations where you might otherwise be forced to do without.

This chapter explores examples of internetworking to reach rare, remote devices. Although most of these examples deal with medical applications, there are many other business uses as well. Consider the need for a distributed computing environment where your files are spread across the world. You can use the Internet to access intelligence in Singapore or London rather than duplicating it at every site. You can even print remotely at a distant site.

Within your organization, there are likely applications from this category. Before you implement redundant repositories, consider the Internet alternatives. Before you concede that a particular resource is too expensive for outlying locations, consider the online alternatives.

Physician Access to the Antibiotic Computer Consultant

The variables involved in prescribing a specific treatment for a patient by a physician can be enormous. Considerations include the patient's medical history, possible bacteria, the least expensive yet adequately effective drug, proper dosage, and possible drug interactions.

To address this problem, Latter Day Saints (LDS) Hospital in Salt Lake City, Utah has built one of the most complex artificial intelligence systems ever conceived for clinical decision making. Running on a Tandem Computer fault-tolerant mainframe, this expert system is part of a hospital-wide information system called Health Evaluation through Logical Processing (HELP).

According to a study published in the *Archives of Internal Medicine* (April 25, 1994), physicians using the antibiotic consultant made better, faster decisions. Unaided, the physicians suggested the best possible treatment 77 percent of the time; assisted, this rate improved to 94 percent. Despite their notorious dislike for computing systems, doctors use this one an average of three times per day. Of the physicians surveyed 88 percent said they would recommend the program to others, 85 percent agreed that the program improved their antibiotic selections, and 81 percent admitted that it improved patient care.

By having networked access to systems such as HELP from remote clinics, other hospitals, or from physician's offices, real-time intervention can occur with a higher degree of accuracy and likelier success. This can be accomplished through the use of various internetworking techniques, including the Internet.

Transport of Medical Images via the Internet

NexSys, the brainchild of Dr. Peter Killcommons in San Francisco, is a subscription-based medical data network reachable via the Internet. By mid-1994, NexSys linked twenty hospitals and medical centers to the Internet.

Functionally, physicians transmit X-rays, magnetic resonance images, or CAT scans to any other medical facilities in the world that can receive them. For this kind of application to be effective, the distant ends must also have sufficient levels of connectivity into the Internet. Chapter Fourteen discusses how to determine the size of the "pipe" that you need into the Internet "cloud."

Provide Remote Computing Diagnostics and Consulting Services

EDI Strategic Services (Medford, Oregon) is a small business consulting firm. Its consultants work from their homes, dial into EDI's Unix-based system, and then telnet to a client location in California or other remote locations to conduct the required work. All of this is accomplished without disrupting the client's day-to-day environment, incurring costly long-distance telephone charges, or the expense of physically traveling to the client's sites.

EDI has a dedicated 56Kbps connection into the Internet, costing them approximately $621 per month. This enables the consultants to reach nearly anywhere on the Internet for a flat monthly fee. The more they use it, the greater the financial benefit in displaced costs.

Conclusion

The need for access to greater computing horsepower is not likely to slow anytime soon. As we have seen, medical imaging systems will increasingly be used by remote physicians. Business people will access information stored in company servers located thousands of miles away. Business-to-business commerce using EDI will increasingly use the Internet as its economical worldwide distribution mechanism. During the summer of 1995, Premenos Corporation (Concord, California), one of the leading EDI software vendors, introduced Templar—a suite of software and services that sits between electronic mail and EDI applications allowing for transfer of information via the Internet. More information is available at **http://www.premenos.com**.

I expect to see many new ways introduced for people to take advantage of remote resources. EDI, medical imaging, and remote client server access are but a few. See if you can identify remote resources that are important to you. Do you ship or receive computer tapes from remote sites? Do you send complex documents via courier? In the not-too-distant future, you may very well be able to handle these communications tasks in an efficient, secure way via Internet! Keep your eyes open.

Part Three

Issues to Consider When Acquiring Internet Services

*C*hapter *Eleven*

UNDERSTANDING

YOUR

REQUIREMENTS

Prior to acquiring internetworking capabilities, it is critical for organizations to understand the issues they are attempting to address within their own companies (reduction of costs, increased effectiveness of the field sales force, and so forth).

Chapter Three discussed some opportunities for using the Internet to enhance your organization's bottom line. This chapter will assist you in continuing the evaluation process by illustrating the costs and effort required to implement Internet services within an organization, as well as some of the "hidden" issues that often impact the success or failure of these efforts.

Once it appears that the Internet or internetworking might be of benefit, you need to determine precisely what that means, as it relates to services from an Internet access provider (IAP).

- Does your organization need a few shell accounts for your salespeople?

- Does it need a dial-up local area network (LAN) connection?

- Do you need dedicated access, and if so, at what bandwidth—56Kbps, T-1, 10 Mbps?

- Are the requirements the same or different in each of your facilities? What about connectivity to suppliers and key customers?

- For which applications do you expect to use these new services (bank rate information, legal services, as a marketing tool, etc.)?

- How much throughput will you need?

- How mission-critical is the data?

- Are you looking to establish a true connection to the Internet?

- Are you interested primarily in access to a select set of your own facilities, customers, or suppliers?

By understanding the nature of the data you want to exchange, you can begin to identify the type of Internet connections that will serve your needs. This may sound difficult, but it really isn't if you know what to look for and where to start.

How many pages do you need to send or receive each day? What is the size of the files that will be uploaded or downloaded? How often do these events occur? How many people are engaged in these activities from the same location?

By assembling this information, you have taken the first steps toward "traffic engineering" your Internet access requirements. At this point, you need to answer an important question: Do you have the technical expertise to design and operate a wide area network (WAN) solution, or do you need to consider outsourcing?

If you or others in your organization can assimilate the anticipated usage information and identify a starting point for Internet access services, you are fortunate and well on your way to enjoying the benefits that the Internet offers. On the other hand, if your organization does not contain this expertise, you may want to hire a consultant to conduct the design work.

A good network engineer who is familiar with the Internet can use the data on prospective usage to design the most cost-effective solution for you in much less time than it will take for you to learn it yourself. Chapter Twelve discusses the selection of Internet access vendors. Chapter Fourteen describes how to compare various service providers and make the best initial procurement of Internet services. It may also prove more cost-effective to use a consultant in this selection process, as the number and quality of Internet service providers continue to change at a dizzying pace.

If you need dial-up accounts or relatively low levels of connectivity serving a limited number of people, the choices are not complex. Alternately, if you want to serve multiple sites with more than a few people using resources in each site, other factors will come into play.

Do you have a network operations center that can handle this new functionality?

Your IAP will probably not monitor the status of servers or portions of your network beyond the router that interfaces with its network. For dedicated access services, this is traditionally the point of demarcation between what the provider will address and what is your responsibility.

How will you maintain the integrity of the networks internal to your organization? Do you have staff personnel with available time for this added task, or should you hire additional employees to perform a network operations center (NOC) function? This job may require some portion of a full-time employee's as well as additional hardware and software monitoring tools, both causing you to incur costs.

In addition, you may want personnel within your organization to perform a help desk or internal librarian role. The Internet is a vast sea of information, resources, possibilities, and barrier reefs. Knowing how to navigate, where to find information, and how to help others—acting as your company's "institutional memory"—can be a tremendous time-saver and can help to minimize frustration by new users. This, in turn, will help you gain better use of the resources and better return on your Internet investment.

Another major potential issue must be addressed: How critical is the security of your on-site computing systems? Do you have an internal corporate security policy? Do you have a network security policy?

Because of its early roots in research, education, and government, most of the initial business users of the Internet were driven by research, engineering, and computing, and came from industries affiliated with the hard sciences (chemical firms, pharmaceutical companies, petroleum producers, etc.).

As the commercial nature of the Internet has evolved, there has been a tremendous burst of interest from a variety of industries, especially finance and services. Finance and service organizations move a large amount of information and are constantly searching for ways to do so more efficiently and cost-effectively.

A good example of this exploration, albeit a cautious one, comes from the securities industry. At the summer 1994 annual Securities Industry Association Information Management conference, in New York City, use of the Internet and the Information Superhighway were the major themes. Many of the leading investment firms, including Goldman, Sachs and Prudential Securities, had already implemented enterprise-wide networks capable of supporting the Internet.

One of the major concerns, however, was the need for effective security measures. This is to be expected from an industry that has historically protected its proprietary corporate information in an ironclad fashion. Yet despite these concerns, securities firms believe the Internet offers a significant marketplace. "We haven't even scratched the surface in reaching customers in today's world," said Bernard O'Neill, a first vice president at Prudential Securities.

The Internet may seem a bit anarchic and threatening, yet businesses are beginning to recognize that these issues can be acceptably addressed.

Internet Security Concerns

The Internet offers access to the most widespread sources of information, people, and remote devices. These resources can be accessed as easily from around the world as from the next room. The beauty of the Internet is that the estimated 25 million "participants" can reach almost anywhere they want. The danger is that there are many whom you do not want to reach your critical intellectual property.

For corporations to become consumers of Internet services on a regular and mission-critical basis, the issues of network security and confidentiality—whether on the Internet or in a corporate network environment—must be addressed.

The greatest threat to a company's computing resources comes not from a stranger but rather from ex-employees or disgruntled employees who know precisely where and how to do the most damage. And, as the network grows and becomes ubiquitous, the number of intruders who break in for the thrill may be replaced quickly by professional spies—corporate or otherwise.

It is critical that corporations understand the security exposures they face and plan for them, and also that they find appropriate tools to implement their security programs.

Fear of Internet security intrusions and industrial espionage continues to grow. In early 1994, "sniffers" were reportedly used on the Internet to capture hundreds of user pass codes. One estimate indicates that more than 1.2 million computers were broken into between 1990 and 1994.

Some of the vulnerabilities that might be exploited to compromise corporate network security are described below.

Open doors

Even before you enter the world of WANs and the Internet, it is important to assess the security of your local network environment. A 1994 survey by Intrusion Detection, Inc., a New York-based software and consulting firm, indicated that out of 35,250 local network users at medium to large companies, nearly 25 percent had no pass codes or easily guessed codes, and 90 percent changed their pass codes infrequently. Law firms were among the weakest industries in terms of local network security, whereas banks and financial institutions seemed much more sensitive to the issue and have addressed it.

Exploitation of known "bugs"

One of the major methods of breaching security—even with the presence of a "firewall"—is to exploit known flaws in computer server software. Since many of the servers today are operating on Unix, this tends to be a major focus point.

In 1994, a security hole in the IBM AIX Unix operating system was discovered in Germany and widely reported across the Internet. The vulnerability allowed remote users to obtain unauthorized root access on AIX hosts, essentially giving them unlimited access to the machines as if they were the primary systems operator. The same flaw also exists in Linux—PC-based Unix freeware available on the Internet. The Computer Emergency Response Team (CERT) is actively working with users to address the problem, while IBM works to fix the hole from its end.

Before you tackle the challenge of Internet security, you need to understand your status quo. As you move into a WAN environment, it is critical that you know your vulnerabilities. This assesment begins with the clear development of your internal network security plan.

Do you have an internal security plan? This may sound like a simple question, but let's explore it for a moment. Do your employees know your facility's office hours? What about off-hours? Who is permitted in the building, when, and under whose authority?

These may seem like intuitive questions, and you expect everyone to know the answers; yet if they are not clearly articulated, an inadvertant breach could occur and be unpleasant for all concerned. It is important to clearly communicate your expectations to your employees—and to your customers or suppliers as well.

Now, let's look at your internal network security plan before we even consider the Internet. Do you have one? Is it written and distributed to anyone who might use your existing network resources? What does it cover? Does it stipulate that pass codes for modems should contain alphanumeric, non-alphabetic, or mixed-case words? Does it indicate words that should not be used as pass codes? How often should the codes be changed? Who is authorized to use your modems, both incoming and outbound?

As you can see, much thought should occur even without considering external network connectivity like that afforded by the Internet. If you do not have a clearly articulated, written set of usage policies for your computing and network resources, take the time to build one. It will certainly give you greater peace of mind to know that your employees are aware of your wishes, and it will probably save you from trauma caused by unintentional breaches of policy.

Developing an external network security policy that covers use of the Internet takes even more time, but it is well worth the effort.

Current Security Tools

Within the networking environment, a variety of tools can be used to implement a security plan. These tools, when used in conjunction with other reasonable security practices, can provide an "acceptably secure" network environment in most cases.

The fees that consumers are willing to spend on these resources are determined by the degree to which they identify their exposure. For example, if a company is primarily interested in protecting electronic mail (e-mail) from interception, a $20,000 per year expenditure may seem outrageous. Alternately, if they are protecting a $3 million accounts receivables database, $20,000 is a bargain.

Surprisingly few companies of any size appear to have a clearly thought-out and well-articulated network security plan that is distributed to key employees. This makes the sale of high-level but costly systems more difficult. Over the next one to three years this should change as network professionals and senior management become more attuned to both the opportunities and exposures represented by wide area networking.

Once a security plan is developed, a variety of tools can be used to implement these plans. They include the following:

- LAN encryption and security tools

- route and packet filtering

- firewalls

- applications layer gateways

- specialized encryption gateways

- adjunct services
    —"secure user interfaces," i.e., Secure Mosaic
    —public key cryptography
    —"smart cards"

The following sections describe each tool's strengths and weaknesses and summarize the major vendors in each category.

LAN encryption and security tools

Many LAN or communications software packages come with encryption and security features. Perhaps the most common are password or security codes. These can work reasonably well if they include non-alphabetical or numeric characters, support mixed case, and are changed relatively frequently.

Unfortunately, this is rarely the case. Codes can be inadvertently displayed in public or they can be intercepted by sophisticated hackers. From an external security perspective, pass codes are a very thin barrier and must be accompanied by other, more stringent measures.

Within most LAN or networking software packages are encryption tools. Companies offering Transmission Control Protocol/Internet Protocol (TCP/IP) software such as Morningstar, ftp, and others, accommodate encryption. This takes considerable maintenance and management by network operations personnel, and it has not proven very effective or been widely accepted as a prime feature of defense.

Although LAN encryption and security tools are inexpensive from an incremental cost viewpoint, they may prove much more expensive when you consider required personnel costs.

Route and packet filtering

Within an internetworked environment, there is a need for a physical piece of equipment (a router) at each site to communicate with other routers across the network. These routers inform each other about the resources and users in each local network that they serve and act as the "traffic cops," directing the flow of information.

It is possible to configure the routers so that certain types of packets (i.e., ftp or telnet) are blocked from either incoming or outbound access. Additionally, certain routes can be enabled or disabled. For example, you may want to receive communication only from certain network addresses. The routers can be configured to do this.

What happens if someone uses a machine from an authorized site but actually is an unauthorized user? They will likely get through. Furthermore, it is possible to use the network to access an acceptable site and continue through it to your destination, all the while appearing as if you were authorized. This is called "spoofing."

Also, route and packet filtering require significant administration. Every time you change the definition of acceptable, you must make entries in all of the affected routers. The changes are universal for your site, meaning that all users have the same access to sites. There are no individual "classes of service."

Route and packet filtering are generally used in organizations with very good technical staff who have the knowledge and time to administer them. As part of a complete network security plan, however, their usefulness seems questionable and will likely be supplanted by more sophisticated tools.

Lastly, routers are not designed to provide a security audit trail. You will not know who tried to break into your system, by what means, or how often. These are important considerations in strengthening your security plans.

Firewalls

The standard view of a firewall consists of a router interfacing with the outside network and connected to a stand-alone workstation, which is then connected on the other side to another router that interfaces with the internal network. The routers on each side use some degree of packet or route screening and use the Unix host to add customizable remote audit logging of security and other related data.

There are several concerns with this type of security deployment. First, three units of hardware are involved, which introduces a real cost ($15,000 is not unreasonable) and multiple points of failure. Second, the software required to implement the Unix workstation may be "home grown" or purchased from a company like Trusted Information Systems (they offer the Internet Firewall Toolkit software).

In either case, firewalls are still relatively primitive and not immune to spoofing. They are a more substantial roadblock to intruders but not a permanent solution to the network security challenge.

Applications layer gateways

Applications layer gateways (ALG) are built on the concept of a "bastion host" serving as a network strong point. Typically, a bastion host or applications layer gateway acts as a point of strict security enforcement, and contains few or no user accounts. The ALG absorbs the risks that would otherwise threaten an entire network.

The ALG does not export any information about its internal networks to the outside world. The only local host to which outside machines can connect is the ALG, and the only outside host that internal machines can traverse to the outside world is the ALG. In this way, there is never a connection from any outside machine to any inside machine except via the ALG.

The ALG acts as the sentry to the local environment, offering classes of service for different levels of users. The classifications can include time of day, day of week, type of services (ftp, e-mail, inbound only, outbound only, etc.), or management level.

Examples of ALG services include the following:

- *ANS CO+RE's InterLock.* Pricing for this service ranges from a minimum of $12,000 to more than $20,000 per year, depending on services offered. Optional services include XWindows, encryption, and Security Dynamics' Smart Card. InterLock is available only as a hardware/software package ported to an IBM RS6000/320H (discontinued as an IBM product in Fall 1993). ANS CO+RE has recently made the InterLock available on Sun platforms.

- *Raptor Technologies Eagle.* Purchase prices for Raptor's product have been as high as $70,000, with leases in the same range as the InterLock. The systems function similarly, but Raptor seems to have a limited marketing budget and has relied on Performance Systems International (PSI) as its principal marketing outlet.

- *Digital Equipment Corporation (DEC) SEAL (Screening External Access Link).* Although SEAL has been around at least five years, DEC announced the service formally in May 1994. SEAL is described by DEC as an umbrella term encompassing custom security consulting, Internet security policy development and rules definitions, installation and configuration of customized software, training, and support services. Although DEC's security services are custom quoted and installed, the base price for SEAL services is $25,000. Digital Consulting, a DEC business unit, is responsible for SEAL.

- *Hughes Information Security Products' NetLOCK.* One of the newest and potentially most interesting entrants into the network security marketplace, NetLOCK is a software product currently offered for use on Sun workstations operating with Sun OS 4.1.X, and the Hewlett-Packard 9000/700 series workstations operating with HP-UX 9.0X or later. The Certification Authority Management Station (CAMS), an additional feature, requires Sun Open Windows version 3.0 or later and Motif 1.X for HP workstations.

    Essentially, NetLOCK has most of the features of the other systems, yet it is not delivered on a preconfigured hardware platform. The user provides the workstation. Pricing for NetLOCK is also different from the others. As a software product, it is offered and priced by the number of workstations with which it connects within the internal network. Prices range from $4,000 for 10 "seats" to $121,000 for 500 seats. These are one-time software acquisition costs.

- *Check Point Software Technologies Ltd.'s FireWall-1*. Another new entry into the security marketplace, FireWall-1 also is provided without the hardware platform. Offered as a software package for Sun OS 4.1.3, Solaris using X11R5 OpenLook GUI, and Sun SparcStations, the FireWall-1 offers one of the better graphical user interfaces available on security systems today. Its features are similar to those offered by other security implementations. FireWall-1's costs are a bit different. The base system is $18,900, with each server or slave for remote sites priced at $4,000. This is regardless of the number of seats behind each of these servers. FireWall-1 is provided by Global Enterprise Services (formerly JvNCNet), an IAP.

Specialized encryption gateways

There is an interesting middle ground between firewalls and ALGs. Some organizations are not interested in access to the Internet, but in communicating cost-effectively with their remote branches, customers, or suppliers without using expensive leased-line network services. This is referred to as "closed user group" or "virtual private data network" services (see Chapter Thirteen for specific details).

Two products address this need: ANS CO+RE's ANSKeyRing and Alternet's LanGuardian. Both systems operate on a PC platform. ANS uses a 66MHz i486 machine running BSDI, and Alternet uses a 50MHz Motorola 68040 with dual Intel 82596CA Ethernet processors, a CEI 99C003 Super Crypt High Speed Encryption Chip, and 4 to 32MB of main memory.

The ANS system reportedly supported 56Kbps access only. Alternet supports both 56Kbps and 1.5 Mbps (T-1) today.

ANSKeyRing is a custom-priced service, and you will need to contact ANS CO+RE directly for associated fees.

The LanGuardian from Alternet costs $5,000 per unit for 56Kbps and $6,000 for 1.5Mbps. An administration station is required for each system (not each site) at a price of $8,000. A $1,500 annual software subscription fee is charged for each system as well. Volume discounts are available for multiple sites. The LanGuardian carries a one-year hardware and software warranty. LanGuardian is used by several U.S. federal agencies that require their contractors to communicate with them via the Internet in a secure, closed user group fashion. LanGuardian currently supports several hundred sites.

Adjunct services

Adjunct services include secure user interfaces, public key cryptography, and smart cards.

Secure User Interfaces

Recently, several companies have announced bundles of security services into existing interfaces, most of them involving Enterprise Integration Technologies (EIT) and RSA Data Security. The announcements typically include an agreement with the National Center for Supercomputer Application (NCSA), EIT, and RSA to develop a "secure version" and so far include NCSA Mosaic, SprintLink II Service (including EIT security deployments), MecklerWeb, iWORLD, and CommerceNet. Also, EIT and RSA recently announced formation of the security firm Terisa Systems.

These are efforts to include public key cryptography in software products, thus permitting the use of digital signatures and encrypted credit card numbers or other sensitive information. These interfaces should allow users to safely transact daily business on the Internet involving their most confidential information.

Public Key Cryptography

Evolved from the Massachusetts Institute of Technology (MIT), RSA is one of the world's leading cryptographic research and development firms and has an extensive array of products and services. These include security reviews, development, assistance, end-user applications, software development kits, algorithm optimizations, literature searches, and cryptographic consulting.

The list of major RSA licensees, developers, and applications is quite impressive. A sample includes, but is not limited to

• Alcatel TITN	Twice CDPD Protocol Software
• ANS CO+RE	InterLock
• Apple Computer	System 7 Pro
• AT&T	Models 4100, 3600, and Secure Video Dock
• Bankers Trust	BT Authentication Services
• DEC	DSSA (Distributed Systems Security Architecture)
• GE Information Services	GEIS Secure NW Services

- HP   Cryptographic Security Module for
                                    HP/9000

- Hughes   NetLOCK

- IBM   4755 Adapter, 4753 Network Security
                                    Proc.

- Lotus Development   Lotus Notes

- Microsoft   Windows for Workgroups, Windows NT

- Motorola   Commercial Secure Telephone Units

- Northern Telecom   X.25 Packet Data Security Overlay System

- Novell   NetWare 3.11 and 4.0

- Oracle   SQL*Net

- SunSoft   Solaris Secure NFS and Secure RPC

- Trusted Information Systems   T-Mail

- Unisys   CTOS

- WordPerfect   InForms

Smart Cards

Security Dynamics of Cambridge, Massachusetts, provides a variety of security enhancements, including the SecurID smart card and Advanced Computing Environment (ACE)/Server security system. In June 1994, Security Dynamics announced a partnership with leading router vendor Cisco Systems to provide a more secure method for users to access distributed internetworked resources.

Security Dynamics focuses on authentication of the user. The SecurID Card is a credit-card-sized unit that generates and displays a randomly generated six-digit user access code, which changes every minute. The server checks pass codes by using a synchronized clock to ensure authorization for use of the facilities. ACE/Server for Cisco began shipping in late 1994 at a starting price of $1,950 and $34 per SecurID Card.

Many tools are being developed to address the issues of security, confidentiality, and fraud over the Internet. The ones described above are but a sample.

The flow of new approaches will only increase as interest in the Internet continues to expand worldwide.

Conclusion

As you can see, defining what Internet means to you and your organization may not be an easy task. You need to consider how it might impact your operations, who it may affect, what skills you currently have and those you may need to hire, and the implications for your information's security. There may be new positions that need to be created, such as corporate electronic librarians or network security specialists. The tasks associated with understanding your requirements are formidable but can be successfully accomplished with forethought and planning. Know your strengths, identify your weaknesses, understand *why* you are implementing Internet, and know how you expect it to be used. In this way, you are much more likely to have a successful experience in the shortest possible time. You also will have the peace of mind of knowing that you have considered the security issues and addressed them in as aggressive a manner as possible. Keep in mind, however, that the Internet is an ever-changing environment, and that security requires continual vigilance. This is also true in general business, yet the global accessibility afforded by Internet requires us to be aware of any potential intruders and that we deal with them properly.

Chapter Twelve

UNDERSTANDING

VENDOR

ALTERNATIVES

It is important to know the vendors available to connect you to the Internet. Several good books can assist you. Some of them are listed in the bibliography at the end of this book. In addition, resources on the Internet can help you, including newsgroups and servers. If you have Mosaic or Netscape, try using Yahoo, ElNet Galaxy, or another search tool and see what you find!

This chapter will give you an idea of the different types of vendors that are out there and what you might expect from them. Each grouping has its own culture, strengths, weaknesses, and potential for growth.

Chapter 15 will help you compare "apples to apples" when trying to select an Internet vendor for a major program. When selecting a provider for dial-up service or when you are just getting started, ask lots of questions and pick the one that is most comfortable.

The State of the Internet Access Marketplace

In 1994, the Maloff Company began conducting research on the size of the Internet access marketplace and relative market shares by companies. The information presented below has been extracted from the company's 1995 report. More information can be found on the Internet at **www.trinet.com/maloff**.

The year 1994 was a very interesting one for the Internet access provider (IAP) marketplace. Maloff's 1993 report excluded information service providers like America OnLine (AOL), CompuServe, and Prodigy from its marketplace estimates. In March 1994, these companies had not begun to offer anything more than electronic mail (e-mail) access to the Internet. By January 1995, they all had promised much greater capabilities, with some offering access to newsgroups, others announcing full IP access (including telnet and file transfer protocol, ftp), and still others beginning to offer World Wide Web (WWW) access through a variety of graphical user interfaces (Spry, Mosaic, Netscape, etc.).

These changes in service offerings make the process of assessing the marketplace more difficult, especially in comparison with 1994. For that reason, two top-ten lists are provided. The listing shown in Table 12-1 evaluates the IAP marketplace exclusive of the information service providers. The listing in Table 12-2 includes the information service providers.

Table 12-1:

Top Ten Internet Access Providers (not including Information Providers)

Company	Annualized Revenue	Market Share
1. UUNet Technologies (U.S.)	$46.78 Million	9.52%
2. Netcom	$31.22 Million	6.35%
3. Sprint	$29.94 Million	5.74%
4. Performance Systems International	$22.92 Million	4.67%
5. Supernet (Colorado)	$10.37 Million	2.11%
6. Advanced Network & Services	$10.30 Million	2.10%
7. CERFnet	$8.00 Million	1.63%
8. BBN	$6.82 Million	1.39%
9. World (Software Tool & Die)	$4.75 Million	0.97%
10.SURAnet (BBN)	$4.35 Million	0.89%

(Based on Annual Revenue "Run Rate" as of January 1995)

Table 12-2:

Top Ten Internet Access Providers (including Information Providers)

Company	Annualized Revenue	Market Share
1. CompuServe	$216.00 Million	20.76%
2. America OnLine	$180.00 Million	17.30%
3. Prodigy	$90.00 Million	8.65%
4. UUNet Technologies	$46.78 Million	4.50%

Table 12-2:

Top Ten Internet Access Providers (Including Information Providers) *Continued*

Company	Annualized Revenue	Market Share
5. Delphi	$44.80 Million	4.31%
6. Netcom	$31.22 Million	3.00%
7. Sprint	$29.94 Million	2.80%
8. Performance Systems International	$22.92 Million	2.20%
9. Supernet	$10.37 Million	0.94%
1 ANS	$10.30 Million	0.91%

(Based on Annual Revenue "Run Rate" as of January 1995)
(Estimated Internet-Derived Revenue Only)

A comparison of Tables 12-1 and 12-2 shows that information providers are the leading Internet access vendors in the United States, largely due to their intense marketing and easy-to-use interfaces. Whether they can maintain this growth and market share as their customers become more sophisticated and demanding remains to be seen. Nevertheless, information providers will be a force in the Internet access business and should not be underestimated.

A similar impact can be anticipated from other industries with large customer bases (e.g., interexchange long-distance carriers, local-exchange telephone carriers, and computer software companies), which have all expressed interest in building on the Information Superhighway.

Categories of Internet Access Providers

Individuals and organizations interested in obtaining connectivity to the Internet have a variety of choices today in terms of classifications of providers. Each has its own strengths and weaknesses.

During 1994, it became quite clear that a convergence is under way that will, to some degree, blur these categories. They remain important as indicators of their origin and as potential pointers to how they might approach the marketplace.

The following sections describe the different types of providers and offer a sampling of providers from each category.

Commercial Internet backbone providers

Commercial Internet backbone providers have established their own multiple node networks in more than one geographic area, specialize in commercial services, and do not rely solely on another IAP for nationwide transport or interconnectivity.

Companies in this category are incorporated businesses with full-time employees. Although the majority are spin-offs from the research and education community, more will probably come from the traditional telecommunications markets, systems integrators, and computer businesses (including the likely emergence in 1995 of Microsoft as a major influence).

Major companies included in this category are

• Advanced Network & Services (ANS)

• Global Enterprise Services (GES/JvNCnet)

• NetCom

• Performance Systems International (PSI)

• UUNet Technologies

Sprint should be considered part of this group as well, as the first interexchange carrier (IXC) to enter the Internet access business in 1992. As a traditional IXC, Sprint is discussed in greater detail under that category of vendors.

Internet protocol resellers

The definition of the IP (Internet Protocol) resellers category has been debated. For the purposes of this analysis, these are companies that purchase access from another organization (such as those listed in the "Commercial Internet backbone providers" section) for the purpose of "reselling" to lower-end consumers.

Most of these organizations focus on commercial access (rather than education) and on a specific geographic area (metropolitan area or state). Some of these organizations have begun to expand significantly to other areas and use leased lines from the major carriers (WilTel, MCI, Sprint, AT&T, and LCI) to "backhaul" traffic from remote nodes to their prime point of entry into the Internet. At this point, the distinction between an IP reseller and a commercial Internet provider becomes less clear.

These organizations tend to be headed by technical people who assisted in Internet activities at a university, government laboratory, or corporation and became entrepreneurs when the Internet market began to blossom.

The range and quality of services by IP resellers is widespread, and you should assess the prospective provider before obtaining services.

Some of the better known or more active companies currently classified as IP resellers include:

- ClarkNet (Maryland)—**info@clark.net**

- DATABANK (Kansas)—**info@databank.com**

- Digital Express (Washington, D.C.)—**info@digex.net**

- InterAccess (Chicago)—**info@interaccess.com**

- MCSNet (Chicago)—**info@mcs.net**

- MSEN (Michigan)—**info@msen.com**

- The Pipeline (New York City)—acquired by PSI during February 1995—**josh/@pipeline.com**

- The Well (Sausalito, California)—**info@well.sf.ca.us**

- World Dot Com (Boston)—**info@world.std.com**

Research and education networks

Research and education (R&E) networks are defined as those wide area networks (WANs) intended to provide Internet connectivity initially to their own community of students, faculty researchers, and staff. Many of these networks were established as a way to collectively participate in grants provided by the National Science Foundation, Defense Advanced Research Projects Agency, Department of Energy, and other agencies. Some of these networks have seen spin-offs become nationwide service providers (for example, ANS evolved from the joint study partnership of IBM, MCI, and Merit on the NSFnet; Global Enterprise Services came from JvNCnet; and, PSI is an outgrowth of NYSERnet, the New York state education network).

Many of these networks have begun to offer access to non-R&E organizations. However, management and organizational focus is normally on the R&E community rather than on fully commercial activities.

In addition, R&E networks can be metropolitan (i.e., BARRNet [Bay Area of San Francisco], state [OARnet (Ohio) or MRnet (Minnesota)], or multistate (CICNet [Midwest]). Almost every state has an R&E network. Those listed below are considered more aggressive in the area of commercial customers:

- BARRNet (part of BBN)

- CERFnet (California)

- CICNet (Illinois, Indiana, Iowa, Michigan, Minnesota, Ohio, Wisconsin)

- Colorado Supernet (Colorado)

- MidNet (Arkansas, Iowa, Kansas, Missouri, Nebraska, Oklahoma; owned by Global Internet)

- NEARnet (New England; owned by BBN)

- NorthWestNet (Pacific Northwest)

- OARnet (Ohio)

- SURAnet (Southeastern United States; ownership by BBN pending)

Bulletin boards and Freenets

Bulletin board providers are technically not Internet access service providers. Hundreds of these organizations are springing up on a regular basis across the country. Most focus on a specific area of geography or topic of interest. Most are reachable via dial-up access and a modem. Once these organizations (which can be one person with a machine in the basement) begin to offer Internet services, they are reclassified as IP resellers or Freenets. A Freenet is a bulletin board system (BBS) that offers some level of Internet access but with minimal service.

Examples of these organizations with Internet access of some kind (normally e-mail and Gopher) include the following:

- Cyberia (Pennsylvania; **adam.viener@cyberia.com**)

- The Daily Planet BBS Maui (Hawaii; **daniel.cohen@tdp.org**)

- DLS Infonet (Arkansas; **jerry@dlsinfonet.com**)

- Real Exposure (New York City; **srovniak@realexposure.com**)

Information providers

Although the information providers have a different culture and perspective from traditional R&E Internet providers, they are a formidable force and will become an integral part of the evolving Internet. Representing an estimated 5 million users today, their numbers will impact Internet usage dramatically.

It is important that all of these companies teach their users "netiquette"— Internet-accepted customs and practices. Netiquette will help ease the transition and make the Internet explosion a more pleasant experience for all concerned.

From a business perspective, it is important to include these providers in your access decision process as soon as they announce the availability of Internet services. Given their marketing muscle, it will be apparent when they enter the fray in full force.

Information providers also face the challenge of holding onto customers. Traditional Internet providers like PSI and UUNet will be poised to take them away if the AOLs and CompuServes fail to live up to expectations. The user marketplace in 1995 and beyond is likely to become quite mobile!

Although the primary line of business for information service providers is the electronic provision of information rather than access to the Internet, they still promote some form of Internet access as part of their services (normally e-mail).

The major companies in this category are

- America OnLine (Vienna, Virginia); phone: (800) 827-6364

- CompuServe (Columbus, Ohio); phone: (800) 848-8199

- Delphi (Cambridge, Massachusetts); phone: (800) 6954005;
  e-mail: **info@delphi.com**

- Prodigy (White Plains, New York); phone: 800-PRODIGY

- The Microsoft Network (Redmond, Washington); phone: (800) 936-3500

AOL has made great strides through the purchase of ANS and by opening up some level of Internet access to its subscribers. It still remains to be seen whether AOL will continue to "grow" ANS and its customer base of dedicated access organizations, or if it will let that base erode while concentrating on its core dial-up business. It is believed that AOL purchased ANS mainly for its network rather than for its customer base.

CompuServe has announced extensive plans to roll out Internet services, including the acquisition of Spry for their graphical user interfaces. CompuServe intends to offer dedicated access services through its private network group and Point to Point Protocol (PPP) services to its broader customer base. Today, CompuServe users can telnet into the company, thus saving on dial-access charges.

In early 1995, CompuServe announced a relationship with Spry's Internet-in-a-Box, replacing Sprint as the vendor of choice, followed quickly by the announcement of the acquisition. Additionally, CompuServe Information Service customers now have access to ftp through the CompuServe Information Manager (CIM) graphical interface.

Delphi has been offering "full" Internet access, including ftp, telnet, and e-mail for the longest time.

Prodigy has introduced AstraNet, a new service on the WWW. The company announced plans for "P2," an enhanced user interface that will be provided to Prodigy subscribers during 1995. Prodigy has also become the first of the information providers to offer a WWW browser to its subscribers. Available free to its membership, the software offers enhanced Web access at no additional charge to subscribers.

Telecommunications carriers

Telecommunications carriers are likely to play major roles in the Internet marketplace during 1995. Telecommunications companies are further divided into two groups: interexchange carriers and local exchange carriers. Internationally, this category includes the postal, telephone, and telegraph (PT&T) organizations and includes organizations that are frequently government-owned or -operated.

Interexchange carriers (IXC). These companies provide long-distance access and include AT&T, MCI, Sprint, WilTel/LDDS, LCI, Cable & Wireless, and a variety of smaller facilities-based companies. Within Canada, Fonorola is considered an IXC.

In the United States, Sprint has been the major Internet player from this group. To date, however, Sprint has offered primarily dedicated-access services, not dial-up. This appears to have been a mistake, as it has given many other organizations (especially information providers) a chance to prepare and compete aggressively. For an organization to effectively compete in the Internet business, it is important to offer a complete suite of services to their target markets.

In addition, Sprint has been the one Internet provider that has actively pursued Internet resellers rather than shunning them as potential competitors.

MCI made several very large announcements late in 1994 about its pending Internet access services. Called internetMCI and part of the NetworkMCI suite, these services will include a full and sweeping set of features, with dial-access, dedicated access, Web services, security services, and more. In addition, MCI has a highly visible technical organization, including Vinton Cerf, widely recognized as one of the founding fathers of the Internet. How effectively it deploys services remains to be seen.

Key companies and what they're up to. The following sections describe activities at AT&T, MCI, and Sprint.

AT&T. AT&T has recently entered the Internet marketplace through an agreement with Bolt, Beranek and Newman, and it has recently purchased several small, related companies, including the ImagiNation Network and Ziff-Davis Interchange.

AT&T has the greatest potential of any organization to make tremendous waves when and where it wants in the Internet marketplace. It had not chosen to do so earlier, probably for at least two very solid business reasons:

- The Internet access marketplace in the United States only recently passed $450 million in annual revenues. It is just starting to hint of a significant marketshare that might cause AT&T to seriously consider entering.

- With a reported 80 percent of the total U.S. point-to-point leased-line market, why would AT&T introduce services that it perceives internally could be self-erosive? AT&T has a long history of permitting products and services to run their life cycle, even if it means missing some portion of a market.

In addition to these powerful financial reasons, AT&T also has the greatest challenge of any potential Internet provider in training its sales and technical support services. It certainly has the means to do so, but the investments are not trivial.

AT&T also has a substantial resource in Bell Labs, and given the anticipated needs for development in areas such as IP over ATM routing, enhanced user interfaces, and sophisticated network security measures, AT&T will certainly be an important player. The key question is when, and with what strategies.

AT&T cannot afford to let IBM, Microsoft, and MCI get too far ahead.

AT&T will likely establish Internet access nodes along its own proprietary network and begin to offer services directly. It may or may not retain connectivity into ANS and other existing Internet backbone providers for redundancy purposes. AT&T also will likely establish a connection and membership in the Commercial Internet eXchange (CIX), both to appear as a "good citizen" and to facilitate exchange of commercial customer routes.

MCI. Since mid-1994, MCI has been sending shock waves into the Internet by hiring some of the industry's most notable people. Among its new hires are Vinton Cerf, former partner with Internet guru Bob Kahn at the Center for National Research Initiatives, chair of the Internet Activities Board, and considered one of the fathers of the Internet, and Phill Gross, former vice president of technology development for ANS and former chair of the Internet Engineering Task Force.

Once MCI enters the market forcefully, the cycle experienced by Sprint is likely to be repeated—a relatively slow start, followed by substantial growth as the customer base begins to sign on. The growth may be more rapid for MCI than for Sprint because of the maturity of the marketplace and MCI's ability to learn from others' mistakes.

Sprint. Sprint first entered the Internet access environment in 1991, when it won the NSFnet's International Connections Manager project to deliver IP services to Europe.

Following this, Sprint announced SprintLink Internet access service in mid-1992. The service was slow to take off because of many of the same problems experienced by WilTel. The Internet was difficult to explain to the sales force and even harder to sell. Sprint's most significant step taken during the past year was winning an agreement with the MCC industrial consortium (Austin, Texas) and Enterprise Integration Technologies (EINet) from Alternet/UUNet.

From a mere 30 connected clients in March 1993, Sprint has grown to a reported 1,200 connections and $29 million in annual Internet access sales as of January 1995.

The EINet relationship provided Sprint with Internet technical abilities that were previously lacking. In January 1994, Sprint was publicly discussing SprintLink II at Communications Networks in Washington, D.C. SprintLink II's design calls for a graphical user interface (GUI) and Digital Encryption Standard (DES) security capabilities. Through MCC's substantial industrial relationships, Sprint has aggressively pursued large Fortune 500-type organizations, and it appears to be succeeding. Sprint will likely build on lessons learned through EINet and develop in-house expertise.

Both Sprint and AT&T, as well as MCI, are expected to leverage their custom tariff offerings (Tariff 12s, SCAs, etc.). In this way, they can attempt to keep a customer already using their voice services as an Internet customer as well—avoiding revenue erosion to competitive service providers.

Sprint has also been aggressive in connecting IP resellers (gateways or back doors). Sprint is the only major provider to make no distinction with standard connectivity and, in fact, actively seeks such potential customers. It is uncertain whether MCI or CompuServe will attack this marketplace. Some IP backbone providers view gateway customers as potential competitors rather than another distribution channel.

As the Internet industry grows, the number of entrepreneurs seeking to enter the IP resale business and capture either a geographic or vertical industry niche will grow dramatically. By permitting these organizations to easily attach, Sprint has created a "feeder" network to build its traffic. Should these entrepreneurs fail, Sprint could consider acquiring their customer bases. Many of the organizations that want to establish regional networks, either as an outgrowth of a BBS or from the ground up, will be looking for these types of connections.

Sprint's major weaknesses are in the areas of sales force and security. At present, Sprint has few experts that can help close all of the business available. It remains to be seen whether the company is prepared to invest in the human resources needed to capture the majority of opportunities. If so, Sprint will continue to be a significant player in the expanding Internet access industry.

All of the IXC providers—AT&T, Sprint, and MCI—share a weakness in lower-end dial-up Internet services. The amount of service and support required from the Internet vendor is greatest with the least profitable customers.

Many of the larger players are understandably reluctant to jump into the low-end business, although they may be forced to do so. Most end-user companies that have not experienced the Internet are looking for a "try it, you'll like it" approach. They aren't likely to invest $10,000 to $100,000 a year with unproven providers offering ill-defined benefits.

The company with twenty sites may start at dial-up but will grow into dedicated access relatively quickly. They will probably look first to their existing vendor for upgrades of service. This "upgrade capture" could be significant for an Internet service provider.

Local Exchange Carriers (LECs). LECs are traditional telephone companies that provide local dial services, intra-LATA long-distance services, ISDN, local leased lines, and other related services. The Regional Bell Operating Companies (RBOCs) are the descendants of the Bell System divestiture, and they continue to be prohibited by the Modified Final Judgment (MFJ) from manufacturing or offering inter-LATA long-distance services in their regions of monopoly. Other, non-RBOC LECs include General Telephone (GTE), United Telecommunications (both GTE and United were partners in Sprint before United acquired the company), Cincinnati Bell, and more than 1,000 telcos throughout the United States. Most of these are referred to as "independent telcos."

CAPS/ALTS are alternate access providers in major metropolitan areas. These companies have invested substantial money installing fiber-optic cable throughout the high-profit business areas of a community. They normally offer an alternative to the local telco for high-cost leased lines. Few offer "dial tone" at this time. The most notable of these providers today are Metropolitan Fiber Systems (MFS) and Teleport. Both offer services in multiple cities.

Among the RBOCs, the most active in Internet services have been Ameritech, NYNEX, Pacific Bell, and US West, although none could be characterized as aggressive in Internet ventures.

US West was the first to actively announce Internet services in 1991, calling it Advanced Communications Service (ACS). Driven by Bill Grant (now with the Minnesota Supercomputer Center in Minneapolis), US West participated on the board of directors for Colorado Supernet (an early research and education network). This gave US West the impetus to announce its ACS services. Although no results have been announced, its sales rate is not thought to be significant. The same challenges that plagued Sprint in its early efforts are apparently compounded by a lack of continued support within US West, despite its early announcements of a "$100 million investment." US West needs to regain its Internet focus and determine the approach that will best serve both its customers and US West.

Both NYNEX and Pacific Bell participated in trials during 1992, using ANS as the inter-LATA transport for SMDS (Switched Multimegabit Data Services). The trials were reportedly quite successful, although neither participant has actively marketed the service. Pacific Bell also joined in one of five federally funded high-performance computing testbeds and is a likely participant as a Network Access Provider (NAP). NAPs are discussed in greater detail in the Service Provider "Meets Points" section in this chapter.

Ameritech also has successfully bid for and been awarded an NAP site. As demonstrated several times, it is anticipated that RBOCs need real-world experience with actual end users before they can successfully introduce Internet access services and capture significant market shares.

Bellcore, the central development center for the seven RBOCs, is exploring all of the "how-to's and wherefores" regarding the Internet and potential services. Given normal business planning cycles, a fully developed and deployed concept is at least a year away. This time could be reduced in the cases of Ameritech and Pacific Bell, but that remains questionable at best.

An interesting effort was launched by MFS in early 1993 when the company inaugurated MFS Datane and brought in the former president of BT TYMNET, Al Fenn. Fenn is responsible for creating a data networking service built around linking MFS's "bypass" cities. By using WilTel's leased-line services, MFS Datanet can offer sophisticated LAN-to-LAN data services. MFS Datanet personnel have already focused on the applications that are likely to be of interest to potential Internet users: large data transfers or remote log-in capability, as well as e-mail.

The RBOCs will become increasingly involved with providing Internet services during 1995. Should Congress lift the restriction placed on these companies through the AT&T divestiture agreement their level of activity will expand considerably.

The newest entrants to the Internet business are the smaller telephone companies. Among those with an interest in the Internet are the following:

- Rock Hill Telephone Company (began offering Internet access in August 1993)

- Shenandoah Communications (began offering Internet access in September 1994)

- Commonwealth Telephone and North-Eastern Pennsylvania Telephone (agreed to offer Internet access jointly in 1994)

- East Otter Tail Telephone Company, Minnesota (begins offering The Internet shortly)

- ComNet, a consortium of nineteen independent telcos in Ohio (will provide Internet access through a connection to an IP provider in Chicago)

Cable television companies remain something of a wild card in Internet access markets. There have been several trials of Internet connectivity through cable television services. In both the Continental CableVision trial in

Massachusetts with PSI and the Jones Cable experiment with ANS in Alexandria, Virginia, it appeared that the hardware to connect the end user through a cable system to the Internet was not satisfactory.

In late 1994, this appeared to be changing. Digital Equipment Corporation announced ChannelWorks Internet Brouter, which was designed to give businesses high-speed access to Internet via standard cable TV systems. At $6,995, this is a bit expensive for most home users, and not all businesses are built in close proximity to existing cable TV systems.

Northern Telecom (NORTEL) recently introduced its Cornerstone Data product line. The Cornerstone Data hub sits between the cable operator's head-end and the Internet, with a Cornerstone Data Port installed at the subscriber's home or business site. No prices were available at the time of this writing.

In both cases, cable TV offers the potential for very high rates of information transfer. Cable TV is likely to become competitive with traditional telephone company for offerings like ISDN (Integrated Service Digital Network) or leased-line access.

Companies with access to a customer base (telcos, cable TV, etc.) will be interested in providing Internet access. Cable TV companies have the greatest difficulty due to a lack of required technical knowledge. Strategic partnering relationships will probably occur among all of these disparate players during 1995.

Government-funded service providers

Government funding of service providers occurs at both the federal and state levels.

Federally funded networks. Federally funded networks include those specific to a particular federal agency, such as the Department of Energy's ESnet or the NASA Science Internet. In general, these networks prohibit use except in support of their specific mission.

From a general business standpoint, you can have an Internet connection provided by NASA, but you technically cannot use it to communicate with your branch offices for business not related to your NASA contract. For this reason, it makes more sense to have your Internet access provided by a service provider not restricted to such a specific-use policy.

In addition, many of the early R&E networks were funded by the NSF or other agencies, such as the Department of Defense. These networks, like

CICNet, NorthWestNet, or WESTnet, must have separate usage policies for NSF-acceptable customers and for those that want to be unrestricted. It is important to determine any limitations that might be placed on your network access and use by your Internet service provider.

State funding for information highways. While the U.S. government has been moving toward funding by specific agencies (i.e., Department of Energy, Department of Defense, or the NSF), individual states have begun to recognize the importance of maintaining technological leadership to be competitive. Louisiana, Maryland, North Carolina, Texas, Utah, Vermont, Virginia, and many other states have begun implementing their plans. These include state information highways that will link state and local government agencies, schools, businesses, and the general public.

The North Carolina network, a $160 million, 116,000 fiber-mile effort, has targeted distance learning, telemedicine, and economic development as its three principal applications. Among its features are the capability to send digital maps of site locations to businesses considering moving into the state and to incorporate the use of the network for employee training programs conducted in real time at a remote community college, as the Freightliner Corporation has done.

Texas has established an Internet accessible online information repository, including job postings and environmental maps.

Maryland will soon offer free dial-up Internet access to all of its citizens. It remains to be seen how useful this will be in terms of contention for lines (i.e., busy signals) or the degree of support.

Service Provider "Meet Points"

For the Internet to function effectively as a conglomeration of thousands of separate networks and network providers, there must be locations where these networks interconnect and exchange traffic. The places these interactions occur are called "meet points."

Meet points determine whether your traffic can get where you want it. A service provider that is not sufficiently connected may not be able to handle your information flow effectively—or at all.

Your service provider can "meet" with others in several ways, and it is to its advantage (as well as yours) to consider establishing multiple meet points for a large network. These meet points include NAPs, industry associations (e.g., CIX), or bilateral agreements between service providers (e.g., the SMDS Washington Area Bypass [SWAB] recently created between PSI and UUNet).

The key is to ask your service provider how it interconnects with others, and if it guarantees that your routes will be accepted by all of the other commercial Internet providers.

Conclusion

As you can see, there are a wide variety of Internet service providers, and a host of others on the horizon that hope to be in the business shortly. In Section Three, we will help you understand how to sort through all of these alternatives and develop a logical method of service provider selection. Keep in mind that the landscape for Internet access will change dramatically during 1995 and 1996. Microsoft Network (MSN) *will* be a player during that period of time. How effective it will be remains to be seen, and I am not ready to believe that Microsoft will dominate the IAP marketplace. There are too many other good alternatives available.

In this chapter, we have tried to give you enough information so that understanding the coming evolution in Internet access will be easier. As new service providers emerge, others are acquired, and some pass into the cyber ether, it is important for businesses to be aware of these changes so that they can respond accordingly.

*C*hapter Thirteen

CYBERSPACE

IS A GLOBAL

PHENOMENON

Although the Internet was born in the United States as part of the Defense Advanced Research Projects Agency program, it has quickly become international. For nearly thirty years, people around the world have participated in the academic and government sides of the evolving Internet. This has occurred through the Internet Engineering Task Force (IETF), the Internet Society (ISOC), and a variety of other gathering points.

The Internet Society can be contacted at 12020 Sunrise Valley Dr., Suite 270, Reston VA 22091; phone: (703) 648-9888; fax: (703) 648-9887; e-mail: **isoc@isoc.org**; WWW: **http://www.isoc.com**.

WELCOME TO THE INTERNET SOCIETY, Internauts

The <u>Internet Society</u> is the non-governmental International Organization for global cooperation and coordination for the Internet and its internetworking technologies and applications.

Figure 13-1:
The Internet Society addresses internetworking issues.

Since early 1990, the United States has been the crucible in which commercial Internet services have evolved. As of 1995, commercial Internet access providers have been springing up rapidly around the world. In some regions, this is a relatively painless process but in others it has been considerably more difficult. In countries like Canada and the United Kingdom, growth in commercial Internet providers has been similar to that in the United States, only occurring several years later.

On February 6, 1995, ISOC released some interesting information on the growth of the Internet worldwide.

A survey was conducted on Internet "domains" (identifiers used as part of an Internet address to identify business type or country) to discover all hosts on the Net. The information presented below was gathered during late January 1995. For more information, see **ftp.nw.com** or **http://www.nw.com**.

The number of host computers found as of January 1995 was 4.851 million. The total grew 26 percent in the fourth quarter of 1994—the largest jump in the recent history of the Internet. Internet hosts in the .com (commercial) domain continued to surge as the largest group. Hosts providing World Wide Web (WWW) service now are the most numerous on the Internet. The study surveyed ninety countries with direct connectivity, as well as the seven transnational domains:

- com (commercial);

- edu (education);

- gov (U.S. government);

- mil (U.S. military);

- org (nonprofit organization);

- net (Internet access provider); and

- int (international).

The following tables illustrate the most active domains, including transnational and national, by growth in the number of hosts (computers) connected to the Internet.

Table 13-1:

Top 31 Country and Global Domains by Size (January 1995)

	January 95 Hosts	4Q94 Increase	1994 Increase	3 yr. % Change
com**	1,316,966	25%	132%	628%
edu**	1,133,502	15%	60%	366%
UK	241,191	24%	112%	1,171%
gov**	209,345	8%	62%	351%
Germany	207,717	23%	77%	569%
Canada	186,722	22%	96%	590%
mil**	175,961	21%	70%	541%
Australia	161,166	20%	50%	409%
org**	154,578	114%	206%	705%
net**	150,299	192%	616%	1,796%
Japan	96,632	17%	86%	1,029%
France	93,041	28%	68%	615%
Netherlands	89,227	20%	98%	599%

Table 13-1:

Top 31 Country and Global Domains by Size (January 1995) *Continued*

	January 95	4Q94 Increase	1994 Increase	3 yr. % Change
Sweden	77,594	22%	83%	318%
Finland	71,372	24%	103%	493%
Switzerland	51,512	-4%	40%	306%
Norway	49,725	15%	57%	387%
United States[1]	37,615	51%	475%	31,155%
New Zealand	31,215	52%	441%	2,698%
Italy	30,697	14%	80%	1,029%
Austria	29,705	25%	92%	793%
Spain	28,446	19%	141%	1,613%
South Africa	27,040	29%	147%	2,805%
Denmark	25,935	75%	181%	1,344%
Belgium	18,699	31%	125%	5,220%
Korea	18,049	24%	101%	1,103%
Taiwan	14,618	25%	83%	1,710%
Israel	13,251	34%	96%	552%
Hong Kong	12,437	18%	52%	2,725%
Czechoslovakia	11,580	58%	153%	Not avail.
Poland	11,477	35%	121%	Not avail.

[1] Most global domains are attributed to the U.S.

** Transnational domains (primarily U.S.)

As of January 1995, 4.851 million host computers were identified on the Internet. Of those, approximately 65.5 percent represented transnational domains (i.e., .edu, .gov, .net, etc.) and the United States; and 32.9 percent represented distinctly international domains. The Internet is truly becoming a global asset rather than belonging solely to any one country.

The .com domains are now the single largest block of Internet host machine addresses, surpassing the .edu sites. The largest individually identified countries in terms of host domains (and excluding transnational domains) are the United Kingdom, Germany, Canada, Australia, and Japan.

The fastest growing domains during 1994 were:

.net	616%	United States	475%
New Zealand	441%	.ORG	206%

The .net domain is used by IAPs and indicates how rapidly the number of these organizations is growing throughout the world. By this count, there are more than 150,000 IAP host computers worldwide. Although this is clearly not the actual number of individual organizations, it is useful as a measurement of the expansion of the industry.

The .US domain is growing in popularity within the United States because it denotes both country of origin as well as the state. For example, "**maloff.dexter.mi.us**" would indicate The Maloff Company of Dexter, Mich., USA.

The .org domain is used by nonprofit organizations. As more and more of these organizations become aware of the Internet's power as a communications tool, we can expect to see continued growth in the use of the .org domain address.

Other domains showing substantial growth spurts during the fourth quarter of 1994 included Denmark (75%), the Czech Republic (58%), and Israel (34%).

Table 13-2:
Growth by Region (1994)

	January 94	July 94	October 94	January 95	4Q94 %
North America	1,685,715	2,177,396	2,685,929	3,372,551	26%
Central/South America	7,392	11,455	14,894	*	*
Europe, West	550,933	730,429	850,993	1,039,192	22%
Europe, East	19,867	27,800	32,951	46,125	40%
Middle East	6,946	8,871	10,383	13,776	33%
Africa	10,951	15,595	21,041	27,130	29%

* Accurate Latin American host counts were not obtained.

Table 13-2:
Growth by Region (1994) *Continued*

	January 94	July 94	October 94	January 95	4Q94 %
Asia	81,355	111,278	127,569	151,773	19%
Pacific	113,482	142,353	154,473	192,390	25%
Total	2,476,641	3,225,177	3,898,233	4,851,873	24%

The European Academic Internet (RIPE) provides monthly host counts that are more definitive. Graphic profiles are now available on the ISOC server in Powerpoint format at **ftp://ftp.isoc.org/isoc/charts/ripe3.ppt**.

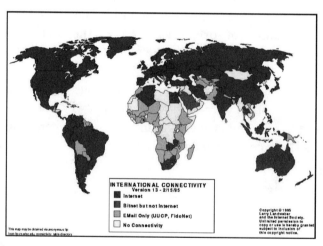

Figure 13-2:
Worldwide Internet connectivity is growing.
Source: Larry Landweber and the Internet Society.

Figure 13-2 shows the types of connectivity throughout the world. Internet refers to those countries that have full use of the Internet protocols. Bitnet is an older university-based electronic mail (e-mail) environment that relies on universities acting as "forwarding" agents. It is rather inexpensive, but as you might expect, is not overly reliable or feature-rich, nor appropriate for general business use.

"E-mail only" refers to simple e-mail capability using the Unix to Unix Copy Program, a method of polling Unix servers for stored information. All of these services can be reached via e-mail from any Internet-connected site.

As more commercial providers emerge throughout the world, the level of connectivity will also increase.

The State of the Commercial Internet Worldwide

The Internet phenomenon is truly worldwide. The following sections take a closer look at the development of *commercial* Internet service providers and services around the world.

Commercial Internet eXchange (CIX)

The CIX is a commercial IAP trade association permitting the exchange of traffic from one IAP to another. It is open to organizations that offer Transmission Control Protocol/Internet Protocol (TCP/IP) or Open Systems Interconnect (OSI) public data internetworking services to the general public in one or more geographic regions. Qualified public data Internet service providers interested in exchanging commercial traffic with other providers on a peer basis can become CIX Association members. An image map of CIX members is also available at the CIX Web site for browsers with image support.

Commercial IAPs Around the World

A partial listing of IAPs by region, excluding the United States and including members of the CIX, is provided below. This listing is current as of May 1995. Many other IAPs are emerging rapidly around the world. Some of these (as shown below) are beginning to offer services in multiple countries. This trend is expected to grow for the next several years.

Multinational/Multiregional IAPs. As the Internet expands, more IAP organizations will extend beyond the boundaries of a single country or geographic region. Table 13-3 presents a sampling of IAPs that are already starting to extend beyond such boundaries.

Table 13-3:

IAPs Extending Beyond Country or Geographic Boundaries

Organization	Region
Ashton Communications	United States and Mexico
CompuServe	United States and International
Globalcenter.net	United States and Canada
HoloNet	United States and Canada
HLC-Internet	International
MCI	United States and International
PSINet	United States and Japan

North America. Clearly, the United States has been the leader in commercial Internet access services. From the beginning of the commercial Internet business, Performance Systems International (PSI) and UUNet Technologies have been the pioneers. Since then, we have seen hundreds of providers emerging across the country. These providers now offer a variety of services—from magazine-like (Global Network Navigator and the WELL) to dial-up and leased-line connectivity to WWW support.

Canada. Canada has become quite active in offering Internet services. Current Canadian providers include: AuroraNet, CA*net, Cyberstore Systems, DataFlux Systems, Electro-Byte Technologies, Fonorola Internet, Internet Direct, and HookupNet. Also, Metrix Interlink, MGL Systems, ONRAMP Network Services, NSTN, UUNet Canada, UUNorth, and Wimsey Information Services.

Canada also seems to be a fertile ground for other Internet-related businesses, including

- Digital Island, which, according to its Web site (**http://www.isn.net/ di/index.html**), is "an Internet sanity, systems consulting, dance and poetry marketing and nifty ideas company based in (beautiful) Kingston, Prince Edward Island, Canada, right next door to a field of dairy cows."

- ONRAMP Network Services (**http://www.onramp.ca**) is an Internet service and Web server provider, hosting real estate properties for sale around Toronto.

- Headquarters Entertainment (**http://www.fleethouse.com/fhcanada/ hqe_home.htm**) provides a master front end to theater-related information on the Internet, as well as specific show and concert information in the Vancouver, British Columbia, area, or in other cities where they have productions.

- Jim Brown-Royal LePage (**http://www.cyberstore.ca/FosTech/ Real_Estate/Royal_LePage/JimBrown.html**) is an Internet service, purporting to be Canada's only coast-to-coast real estate broker, with over 5,000 agents.

- The Electronic Commerce Association (ECA) is a nonprofit organization established to advance electronic commerce and business use of technology in Canada. The association has more than 400 members from the public and private sectors. The ECA has regular seminars on such topics as electronic document management, commerce on the Internet, and Electronic Data Exchange. Discussions focus on available technologies and their impact on how business is conducted.

Mexico. Mexico has been somewhat slower to embrace Internet entrepreneurism.

Pixel Internacional S.A. de C.V. (PixelNet) claims to be the first Internet commercial IAP in Mexico, offering e-mail, Gopher, WWW, Usenet news, local news, and other services to businesses. PixelNet is headquartered in Monterrey with presence in Mexico City and Guadalajara. The company plans to extend service to others cities in Mexico.

Atlantic and Caribbean Island Nations. Interest in the Internet is growing in the island nations of the Atlantic Ocean and the Caribbean. Lynx is an IAP serving Bermuda. Other IAPs are attempting to establish themselves in Jamaica, Barbados, and the Bahamas.

Central and South America. Increasing numbers of organizations in Central and South America are looking to become IAPs or to assist local businesses' use of WWW and other Internet-related services.

Two early entrants are RACSAnet in Costa Rica and Asociados Espada C.A. of Venezuela. In addition, local telephone companies are likely to become access providers. Already, Embratel in Brazil offers Internet access. How these telephone companies provide access, at what rates, and whether they permit competition (including resale of their Internet services) is undetermined. Global

Enterprise Services/JvNCnet in the United States also has a direct link into Argentina, offering Internet access services through an Argentinean provider.

For Central and South America to prosper, an open and lightly regulated Internet access environment is necessary to foster competition and produce the best results for the business community. Increased competition drives creativity and will help South America become an even more integral part of the global economic community.

Europe. The European Internet access market is quite robust. Among the countries showing tremendous innovation and movement toward full commercial use are the United Kingdom, the Netherlands, and Germany. In addition, there are pan-European networks like EUnet and the newly formed EuroNet Internet.

According to Dataquest, Inc., personal computer shipments to Europe reached almost 3.5 million units during the first quarter of 1995. This is an increase of more than 28 percent from the same period a year earlier. For the first time in years, European PC shipments and their rate of expansion exceeded the growth in the United States. Home PCs in Europe grew by more than 44 percent during the first quarter, compared with a 24 percent gain in the market for office PCs. The expansion of PCs is a prerequisite for Internet use and growth.

Germany. Germany possesses one of the most formidable business economies in Europe and, along with the United Kingdom, signals how readily the use of the Internet as a business tool is being accepted in Europe.

Among the Internet-related businesses in Germany today are

- Netplace Internet Consulting, offering WWW services and Internet consulting in the Munich area

- Contrib.Net, offering full Internet access in most major cities of Germany for fixed rather than usage-sensitive fees

- PFM News and Mail, an Internet provider in Mainz/Wiesbaden

- Germany.net, a free Internet provider and WWW online service

- Nacamar, a commercial Internet provider in all major cities in Germany

Other German IAPs include Individual Network, Internetworking Systems, MUC.DE, Spacenet GmbH, and Touchnet GmbH.

Because of the robust German economy and the large number of new PCs shipped during the first quarter of 1995 (848,300), the country can expect business interest in Internet use to skyrocket during the next several years. This will bring new entrepreneurs to provide Internet Protocol access, Web services, security, and consulting.

United Kingdom. The United Kingdom is another bellwether country. Already activities and interest similar to what is occurring in the United States, Canada, and Germany are happening in the United Kingdom.

Some early U.K. entrants include

- Frontier Internet Services, based in London, offers various services including IP dial-up, personal Web pages, company Web pages, and WWW advertising.

- U-NET is an Internet access and service provider based in Warrington.

- The Electronic Telegraph provides a complete copy of the United Kingdom's *Daily Telegraph* free to Internet users.

- Milestone SuperStore offers products and services to the Internet community, including the United States, Europe, the United Kingdom, and worldwide markets. Flowers, car audio, travel house, car insurance, and a bargain basement are among its offerings.

- UK Online is creating a new medium for information and entertainment. Clubs, lifestyle magazines, news services, shopping, Internet access, and e-mail are all part of its services.

- London Calling Internet is an independent, cooperative group offering an entertaining and informative place to visit with easy access to services (many related to London and the United Kingdom), leisure-oriented editorials, and new items available through the Net via mail order.

Other IAPs serving the United Kingdom include BTnet (British Telecom), Cerberus, Demon Internet, DIRCon, PIPEX, and Total Connectivity Prov. Ltd.

Other European Activity. Other European countries that are most active on the Internet are France, Italy, the Netherlands, the Scandinavian countries, and Russia. Many other countries are also in early stages of commercial Internet service development. Table 13-4 shows some of the major known IAPs in these countries today.

Table 13-4:
Other European IAPs

Organization	Country
Internet Way	France
Galactica	Italy
I2U	Italy
ITnet	Italy
IUnet	Italy
Internet Way	France
Internet Exchange Europer	Netherlands
TOPNET	Netherlands
XS4ALL	Netherlands
RELCOM	Russia
Sovan Teleport	Russia
Nordic Carriers	Scandinavia
UNINETT	Norway
Powertech Information Systems	Norway

In terms of PC growth by mid-1995, Norway, Finland, and Sweden experienced rates of 60 percent, 46 percent, and 40 percent, respectively, compared to the first quarter of 1994. Italy's 283,000 units was an increase of 34 percent over the year before, and second in volume only to Germany. The Netherlands shipped 233,000 units and grew at a rate of 39 percent. With this degree of growth in PCs, businesses will be looking for ways to make them pay off. The Internet is clearly one of the directions they will be exploring.

Asia and the South Pacific. Japan seems to be embracing the Internet most aggressively in Asia. I found the following IAPs using a Yahoo search and the keywords "Japan" and "Internet": Fujitsu, Global OnLine, IBM-Japan, IIJ, InterCon, and InternetKDD, as well as NEC, RIMNET, SpinNet (AT&T Jens), TokyoNet, TWICS Kabushiki Kaisha, and Tokai Com.Plat.Net.

These resources appeared from that same search:

- Language Engineering Corporation (LEC) provides English-to-Japanese desktop translation software, Internet e-mail translation services, and natural language processing development services.

- TKO Personnel, Inc., specializes in recruitment and careers in Japan and the Asia-Pacific region. Job applicants can view job descriptions online, complete with salary range. Employers have access to an active list of bicultural candidates and their qualifications in the semiconductor, software, and telecommunications industries.

- Internet Shopping Mall offers Japanese hypertext mark-up language (HTML) creation, as well as a Web space for Japanese and local Japanese community services in San Jose, California.

- INFORUM Home Page is designed to improve the quality and quantity of information about and from Japan and to promote and encourage use of the Internet among Japanese corporate, academic, and governmental organizations.

- Using Japanese on the Internet contains various resources, links, and guides to support using Japanese on the Internet.

- Internet Guide to Japan Information Resources is an experimental project.

- GNJ Spectrum is a bulletin board system (BBS) offering Internet, OneNet, OneNet Japan, and Pride International Network gateways to users in Japan.

- Japan Edge (The Internet Edge Culture Archive of Japan) is the first Japanese-edge culture archive. This archive introduces Japanese street/underground culture information.

China. There are IAPs in mainland China today, but none are commercial. The Institute of High Energy Physics of the Chinese Academy of Sciences (CAS) is connected via both the Energy Sciences Network (U.S. Department of Energy) and KEK in Japan. The Networking and Computing Facility of China in Beijing connects several institutes of CAS plus Beijing University and Tsinghua University in a metropolitan area network (MAN) that is connected to SprintLink in Stockton, California.

For more information on current Chinese networks, contact **zhengc@cnd.org** (Cindy Zheng).

Hong Kong. Hong Kong has been exceptionally active for a small country. One of the major providers is Hong Kong Supernet, which provides coverage to Hong Kong, China, and other Southeast Asian countries.

One recent innovation, in an attempt to address the needs of the business community, is an Internet-to-fax program. Through this project, you can now reach those in Hong Kong who have access to a fax machine but no e-mail. For more information on this experiment, access **http://linux1. balliol.ox.ac.uk/fax/faxsend.html** or send e-mail to **Pindar.Wong@ hk.super.net**.

Another interesting program is the Hong Kong Business Directory, a free service on the WWW that lets Internet users all over the world source products, find manufacturers, locate importers and exporters, and find hotels, services, suppliers, buyers, and even individuals in Hong Kong.

Because many companies from China, Taiwan, Korea, Japan, and Singapore also have branch offices in Hong Kong, users of this directory can reach a large number of companies from those countries as well.

The directory contains more than 123,400 businesses, and it can be searched by keywords. Most entries are company or individual names only. Some entries have additional information such as product lists or catalogs, which the search engine also examines. Entries with graphic catalogs available are clearly marked.

In addition, users can also send "inquiries" directly to any company free of charge by simply filling in a form.

Another service, multiple inquiries, allows users to inquire about more than one company at one time. To avoid potential abuse of this service, there is a charge and users must preregister with FarEast.com, the publisher.

Further information can be obtained by e-mail to **enzo@FarEast.com** or at **http://FarEast.Com/HongKong/directory.html**.

Other Active Asian Countries. Throughout Asia, the Internet is gaining in popularity. Other Internet providers from the region are I-Net Technologies and Kornet in Korea; Singapore Telecom and Technet in Singapore; and HiNet (formerly DCI) in Taiwan.

Korea, Singapore, Taiwan, and especially India will probably take advantage of the Internet for commercial use. Many of these countries have personnel that travel to other locations to provide contract engineering or design work on a temporary basis. In the future this will be accomplished via the Internet without the need for extensive travel.

Middle East. The most active country in the Middle East has been Israel. A variety of Internet-related software products are under development in Israel, and its geographic isolation makes the Internet an even more important tool for its future economic prosperity.

Interest in commercial Internet services also appears to be growing in Egypt, Saudi Arabia, and the United Arab Emirates, although few IAPs have yet emerged.

Some of the providers serving the Middle East are NetVision and Trendline Information & Commercial Services in Israel, and Emirates Internet in the United Arab Emirates.

Australia and New Zealand. Australia has been a hot area for commercial Internet growth during late 1994 and early 1995.

Current active Australian IAPs include AARNet, Connect.com.au, Corinthian Internet Services, Internet Access Australia, MagnaData Internet Services, and The Message eXchange.

AARNet was the original research and education network in Australia. It operates the Australian Network Information Center which assigns Internet addresses and domains within the region. AARNet provides services to value-added resellers—organizations that resell Internet access and services to third parties. AARNet funds and maintains the Australian Computer Emergency Response Team (AUSCERT) for handling network security alerts and advisories. AARNet claims to have the largest transPacific telecommunications link to the Internet.

AUSNet Service Pty Ltd. purports to be Australia's only independent Internet service provider with a private backbone around Australia and direct links to the United States and the United Kingdom.

NetSpace Online Systems, of Victoria, has provided Internet access services since 1991 in a number of guises (the most prominent being MacInsanity and Insane Public Access Internet). Since leaving the nonprofit group APANA (Australian Public Access Networking Association) in February 1995, the company has focused on commercial clients. In addition to providing Internet connectivity, NetSpace Online provides Internet consulting services, training, and WWW authoring aimed at home and business users.

Africa. Internet access in Africa has come about more slowly, with most of the growth occurring in South Africa. Given the state of most public telecommunications systems in Africa, it may take a longer time for commercial use to catch on here than in other parts of the world. It is possible that direct satellite links may help.

Known IAPs in Africa include InfoTek, The Internet Solution, and TICSA in South Africa, and Internet Africa in Zaire.

The Internet as a Global Economy

The Internet is no longer the domain of the United States alone. The Internet is a global phenomenon. It helps organizations conduct business remotely. The Norwegian company that uses a rock mechanics expert in Ontario, Canada to assist with oil explorations in South Africa is but one example.

In addition, entirely new businesses are arising. Language Engineering Corporation (LEC) in Japan provides English-Japanese translation services.

Global Translation Systems (Chapel Hill, North Carolina) provides large-scale and machine-translation projects for corporations in the fields of telecommunications, computers, consumer products, and others. They work principally in English, Spanish, French, and German and have also conducted work in other languages. Final documents are delivered in electronic media and/or hard copy via fax, courier, Internet, or direct modem transfer—at the client's preference. Global's Web site is **http://www.interpath.net/~global/**.

Another new business opportunity was uncovered by @pangaea.net. This organization provides access to key international business contacts and information on associations, events, and news—all focusing on international business. Visitors use this service for immediate access and contact with thousands of overseas suppliers, distributors, research companies, advertising agencies, manufacturers, customs agents, freight forwarders, and finance companies.

As part of this service, @pangaea.net is developing an online Global Business Directory and an international business match-making service called Interactive Global Marketplace™. The company is looking for internationally minded firms worldwide to list. Further information about @pangaea.net is available via phone at (212) 678-8500 or e-mail at **pangaea@panix.com**.

Translation services, geologic mining information transfers, marketing planning, corporate mergers, sales of goods and services—all of these are happening on the Internet today around the world. The Internet is truly becoming one of the tools that helps the global economy to function. We have the capability to make contact, exchange ideas, and do business with less concern for time zones and language barriers than ever before.

It is critical for businesses to understand how the tools offered by the Internet can directly benefit their organizations. It is even more important that businesses express their desires to government regulators to ensure a fair and robust Internet access marketplace exists in their nations. Without this freedom and "buyer's market" environment, businesses operating in restrictive countries will be at an increasing disadvantage. This may lead those companies to contract with providers in other nations as a way around this problem. For example, a company in Zimbabwe could provide its documents to a cybermall in London or Toronto—and nobody would know the difference or care!

Governments must understand the true globalizing effect that the Internet is having and recognize that closing borders is becoming more and more difficult. The solution is to understand the changes that are under way and embrace them. The ultimate beneficiaries will be their own domestic businesses and populations.

Conclusion

As you can see, the Internet has become a truly global phenomenon. This impacts us all in several ways. First, multinational companies now have the ability to communicate more effectively than ever before with their international facilities and partners. Second, countries that have not been viewed as in the main stream of world economics now have the ability to position themselves in ways previously not possible. Last, through the use of Internet's interactive abilities, we have the ability to break through cultural barriers and create understanding on a worldwide level. The impact on how we conduct business and teach our children will be significant. It is important that we, as users of the technology, be the drivers rather than simply letting the hype and technology drive us. Let's use these wonderful tools to enhance all of our lives!

Chapter Fourteen

AN ALTERNATIVE
TO PRIVATE
DATA NETWORKS

More and more organizations are either exploring or actually implementing closed user group internetworks to help them better interact with their own branches, customers, suppliers, or colleagues. This approach can supplement or replace traditional point-to-point leased-line private networks.

As far back as the 1960s, large companies became aware that it was less costly to pay the telephone company or a long-distance carrier a flat fee per month for a communications "pipe" between two locations than to continue to dial direct all of the time. When there was sufficient voice, fax, video, or data traffic between two specific sites to justify a leased line, this was called the "crossover point."

These private lines connected two points. Other sites must be connected with an additional pair. A single private line could provide "multi-drop" functions connecting locations like a string of beads, yet it was, in reality, a series of pairs linked together.

Private lines are mileage-dependent, meaning that your fees are determined by how many miles are between the two points you want to connect. A typical voice-grade private line capable of carrying 56kbps easily costs several hundred dollars per month, and can cost more for greater distance. Throw in international connectivity, and suddenly the costs can exceed several thousand dollars per month.

If an organization consisted of five locations, all needing frequent communications with each other, it would require at least five private lines of varying costs based on the distance. In addition, the company must monitor the information transported over the circuits, as the carriers typically do not. This adds to the personnel and equipment costs.

As you can see, this can get expensive very quickly. Other issues present problems. Point-to-point circuits link only those two locations. Costs probably prohibit connecting your smaller locations, your suppliers, or your customers, although it may be valuable to connect these sites as well. Such companies need a cost-effective, efficient fashion.

Security is one apparent advantage of a private line network when compared to the Internet. Given that the private network is physically closed, the risk of intrusions is lower. But private networks are not as secure as they may appear.

Wire tapping is an inevitable spectre. Certainly this can occur, but it takes tremendous effort and is easily done only by true professionals.

A point of vulnerability exists in your telephone carrier's point of presence (POP). Anyone with knowledge can intercept information within the POP. Most telephone companies take great precautions to provide physical security; nevertheless, the risk remains.

Lastly, the greatest threat to security is always from within. Your own personnel know where and how to hurt you the most if they want to do so.

Planning for security and confidentiality is crucial. Do not be lulled into thinking that a private network alone is sufficiently secure, or that the Internet cannot be made satisfactorily secure. Explore your options and determine what is best for you based on facts and analysis. Don't leave open any back doors, and don't miss a valuable opportunity.

The remainder of this chapter presents examples of how to use the Internet for internal company purposes, communication with suppliers or customers, and as a supplement to or replacement for a point-to-point private network.

Transport EDI Information More Cost-Effectively

EDI is a practice used by many businesses whereby standard forms, such as bills of lading, orders, or inventory, are automatically transmitted between computers. Many times no human intervention occurs.

Suppose you want to place an order for ten million widgets. You fill in an electronic form on your workstation, which in turn sends the information to your mainframe or one of your client/server computers. The system searches its databases and finds that Acme Widgets is your principal widget supplier. It sends a message to Acme's computer. Acme accepts the order, issues a written confirmation notice that will go out in tomorrow's postal mail, and transmits the order to all of its departments that have a need to know (inventory, shipping, billing and accounting, sales, etc.).

Many companies use this practice today. The communications methods, however, vary widely. In fact, companies such as Premenos in California and Sterling Software in Ohio act as intermediaries between EDI interactions and ensure their proper receipt.

In most cases, companies using EDI can choose between using direct-dialed long-distance service; "value-added carriers" such as TYMNET, Advantis, or SprintNet; or "leased-line" long-distance circuits physically connecting the sites permanently. Direct-dialed long-distance can be quite expensive, particularly when it involves international locations. It is both usage and destination sensitive—the more it is used, the greater the cost.

The Internet offers an interesting alternative for EDI. If the participating locations have Internet access, the data can be handled just as easily as with any other method. In fact, given the declining cost of "leased-line" Internet connectivity, a 56Kbps connection into the Internet is likely to be quite cost-effective.

At present (and this changes rapidly), you should be able to find an Internet access provider (IAP) that can offer 56Kbps for $300 to $600 per month, plus the cost of the local telephone company circuit needed to connect your location to the service provider's POP. The average 56Kbps price in the United States as of January 1995 was $550. The telco cost varies among local telephone companies and depends on distance. Another $150 to $250 per month is not out of line. So, for a cost of about $650 per month (flat rate, no other usage charges) per site, you can connect to the Internet and exchange EDI information with any location also connected to the Internet worldwide!

It's very easy to look at your cumulative long-distance bills, identify the calls to your EDI counterparts, and compare the costs. Clearly, your EDI partners will need to "play" in the Internet world as well, but I suspect they'll be willing if you push the issue. After all, it's to their benefit to keep you as a satisfied customer.

The "how to" of this application is simple. You need not do anything differently except for the transmission.

Evaluate the different providers of Internet access services in the regions of interest to you, and get the best (not necessarily cheapest) dedicated access to the Internet.

"Have Net—Will Travel" Virtual Office

One beauty of the Internet is that you can control your lifestyle yet still earn a living. Imagine living on a farm at the top of a mountain, yet having regular contact with your employees, coworkers, or bosses worldwide. I know of many people who do this today.

As an employer, you can now hire people in remote locations who are not willing to move to your major site. O'Reilly and Associates does this quite frequently. It works exceptionally well with skilled knowledge workers. In the past, perhaps you couldn't hire particularly desirable workers because of their family commitments or other "roots" to specific locations or because the potential hires simply did not want to move to California or New York. It didn't suit their lifestyles.

Now, by using the network, you can often have the best of both worlds. Clearly, this will not work in all cases. Employees who act in a regular hands-on, supervisory role often must be on-site. For employees who require a great deal of management and supervision, it isn't desirable. However, for the many people who are task—or project—oriented, it may work quite well. This list certainly includes software developers, strategic planners, and product development personnel. It may even include legal and accounting staff.

When used in conjunction with telephone and occasional supplemental face-to-face meetings, remote work environments using the Internet as the communications nervous system can be quite beneficial.

This application is also easy to implement. Assuming that your organization has connectivity at one or more of its principal sites, the remote employee needs an Internet access account and an appropriate computer and modem for connection. Internet accounts can be obtained from a variety of providers. If your employee is in an area with local Internet access, the fees are likely to range from $20 to $35 per month plus $1 to $3 per hour of usage. If your employee needs to use an 800 number for access, the hourly fees could range from $5.40 to $9.50 per hour. The flat monthly fee should remain around $20 to $35.

Connected, remote employees can send e-mail to anyone—both internally within the company and externally. They can use Mosaic or Netscape (or many similar tools) to access the company's various computing resources as if they were at the site. They may even use telnet as a remote log-in capability.

Utilize "Groupware" Software Across Your Organization

An interesting phenomenon of the past year is the advent of groupware software packages, such as Lotus Notes. These programs are designed as "shared" software programs, in contrast to the usual individual packages. Groupware programs are designed to communicate the actions of various individuals to the rest of the team so that all are up to date on activities.

For example, anytime anyone in an organization sees a client at a cocktail party or baseball game, receives a telephone call from the client, makes a presentation to the client, or receives payment from the client, a notice appears in everyone's electronic mailbox alerting them to new information. No one is out of the loop. The quality and integrity of information is maintained.

This approach works exceedingly well in a single location. What if key people are distributed across the country or the world? By using the Internet as the wide-area linkage, all appropriate personnel can participate in project management as if they were at the same location.

Consider the implications for major projects. You may not need to move employees among sites, and you may increase efficiency.

Another example of groupware's usefulness is an application by the Chicago Research and Planning Group (CRPG), a 120-member organization of Midwest information systems executives. The CRPG uses Notes to post a catalog of training courses offered by members and vendors. It also uses Notes as a bulletin board service (BBS) to post meeting announcements and as a forum for members to share views on emerging technologies and service providers. Lotus provided the CRPG a free copy of Notes in December 1993, and by June 1994, 70 of the 120 top IS executives were using Notes.

By using a Notes platform rather than an open discussion group, such as a Usenet group, these chief information officers have a greater sense of confidentiality and assurance that the participants are part of their organization.

In extensive interviews with more than fifty Notes sites, International Data Corporation (IDC) found that the three-year return on investment (ROI) for Notes applications ranged from 16 percent to 1,666 percent on an average investment of $240,000. The average three-year ROI was 179 percent. These paybacks were largely attributable to time saved completing projects and solving problems. In some cases, the payback was credited to decreased need for mainframe computing cycles.

Frito-Lay and McCormick and Company are another good example of groupware use. These two companies trade inventory information using a replicated Notes database. In early 1994, Frito-Lay built the Notes application to function similarly to EDI.

Although this particular application currently runs over dial-up connections, it could not be extended economically using the Internet. Prior to the dial-up access, the two companies had used a commercial EDI value-added network at a fee of roughly 50 cents per transaction.

Another interesting innovation was developed by the Walter Shelby Group in Bethesda, Maryland. John Buckman was developing TILE, which converts Notes to hypertext markup language (HTML). TILE will permit organizations that use Notes to translate it directly into the HTML format used by the World Wide Web. For those with a Mosaic-like interface, check out **http://www.shelby.com/pub/tile**.

Groupware programs are a relatively new innovation. Several groupware conferences exist; you might gain insight by visiting such shows and exploring how groupware might be useful to your organization.

Once you have determined that groupware works for you, your systems administrator needs to ensure that the data streams can work over your Internet connection, and you are on your way!

Incorporate Desktop Video into Your Communications Channels

Do you need to "see" who you are communicating with in real time? Or do you need to see objects? In the very near future, you will be able to establish a video window on your workstation, and still display documents, video, or other information to discuss with your distant colleagues.

The concept of video communications is not new. In fact, AT&T introduced Picturephone at the 1964 World's Fair. As you can probably tell, it still is far from ubiquitous in our homes. One main reason it was not adopted more readily (aside from costs) is that no one wanted to be first. Whom could you call?

Several companies are introducing relatively low-cost video services, including products from Intel, InVision, and Northern Telecom. These units include the hardware, small workstation camera, and software. The price of several thousand dollars is becoming affordable to many businesses.

The key question remains, however: Why do you need to see the other party? Here are a few possible scenarios where images—even less than full-motion broadcast TV quality—might apply.

How about personnel interviews? Often we conduct screening interviews over the telephone, but have no idea how an individual presents himself or herself in person. By using a video interview, corporations may be able to reduce the number of people they bring in for visits but find are not fully qualified because of their demeanor or how they conduct themselves when in full view.

How about strategic negotiations? If it isn't possible to travel when needed—especially internationally—perhaps a video conference can be of assistance.

Although video has many marvelous qualities, it will not displace travel, voice, or written communications in the near future. It's important that we identify areas where it can fill existing gaps and be of immediate benefit.

Conclusion

The concept of the small "i" internet is important. The Internet with its wealth of people, computing resources, and databases may not be appropriate for all companies. Many wish only to be able to better interact with their own customers, suppliers, or branches. Understanding how the Internet may be able to assist you in this process can help you save significant investment capital, and therefore enhance your overall bottom line and profitability.

Chapter Fifteen

COST JUSTIFICATION
OF INTERNET
INVESTMENTS

Understanding your requirements, and leading to cost justification of the Internet, is a process designed to provide comparative analysis between anticipated results and required efforts. This is accomplished through a systematic analysis of your current operations and projections of possible impacts, and it will lead to a much more satisfying business decision that can be clearly communicated throughout the organization's management chain.

To effectively conduct a cost-justification analysis, you must have

- an understanding of existing expenditures (what you do today)

- possible new sources of revenue accessible through the Internet (new customers, more revenue from existing customers, or the ability to better keep current customers)

- potential alternatives to your status quo

Without spending the time to analyze your current environment, it is nearly impossible to make a solid case for any new business tools, let alone ones as mysterious as those offered via the Internet. You need to slice through the mists and determine the real, likely tangible impact the Internet might have on your organization's operations. What will it cost? What benefits will it provide—both hard numbers and intangible benefits? Who will it affect? What are the risks, and how can you minimize them?

It is also important to evaluate the risk of *not* implementing an Internet solution. For example, if your competitors aggressively market their services over the Internet, will this erode your market share? Perhaps you have been unable to hire people you want because they do not want to relocate. By using the Internet and "telecommuting," everyone could be satisfied and a mutually beneficial relationship created. Should you decide the Internet is not for you at this time, you may lose out in other ways. It's worth some time to consider this carefully.

The Internet is not a panacea for every information flow challenge or a solution for every ailment. It is important to consider Internet services from as many angles as possible, to ensure that you are investing wisely. Few businesses can afford to buy a product or service simply because it is the latest technology (the high "gee whiz" factor). It must increase revenue or reduce expenses, and in either case, it must contribute to an enhanced bottom line. One illustration is the re-engineering of existing applications from closed, proprietary environments to "open standards," often called "business transformation." Alternately, you might find that building additional applications (i.e., desktop video conferencing or enhanced intercompany information repositories, servers) are a higher priority with greater payback than changing the basic infrastructure.

These decisions require an analytical approach to the status quo and the potential trade-offs presented by Internet alternatives. Real-world examples can help you identify the potential value, and make the best choices at this point.

Internet Costs

A frequent miscalculation by many looking into the Internet is expecting that the only cost is the Internet service provider. A range of obvious recurring and one-time costs are involved, as well as a variety of costs that are not so readily apparent. This chapter sheds light on *all* of your potential costs.

Prices for Internet access service vary widely. Dial-up services cost $10 to $35 per month, plus $1 to $3 per hour for usage. Dedicated access (leased-line) services normally start at a minimum of 56Kbps, with prices ranging from $5,000 to $16,000 per year *per site connected*.

Your organization could have a single Internet-connected site, while all other facilities use a private network for Internet access through the main location. Or you may want each of your branches to connect to the Internet locally. This becomes a performance and cost issue. Some Internet access providers include equipment and software, but others do not. It is important to compare "apples to apples" so you have a clear picture of your potential costs in all locations.

Then come the other costs, including some that might be hidden, including the following:

- Local or long-distance telephone company charges (dial-up costs or "tail circuits" for leased lines between your company locations and the Internet service provider's Point of Presence [POP]). These range from pennies per call to $5,000 per year or more, per connection. Tail circuits are mileage dependent in most locations, so costs will vary.

  For example, in the Chicago area there are "timed message units" for local data calls. The costs vary depending on your distance from your service provider. They can be as low as a few cents per minute, but they can add up rather quickly. Leased-line services are typically charged by mileage and can vary quite a bit depending on the local and/or long-distance telephone companies that participate in the connection. In many instances, the tail circuit can be as costly as fees from the Internet access provider.

- Additional hardware needed (routers, csu/dsu, cabling, etc.). These costs can start at a few thousand dollars per year, and climb rapidly, depending on the services. Clearly the impact is directly related to the method of pro-curement—direct purchase, length of amortization, lease, etc.

- Additional software needed, such as a Transmission Control Protocol/ Internet Protocol (TCP/IP) and "user interfaces" for electronic mail (e-mail) or network navigation. This includes both systems software, such as TCP/IP, Novell NetWare, and others, or applications software such as Lotus Notes. Cost for these packages typically start in the hundreds of dollars and can climb, although site licenses and other forms of bulk purchase arrangements can help. You may need more than one copy of some packages, an organization or site license, or a package that can operate with your local area network or workstation environment.

  You may also want to standardize on a particular user interface, like Mosaic, Spry, or Netscape. These actions may have costs, not only in procurement of the software but also in administration of standards. You may find it easier to select one common interface than to support multiple ones.

- Modifications to your internal LAN. For example, you may have to use equipment to translate X.25 into TCP/IP. It is difficult to estimate these costs, as they are so specific to each organization.

- Establishment of an internal Internet "help desk" to train and assist users in how to gain the maximum value from your Internet investment. Depending on the size of the organization, this can quickly evolve into a full-time position, by one or more individuals. The number of internal "consumers" that a help desk can serve is hard to estimate and depends on the technical sophistication of your staff. A rough estimate is one Internet help desk person for between fifty and one hundred active Internet users. Revise this estimate based on workload and effectiveness.

- Internal Network Operations Center services. Who watches the network, ensures its integrity, and coordinates with outside vendors? You may outsource this function to another company or do it yourself as part of your existing network administration efforts. Either way, it is a real cost in terms of personnel effort, additional workstations, and software, with the price tag depending on the size and complexity of your operation.

- Establishment of internal network security policies and plans. How much will you lose if your intellectual property—your customer records, new product plans, and such—are compromised? Securing your LAN is costly, involving such services as packet and route filtering in your routers (inexpensive) to full applications layer gateways that cost $20,000 per year or more per Internet connection. If you have more than one Internet-connected site, you will require some form of protection—designed to provide *acceptable* levels of security risk—at each site.

All things considered, an organization will spend

- from $10,000 to $50,000 per year *minimum* for a 56Kbps connection into the Internet

- from $24,000 to $70,000 per year *minimum* for T-1 service (1.5Mbps)

These costs depend on the number of users in an organization, the nature of their use (heavy file transfers or mostly e-mail), distance from a service provider's facilities (tail circuits), and the choice of server providers available (Which providers offer service in your area, and which services do they provide locally?). You need to find a substantial amount of "trade-off" dollars and business functionality to justify these levels of expenditure.

Now that you have at least an idea of the costs of Internet connectivity, you need to explore the direct tangible benefits to your organization. Perhaps the best way to do that is to explore cost-justification techniques and examples of how others have faced the same questions.

Cost Justification Using Specific Business Issues

To illustrate how to conduct a cost-justification analysis in your organization, it helps to use a pattern. This example explores the specific business issue at hand, the identifiable quantifiable costs associated with the issue, the design implications for an Internet solution (What kind of services do you need? Dial-up? Leased-line access? How much bandwidth?), and the associated benefits.

Before you can evaluate the viability of the Internet as a solution, you need to clearly articulate the business issue. A business issue is not file transfer protocol (ftp), telnet, or e-mail. A business issue is not Mosaic, Gopher, Netscape, or World Wide Web.

A business issue might be

- the need to reduce corporate expenses by 15 percent

- the need to reduce customer turnover from 17 percent per month to 3 percent per month

• the need to find a way to double sales without a concurrent increase in expenses

Many examples of business challenges exist. The key is to find an area you believe can change in a positive way through a more efficient method of communications.

Replacing courier costs with Internet

Our example investigates how a mortgage banking company supplemented and displaced some courier services with interactions conducted across the Internet. Costs previously were unchecked, and personnel were becoming dissatisfied.

Business Issue. The Southeastern Banking and Finance Company (a fictitious company) needed to reduce the cost of software update distributions to its 500 branch offices. The previous solution used overnight courier services. The packages included software updates of custom forms for company laser printers.

Once you identify a specific business issue, you must then identify all costs associated with that issue and determine how they are impacted by a change. Remember, the rationale of "because we've always done it this way" doesn't cut it anymore. You need to be clear why you conduct business in this manner and see whether any better ways might be considered.

Quantifiable Costs. With an average cost of $15 per package for shipping, plus an estimated cost of $3 to copy disks, print labels, stuff envelopes, and label each package (representing a per-unit cost of $18), a per-update cost to reach all 500 sites is $9,000. It takes the company's employees an average of five minutes per package to fill out the required forms, assemble the materials to ship, and prepare the package for shipment. Updates are issued twice each month, resulting in a total annual cost of $216,000.

After identifying this range of costs for this business problem, you need to gather information so you can design an internetworking solution and see whether it is cost justified. To do this, you must determine the volume of information involved. This could be number of pages or the size of a data file (number of bytes).

Remember, when you are trying to assess how much bandwidth you need, you must multiply bytes times eight to calculate the number of bits. This is important because bandwidth is characterized in bits per second.

Volume of Information. The software shipped from the sample company by courier is an average of 2MB. In addition, other written documents of up to 1MB data file size are occasionally included in the packages.

"Mission Criticality." Another key factor is the degree of urgency. Is the information you are transporting critical to the functioning of the operation, or will it make litte difference if it takes a few hours?

In the case of the sample company, it is important that all sites use the same laser printer formats for corporate consistency. Therefore, all sites must receive the updates within twenty-four hours. The company places a high value on corporate consistency and image. Using different forms at the same time is unacceptable.

It is important to recognize that certain functions, such as the distribution of courier packages or sending faxes, may go on in several different locations of your business many times a day. You need to have a handle on these occurrences. How often does this process or activity occur—once an hour, once a day, once a week, or some other time variable?

Frequency. This particular application is occurring twice a month at the sample company.

Business Issue Summary. Once you identify the nature of the issue, quantify its potential value, determine the amount of data to be communicated, and know the degree of criticality and how frequently this process occurs, you can begin to engineer the size of the Internet "pipe" you might need.

Internet Connectivity Requirements. In review, you need to send a 2MB to 3MB file to 500 sites twice each month, and the information must reach all sites within a 24-hour period.

A 3MB file is equal to a 24Mb file. A conservative estimate puts the amount of information at 30Mb (this includes additional header and overhead information required in the data transmission). Given the anticipated load from additional applications, you could accomplish this using a dedicated connection to the Internet, and broadcast the information to all 500 sites in one transmission.

If this is the only application, alternatives such as batch and dial-up services or data compression may reduce the requirement for bandwidth. In actual environments, carefully explore all options before implementing any solutions.

For the traffic level in this example and assuming no other applications, a 56Kbps dedicated connection at the headquarters site is sufficient. Each of the 500 remote sites needs a minimum of a 19.2Kbps dial-up host connection from an Internet service provider. This permits remote sites to dial into a local service provider and download the information to their computing environments at their convenience.

Internet Connectivity Costs. For the corporate headquarters, the cost should range from $12,000 to $20,000 per year. This includes the router (the Internet "switching" mechanism), CSU/DSU, average "leased-line tail circuit" costs to get from the service provider's site to your facility (dedicated connections only), and Internet service provider fees.

For the field offices, 500 dial-up accounts averaging four hours per month at $6 per hour for 800-number service would cost about $144,000 per year. This assumes that each office already has a computer, appropriate modem, and communications software. It is likely that you can find a local dial-up provider (rather than an 800 number service) for about $20 per month, reducing this cost to about $120,000.

Other Potential Costs. Internal LAN modifications, additional internal network operations and monitoring costs, establishing an internal help desk and continuing internal training all can add up quickly, and will be specific to each organization. Costs could run as high as one or two full-time employees ($40,000 plus) as well as one-time equipment and software costs of several thousand dollars. The larger and more complex your organization is, the greater the need—and therefore the costs—for these functions. It is important to include these costs in your plans.

Last, consider security of your "intellectual property." Costs to ensure network security can range from $2,000 to $25,000 per year. It may be sufficient to secure only your main location, or you may require security at outlying sites as well. In this example, only the headquarters location ($25,000 per year) needs security.

Bottom-Line Analysis. Based on the Southeastern Banking and Finance Company, here's a comparison of the impacted expenses to the anticipated costs.

Impacted Expenses

$15 per package for shipping plus $3 for copying disks, printing labels, stuffing envelopes, etc. =	$18 per-unit cost
500 total sites affected x $18 =	$9,000
24 times per year (twice a month) =	$216,000 per year

Anticipated Costs

Headquarters Connectivity	$20,000
Field Office Connectivity	
500 Accounts	
4 hours use per month	
$6 per hour usage fees	
Total Field Connectivity	$120,000
Personnel Costs	$20,000
Anticipated Hardware/Software	$4,000
Security	$25,000
Summary Total	$169,000

Total Impacted Expenses	$216,000 per year

Total Anticipated Costs	$169,000 per year

The costs could be much lower after specific analysis and engineering design work are conducted.

Conclusion

As you can see, Southeastern Banking can anticipate a savings of $47,000 per year. This is a reduction of the per-unit cost from $18 down to $14—a more than 20 percent reduction. In addition, a variety of intangibles make the Internet an even more attractive alternative.

- Updates can be delivered more quickly. The new software can be loaded the same workday it is received. Also, there is no additional delay for the package to be received, unpacked, and implemented, nor is there delay due to weather problems, traffic, or other such unforeseeable events.

- Updates can be delivered directly to the destination computers, requiring only minimal additional work as opposed to unpacking and loading physical storage media.

- Corrections and additional "mini-updates" can be sent far more affordably; distributions no longer cost $18 per package minimum.

- Clerical personnel can accomplish other tasks in the time they have recovered, and their morale has improved markedly.

- E-mail is now available to branch offices at relatively minimal incremental costs, and remote employees are beginning to feel much more "in the loop" with immediate communication of company "happenings." Shorter documents and queries can be sent for negligible costs.

Not all courier services costs can or are likely to be displaced. That is why it's important to do a detailed justification analysis *before* you set your expectations. Other applications are likely to occur once you have established connectivity. Anticipate this event both in your costs analysis and in your benefits considerations.

By considering the specific business areas where you believe the Internet might be of value, the investments required to implement Internet solutions, and any trade-offs that might occur, your organization is more likely to experience positive change and avoid unnecessary disappointments. This process requires time and effort on your part, yet it is certainly worth it.

I strongly recommend that you attempt to cost justify any major changes in the way you conduct business, especially if they require an investment. When justifying Internet use, consider all of the ways your organization exchanges information today: telephone, memo, fax, data disks, personal visits, courier packages, letters, invoices, Electronic Data Interchange, and so on. Think about who initiates the communications and who actually sends them (you, your secretary, another employee?). Then consider why it is done this way. Lastly, investigate the costs associated with these practices and communications.

Are there better ways to conduct the information flow of your business? Are these alternatives more efficient? Are they faster? Do they involve fewer people? Do they result in a broader reach to the marketplace?

As you have seen from the example, these modifications may be substantially nontrivial—resulting in impacts of millions of dollars. In today's business climate, that's hard to ignore.

You might also have guessed by now that this is not a one-time process, and the Internet is not the only viable tool to consider. As part of a continuing information management strategy, the Internet and internetworking will play a key part in the success of the world's best organizations well into the next century. Continued evaluation and vigilance concerning new concepts, new services, new products, and new vendors offer substantial benefits to you and your organization.

To help you, a cost-justification worksheet is provided in Appendix A. This worksheet will help you step through the process and includes samples of areas you need to consider both in your business and in evaluating Internet alternatives. The worksheet will also help you conduct a benefit-to-cost ratio analysis.

*C*hapter Sixteen

You may feel that you are ready to explore the use of Internet services as a tool for your business. By this time you are comfortable with the business applications that need to be addressed. You have identified, at least with a first look, the likely costs associated with an appropriate Internet solution, and the numbers look good. Now what do you do?

Have you read Susan Estrada's *Connecting to the Internet*, and are you ready to pick a vendor? Have you investigated the national providers like Performance Systems International, UUNet, Netcom, Sprint, or MCI? Have you considered America OnLine, CompuServe, Delphi, or Prodigy? Have you sought out local Internet access providers in your area?

Once you have identified a potential group of providers, are you sure you know what to ask them? How do you ensure—to the best degree possible—that this is the *right* vendor for you?

For an individual user, I suggest you try a vendor's service *before* making a long-term commitment. For large organizations, I recommend you develop a Request for Proposals (RFP). This is a time-consuming task that involves thinking through all aspects of your procurement, then communicating them to a list of prospective vendors. In the RFP you indicate the format of their responses, required content, and a deadline for responding. This way, you cut through all of the nuances, buzzwords, and confusing pricing approaches, and you can truly compare services based on vendor responses.

This may sound like a great deal of effort. Just wait until you compare performance, suitability, and pricing of integrated services digital network (ISDN), switched multimegabit data service (SMDS), InterFrame, LANdial, or 56Kbps leased-line services.

As a business, your objective is to find the tools that work most effectively for you. This method lets you take control of the procurement process rather than letting the vendors dicatate to you. It is also valuable to the better vendors, because you will have a much clearer view of your own requirements than had you called and asked for "Internet service, please!"

Developing an RFP

At a minimum, the RFP should contain the elements listed below:

- *Summary statement of the request.* Briefly, the summary statement should identify what you want to accomplish.

- *Description of the requesting organization.* What is the organization's business? How large is the organization by locations, people, or revenues? How many locations, departments, and people will be impacted by the anticipated Internet solution?

- *Description of business application.* This item should identify what you are trying to accomplish functionally.

- *Description of the current computer networking environment.* Does your current environment consist of no data networking, dial-up directly using modems, electronic mail services (AT&TMail or MCIMail), value-added services (Advantis or SprintNet), dedicated access services (frame relay or leased lines), or existing Internet access? What are the issues or problems associated with the current environment?

- *Description of required services.* With this item you need to be as specific as you can. How many locations do you want to connect? Which locations (include the sites' addresses and telephone numbers)? What bandwidth or type of service is required at each location? Do you seek specific performance requirements (i.e., availability [the amount of time the connection is "up"] and latency [the potential delay in transporting data, etc.]).

- *Description of vendor's responses.* This item lets vendors describe their services and what their fees include. Vendors must specifically state whether their services include certain equipment and software and define the level of support. You may want to ask vendors to describe any other equipment or services that you may need for proper functionality. For example, you may need to obtain serial link internetworking protocol (SLIP) software to use an access provider's services, or you may need to reconfigure your local area network mail package to use a dedicated Internet connection.

The RFP is your chance to make the vendors work for you and to share their knowledge of what it will take for a successful Internet implementation.

- *Cost factors.* Ask vendors to be very precise regarding this item. It is most advantageous if you create a pricing matrix and require that the vendors respond in that format. A sample matrix is presented in Table 15.1.

Table 15-1:
Sample Pricing Matrix

Location	Telephone Number	Bandwidth	Monthly Fee	One-time Installation Set-up Fee
Ann Arbor, MI	(313) 426-xxxx	56Kbps	$687	$1,500
Albuquerque, NM	(502) 361-xxxx	Dial-up	$35	$100

The matrix makes it easier for you to compare prices among the responses.

- *Number of copies.* Specify the number of copies you want of each vendor's reponse. This makes it easier for you to distribute copies to your evaluation team.

- *Vendor alternatives.* It is always useful to include this item because it lets vendors tell you why they believe your approach is wrong, or at least might be modified. This lets them be creative, and that can turn out to be quite valuable.

- *Response dates.* Establish a clear calendar of events and tell the vendors in the RFP. This includes the dates of any "bidder's conference," deadline for submitting written questions or requests for clarification, deadline (including time of day and location) for receipt of written responses, acceptable format for responses (written, electronic, etc.), announcement date for "best and final" responses (if any), announcement date for awards, and anticipated implementation dates.

A bidder's conference is normally held shortly after the RFP is issued. The conference permits potential bidders to gather and hear the same information from your organization. It is traditional that any questions answered, either at the meeting or subsequently, be communicated in writing to all interested parties. A bidder's conference is normally used only for larger, complex procurements.

For some procurements, you will get a large number of proposals and may want to select a small subset (normally three or four, at the most) of the responding vendors to bid again with their "Best and Final Offer" (BAFO). Here the vendors must sharpen their pencils and tighten their proposals.

Evaluating Responses to the RFP

To evaluate the various responses as fairly and objectively as possible, it is useful to develop a "weighted factor analysis."

You start by listing all of the criteria that are important to you. The factors generally fall into the groupings described below:

- *Administrative.* Were the responses received on time, in the proper quantities, and in the proper formats? Was the vendor "fully responsive" to the request, or was information omitted?

- *Functional.* Does the proposal answer the request, and how well?

- *Organizational.* How credible is the bidding organization? What is its track record? Are references included, and how did they check out? Did you contact other customers of this vendor that were not provided as a reference? How did they compare? What is the vendor's financial state? How durable is it likely to be?

- *Pricing.* How does the price level and structure compare to those of other bidders? What type and length of commitment does the vendor require? What degree of "up-front" costs versus monthly charges will you incur?

- *Service and relationship.* What kinds of support services can you expect? Does the vendor have a 24-hour help desk? Does the vendor recognize what you need and try to assist, or does its staff appear uninformed, arrogant, or intimidating? Remember, this is your money and you have a moral imperative to spend it with people with whom you can relate well, if possible.

After you have identified the characteristics to evaluate, establish a "weighting" scale. Is this particular factor the most important or of lesser importance? For example, if you need 56Kbps throughput and the vendor primarily offers dial-up accounts at a maximum of 14.4Kbps, this should weigh fairly heavily in your evaluation and would have a high multiplying factor. If you are using a scale in which one is of least importance and five is of greatest importance, this category would likely be a five. On the other hand, a detailed user's manual might be nice to have, but probably won't make or break the success of your Internet effort. This might be weighted as a multiple of one.

Once you have listed each of the criteria and assigned a weighting factor to them, you have essentially created your evaluation sheet. You will need one sheet for each proposal and a complete set for each evaluator. You can enter the numerical scores into a spreadsheet and see how the evaluations turned out.

At this point you can assess intangibles and begin deciding whom to invite to a BAFO step (assuming you have no clear winner).

After the evaluation stage comes contract negotiations. This is when you fine-tune the prices and deliverables as much as possible. During this phase, you will get a much better sense of your future working relationship. Now, everyone is playing hardball. If there will be future relationship and flexibility problems, they may begin to show up here.

Using an RFP can be a tremendous help in comparing "apples to apples" instead of "apples to oranges." In addition, you may find a need to use related documents, such as a Request for Information (RFI) or a Request for Quotations (RFQ).

An RFI is used when you are unsure of your specific requirements and want vendors to respond with information but perhaps not a fully developed proposal. RFIs may even explicitly state that prices are not to be included and that they will be expected when the later RFP is issued. If you are a vendor, recognize that you may still have a chance to be the "sole source" provider if your RFI response is superior to others submitted. For this reason, you should respond as professionally as possible to an RFI.

RFQs are used when you know precisely what you want, and the major deciding factor will be price. RFQs are straightforward and easy to issue but leave vendors little room to be creative. It does, however, establish an easy apples-to-apples price comparison model.

Conclusion

Whichever tools you use, it is important to be able to compare and contrast the various services and relate them directly to your needs. Failure to clearly think through your wants prior to requesting quotations from vendors will lead to confusion and could impair the effectiveness of your Internet solution.

Part Four

REARVIEW MIRRORS

AND ROAD MAPS

FOR THE

INFORMATION HIGHWAY

*C*hapter Seventeen

LESSONS LEARNED,

OPPORTUNITIES

AFFORDED

The Internet has existed for more than thirty years, yet within the past several years it has become an "overnight" sensation. Why has this happened now, and what can we learn from the way the Internet has evolved to become the successful entity that it is today?

For most of its existence, the Internet was an amalgamation of networks, principally funded by governments, used by researchers, students, academic faculty, scientists, and government employees. With the emergence of online information providers (America OnLine, CompuServe, and Prodigy) and electronic mail (e-mail) services from the likes of MCI and AT&T, people began to learn the value of going online. In addition, bulletin board services (BBS) began to spring up in many locations.

Many of the previously research-and education-oriented networks began to offer Internet access to their alumni, the general public, and businesses. This was accomplished through a modification in their "acceptable use policies" or by spinning off a new commercially oriented company. Performance Systems International (PSI) evolved from NYSERnet (the New York State research and education network). Advanced Network & Services (ANS) was an outgrowth of the National Science Foundation Network (NSFnet) program.

In most cases, when government money was invested in a network service provider, that network was prohibited from providing services to organizations or people not related to the funding source's mission.

This may seem complicated, but it is an important point. As an example, the NSFnet could not provide Internet services to General Motors (GM) for activities other than appropriate research or collaboration. If GM used its network access to collaborate with researchers at the University of Michigan, that was fine. If GM wanted to use its NSF-funded Internet connection to conduct business with Toyota in Tokyo, however, it could be argued that the NSF was providing GM with an indirect subsidy.

This issue led to the establishment of Acceptable Use Policies (AUPs) for each network provider, and it further helped stimulate creation of the entire commercial Internet provider community.

Organizations like PSI, ANS, UUNet Technologies, Netcom, Global Enterprise Services, and BBN Planet Internet Services have emerged to meet this demand.

What Can We Learn from the Internet's Evolution?

The evolution of the Internet has taught us a lot about communications technology, and more.

- Government catalyst programs can work. The NSF, Department of Defense, Department of Energy, and assorted other agencies in the United States and internationally have funded network-related programs for years. As a result, a vibrant industry is emerging that will generate billions of dollars of income to companies throughout the world by 1996.

- Would the Internet have happened without government support? Probably not. Each long-distance vendor would have tried to capture the market with its own proprietary language and model—somewhat like SNA or DECnet. Would the vendors be able to intercommunicate? Probably not very easily.

  Because of government "seeding," a new community of independent commercial service providers is growing, and a breeding ground of new Internet talent is coming up through universities, high schools, and now even elementary schools. All of this has happened because of some well-placed taxpayer dollars. People like Steve Wolff at the NSF should be congratulated for their tireless efforts and perseverance in the face of an opinionated, talented, and at times fractious community.

- Government needs a clear "exit strategy." A lesson from the evolution of the Internet is that government funding must have a specific purpose, and when the commercial community can support that purpose as well or better for appropriate fees, the government needs to make an orderly withdrawal.

  Given the uncertainties of the new commercial Internet marketplace, the NSF seems to have done fairly well in this regard, although its plans for departure could have been a bit clearer and executed a bit sooner. This, however, is an observation made in hindsight.

- Organized chaos can be more creative than proprietary development efforts. The Internet, through the Internet Engineering Task Force (IETF) and other related working groups, offers one of the few international, multidiscipline working groups of its kind. People from all over the world can collaborate on new ways to exchange information faster or more efficiently.

  Driven by visionaries like Vint Cerf and Bob Kahn, the IETF is responsible for all of the underlying electronic "gears and cogs" that make the Internet work. Other protocols and approaches are touted as a replacement for Transmission Control Protocol/Internet Protocol (TCP/IP)—the Internet standard—yet nothing else seems quite as good or quite as open.

  Even today, IETF colleagues are working on the release of Transmission Control Protocol/Next Generation (TCP/NG). Perhaps you get a hint as to what TV shows these folks watch when they are not building networks?

  This global "stewing pot" enables talented people worldwide from academic, government, or business organizations to exchange ideas and fine-tune their approaches. It works because of its openness.

- "Give a little; get a little" is an important and successful approach to business. Once you are involved in the Internet, you will rapidly find many resources of value to you that were placed on the net free of charge. It is expected that you will return the favor and provide useful information for new interested people. This may be in the form of white papers, general information, newsletters, or software.

  If we all act in this way, the Internet will become increasingly rich. On the other hand, if the equivalent of an Internet "locust storm" were to occur and people took but never gave . . . . Well, you can see the importance of learning the Internet culture and participating in it rather than just consuming.

  Remember, the Internet isn't a business. It is a community, and if you have gotten this far, it's probably your community now too.

- Technology has developed at a much faster pace than our ability to apply it easily to business functions. Within the Internet, we have done an exceptional job of using evolving technology to move bits of information faster and more accurately. We have not yet done a very good job of tying this movement of information to valuable benefits within business. This is the next challenge. Businesspeople need tools to meet their needs, not technologies looking for a place to land. We still have much work to do in this arena.

- Political borders are largely irrelevant in the new Information Age. For all of my life, I recall thinking in terms of political boundaries. If you want to make a telephone call outside of your home state, you need to know the area code as well as the number. If the call is outside of North America, you need to know the country code as well. Sending a letter? Postage differs depending on the destination. Even traveling from one country to another requires a passport and proof of citizenship.

  In cyberspace there are few borders. You can use the World Wide Web to navigate among servers without any concern about where they are located. Information on a server in New York may refer you to another server in Finland and still another in California. You probably do not know or care about their locations. The fact is that the process works, and it brings us all closer together than ever before.

The more artificial barriers that we can destroy, the better. Having our elementary schoolchildren establish electronic "pen pals" in other countries will go a long way toward teaching us that we are really all one people, just trying to get by and enjoy life.

- We are all citizens of cyberspace, and we must follow codes of conduct for it to be a pleasant place to work and play. For the Internet to function, participants must accept codes of conduct. There will always be organizations that intentionally breach the rules—like sending out an advertisement message to thousands of unrelated newsgroups.

    Yet, if new organizations coming onto the net take the time to understand what is considered acceptable practice and what is not, everyone will function much better. Even if an intentional breach is successful, in the long term the intruder will create more enemies than anyone needs.

    Take the time to understand how to participate. Hire someone to help you if you need to. By doing so, we will have perpetuated one of the fragile gems of the Internet.

Conclusion

Let's preserve this remarkable culture to pass on to our children. Whichever tools you use, it is important to be able to compare and contrast the various services with one another and relate them directly to your needs. Failure to clearly think through what you want prior to requesting quotations from vendors will lead to confusion and could potentially impair the effectiveness of your Internet solution. A written RFP can help you gather your thoughts and communicate them clearly to all of your prospective vendors. In addition, you will have the comfort of knowing that you have done as through a job as possible to meet the needs of your organization. It may take a bit of time, but it will be well worth the effort.

Chapter Eighteen

SILICON SNAKE OIL

OR LINIMENT

FOR THE MIND?

As the hype surrounding the Internet continues to grow, the easily anticipated emergence of naysayers also occurs. It is important to hear their arguments, consider them, and if they are valid, address them.

One of the leaders in this movement is Clifford Stoll. Famous for his book, *The Cuckoo's Egg*, Stoll has put forth his concerns and laments in *Silicon Snake Oil—Second Thoughts on the Information Highway*.

Objections to the growing use of the Internet by both businesses and recreational users fall into the following categories:

- Computer networks create isolation from people and cheapen human experiences.

- Computer networks work against literacy.

- Computer networks will undercut schools and libraries.

- The Internet is a nonexistent universe ("a soluble tissue of nothingness," according to Stoll).

- The Internet is insidious, can take control of our judgment, and will cause people to waste enormous amounts of time.

- Computers force us to make things with our minds and prevent us from making them with our hands.

- The Internet does not work well for all forms of communications and may be too anarchic and too slow to be of benefit to business.

Interestingly, some of the people playing devil's advocate on the Internet, including Stoll, come from the Internet environment themselves. In some ways, they seem to be saying this playground was fine for them but the unwashed masses do not belong there. To me, that borders on intellectual elitism and is the highest form of hypocrisy in the truly open, unbounded, unmanaged world of the Internet. Our world is what we make of it, whether it is corporeal or in cyberspace.

Let's consider each of the arguments against the Internet and see whether there is reason for reconsideration and vigilance.

Computer Networks Create Isolation and Cheapen Human Experiences

Computers are nothing more than very sophisticated and fast number crunchers. They do precisely what we tell them to do—even when it happens to be wrong.

You cannot blame your Mac or Windows machine for your failure to properly allocate your time. Cars run over people of their own volition only in Stephen

King novels. Guns rarely shoot people—people do. And computers? They do not purposely isolate us.

Throughout history, people have fought and perished so that they and their children might choose where and how they live. Now we have the freedom to live in St. John's, Newfoundland; Des Moines, Iowa; or Sao Paolo, Brazil; and to conduct business as if we were in New York or Paris. Physical space isolates us less than before—not more—because of the Internet!

Time zones are less constricting as well. You can send me an e-mail message at 3 a.m. Detroit time and I will receive it when I check my mail in the morning on the East Coast. You can also access my home page at 9 a.m. in London and get a copy of my Internet Access Providers Marketplace report, even though it is only 3 a.m. in Michigan. It seems to me we are closer than we have ever been—not more isolated.

Just as it is possible to use any tool to excess, so too it is possible to spend most of your waking hours "surfing the net" to the detriment of family, business, or other personal obligations. You cannot blame this on the Internet. It is too easy to make excuses for our behavior and to place blame anywhere but where it belongs.

As business managers and as employees, we have an obligation to consume organizational resources wisely. As parents, we have a responsibility to teach our children proper use of tools and moderation. The Internet is not even the messenger—it is the horse he rode in on. Let us not shoot the messenger's horse!

Computer Networks Work Against Literacy

It has been said that unlike typed or written letters, e-mail discourages contemplation and reflection. The ease with which you can respond to an electronic message is too tempting and therefore subject to more mistakes in spelling, composition, and thought.

Once again, computers are tools. Learning how to use them and their networked umbilical cords is another issue entirely. I believe computers and networks force us to become more literate. Letter writing has become somewhat of a lost art. By encouraging people to learn to type (many did not know how before they went online), we add to the functional capabilities of our global society. Now, as with any new or re-acquired skill, there will be mistakes. I am quite willing to tolerate a few mis-keyed letters in an e-mail response. I am less tolerant if it is an initial posting that someone had time to ponder. And I am even more distressed when it is in a formal business communication such as an invoice or proposal.

How we communicate in cyberspace is part of the never-ending process of image creation and enhancement. You cannot be seen or heard on the Internet. All you have to create an impression is your words. How you publish them, where, to whom, and in how timely a fashion will contribute to your cyberspace persona.

To assume or imply that the Internet and computers contribute to poor grammar and ill-advised commentary misses the point of origin. When all is said and done, we have no place to point other than at ourselves—however well or weakly we have performed.

Computer Networks Will Undercut Schools and Libraries

The argument offered here is that computers cannot provide the direct experience of human interaction, warmth, the thrill of discovery, or other training in essential skills like reading, teamwork, or societal values. One-on-one interpersonal interaction is always preferable to mechanized training methods. Libraries need to retain the human touch and the manual feel of old-fashioned card catalogs.

In addition, there is a growing groundswell of concern about schools and universities spending money and resources on computers and networks as a panacea to what ails the systems.

On the surface, I find little with which to argue. Dig a bit deeper, however, and you'll find more avoidance behavior and seduction by nostalgia. No computer can replace a human smile, a hug, or a well-timed "Attaboy!" No computer can replace the need for some forms of "hands-on" instruction, which offer the ability to adapt and relate to the student and at the same time provide the benefits of the instructor's experiences. I cannot foresee a time when human teaching is entirely supplanted by computers or other mechanized systems.

On the other hand, computers do a wonderful job of administering repetitive tasks. They can increase difficulty levels as a student progresses, and they can reinforce previously learned information. This should not be an "all-or-nothing" environment. Rather than dismissing computers and networks as a teaching tool, efforts should focus on understanding where and how well they work in specific environments. As parents and teachers, we should not accept blanket statements from schools about how computers and networks will be used. We should ask the tough questions. We should know who in the school is responsible for ensuring that teachers and staff know what these tools can do before the curriculum is rolled out. Schools should develop specific programs that take advantage of these tools rather than open their availability for ad hoc experimentation. We should all ensure that we deploy what we need—not what is sexy.

From a business perspective, how schools incorporate computers and networks in their programs will directly impact the skills of future employees, decision makers, and public officials. As businesspeople, we need to encourage schools to emphasize functionality and use rather than either eschewing technology as inherently evil or embracing it as the latest directionless fad.

The Internet Is a Nonexistent Universe

If the Internet is a nonexistent universe, then so too are television, radio, books, telephone, and astronomy. We cannot touch, feel, or smell any of the communications offered by these media, yet they seem real enough to us. We cannot be certain to whom we are speaking on the telephone, nor can we be absolutely positive that the voice we recognize is who we believe it to be.

The Internet is as real as any other communications media. It also is multidimensional. Through the Internet, you can exchange e-mail messages with your children or colleagues, you can access information on the weather in Brazil, you can offer your organization's goods or services for sale, and you can find specialists working in your area of interest regardless of where they live in the world.

Thousands of businesses use the Internet today as an adjunct to their existing business practices. To claim that there is no "there" there is like suggesting that Saturn does not really exist because we have not actually been there. We use our senses to relate to the universe around us. Computers, networks, microscopes, and telescopes simply are tools that help extend the range of our senses. To denigrate them is to deny the possibilities that they represent.

The Internet Is Insidious

"The Internet is insidious. It has the ability to take control of our judgment, and it will cause people to waste enormous amounts of time." I call this the electronic zombie theory. Personification of computers and networks as a vehicle for mass mind control is absurd. This is not to suggest that these powerful tools cannot be abused by unscrupulous people. They can and have been. Specters of subliminal projections being used to sell soft drinks come to mind. It is precisely the awareness of these possibilities and the concurrent positive use of the technologies that will help us protect ourselves from misuse.

Technology is neither inherently good nor bad. It is simply what we make of it. Computers do not waste time; people do. We have the choice whether we want to surf the Net for hours at a time or permit our children to do so. The same is also true for watching television, reading romance novels, or playing poker. The important lesson is to understand your alternatives and make the choices that work for you.

Using Our Minds, Not Our Hands

"Computers force us to make things with our minds and prevent us from making them with our hands." Computers do not prevent us from doing anything. We can still weave baskets or carve wood with our hands. We also can expand our minds through contact with people around the world whom we otherwise might never meet. As with everything else, some of these experiences will be positive and others not. That is not the fault of the medium.

We live in a complex and diverse world with many tastes, cultures, and customs. The wondrous part is that we can begin the exploration from our homes or offices. It is then up to us to follow that with a real visit. My consulting work has taken me to Canada, Brazil, Norway, and Germany. I initiated all of these contacts through e-mail. All of the details of my trips have been discussed via e-mail before my visits. In some cases, I have even submitted invoices electronically after returning home.

We have always created with our minds. Where do we think the inspiration for those paintings, sculptures, or novels came from? Simply because we have added new methods to our palette does not mean that we have forgotten how to apply them.

Our hands and minds are inextricably connected. The computer and the Internet help us expand the spheres within which we can create.

The Internet Does Not Work Well for All Forms of Communications

"Can you name one form of communication that works well for all communications?" Voice telephone works great for interactive conversations but is weak for documentation. Personal travel works well, too—when there is time to go everywhere you need to be. Written letters and documents are wonderful for a record of communication, but they lack emotional trappings and subtlety. The Internet is another communications vehicle. It is not the Golden Fleece. It works well when you understand its limitations and capabilities.

The Internet is still in its infancy, both as a technology and as a business tool. Because the Internet is a "network of networks," each Internet Access Provider relies on others to carry the traffic of each of its customers. As the Internet grows larger and more substantial companies become IAPs, they will continue to upgrade their communications capacity and diminish the slow response time that bothers some users. This means that your messages will move through the Internet as fast as your modem or network router can send them.

Congestion can also occur at the specific server or information source that you have contacted. Some sites, like **www.yahoo.com**, are so heavily used that your response time may be from many seconds to minutes. This is likely to be a temporary phenomenon. As the Internet becomes more attractive to businesses, servers like Yahoo will either charge a fee or accept corporate sponsorship as a way of keeping up with demand. Delays will inevitably occur—they just won't last long. Because the Internet is becoming competitive, many entrepreneurs will look for popular areas of interest to build upon.

Conclusion

Critics of the Internet make the point that our cities were not destroyed by atomic bombs or plagues; they have been devastated by urban flight. It was television that caused the demise of neighborhood cinemas. MTV and megastars have weakened the appeal of amateur musicians and local bands. Interstate highways devastated passenger rail service, and airlines have made passenger ships obsolete. In the same way, our library system is now at risk of becoming the next dodo because of the Internet.

Urban flight did not destroy our cities. In fact, despite a few fiscal miscues, I cannot think of any city in the industrialized world that has simply vanished other than through acts of war or disease. Boston, New York, Baltimore, Washington, Chicago, Los Angeles, Toronto, London, Sao Paolo, and Tokyo still exist quite nicely, thank you. In fact, many of these cities are experiencing a rebirth, as people renovate homes in inner cities and move back to them.

My home town of Baltimore has experienced such a rejuvenation. While I was growing up, the last place you wanted to go on a weekend or on a summer evening was downtown by the waterfront. Now, myriad events and festivals take place around Harbor Place in the Inner Harbor area, and the new Oriole Park at Camden Yards baseball stadium packs them in (when the "professionals" aren't on strike!).

Neighborhood cinemas have fought the rise of the megaplex theaters more than the challenge of television. Again, I remember neighborhood theaters surviving long after television. The more inventive ones still survive today. After all, the ultimate ballot box are the receipts from customers. Fail to keep up with the demands of the public, and the public will vote with its tickets.

MTV and megastars have killed off local bands? I don't buy this one. Just because our children can see a music video on television does not mean that they no longer want to dance or party with others. From what I can tell, local bands are just as prevalent as when I played guitar in one back in the 1960s.

Our society is what has changed. I no longer see many dances, mixers, or teen centers sponsored by community associations or religious groups. This is partly to blame on concerns over increased violence, insurance liability, or the availability of adult chaperones. Our institutions change for a few simple reasons. Everything is subject to evolution.

Interstate highways and airlines did not signal the demise of passenger rail service or luxury liners. Our way of life changed. With the construction of interstate highways, we can set our own schedules for travel rather than being subjected to those offered by the railroad. We can carry five people in one car for the same price as carrying one. On a train, we would pay for five seats. When traveling by car, we can stop and see the sights along the way rather than seeing only train stations. Passenger ships were the only way to cross the oceans for hundreds of years. We did not choose that mode of transportation— it was all that was available.

With the advent of air transportation, we have new choices. Not all such choices are so quickly embraced by the traveling public. If faster were always better, we would be traveling on the SST and Concorde instead of flying in DC-10s or 747s. Because of its expense, the Concorde comprises a very small percentage of transoceanic flights today. What will happen when the new rocket planes under development become available to the public? The public will vote with its wallet.

So are our libraries ready to fold because of the Internet? I think not. Libraries serve not only a function as a repository of information but also as a meeting point for the human exchange of ideas. Libraries must learn to understand and embrace new approaches and technologies and increasingly assume the role of facilitator. The key to survival is the ability to adapt and remain useful.

Enchantment with nostalgia and the attempt to rigidly hold onto the past is the quickest way I know to achieve obsolescence. The moment we stop growing—as people, businesses, or services—is the instant our replacements will begin to take hold.

I understand the uneasiness with which some people regard the Internet. Many seek the "magic bullet" and fail to recognize that it is always a mirage. Little can be achieved without significant thinking, planning, and hard work, no matter what the endeavor. The Internet is but one tool in the struggle to realize our dreams. The Internet cannot dominate us. The Internet cannot force us to take actions we do not want to take. The Internet cannot make sales for us. The Internet cannot solve the problems that afflict our businesses. The Internet cannot corrupt our children.

We can either cause these events to happen, stand by and watch them occur, or prevent them from occurring. It is our choice! Recognize the choices that confront you and make them as wisely as you can.

*C*hapter Nineteen

WHAT DOES

THE FUTURE

HOLD?

The Internet is already on its way to becoming the most important tool for international commerce since the invention of the
airplane and the telephone. Consider how large a step it was to
be able to meet for business discussions in a matter of hours as
afforded by air transportation, as opposed to steamship travel
that might take days or weeks.

Then consider the benefits of real-time, high-quality voice communications as a replacement for telex or TWX services. I still remember paper tape used as a record for telex transmissions. Transatlantic and transpacific fiber-optic routes helped to change all of that.

Now consider what high-quality, highly distributed data communications will likely do to the masses. The Internet has the potential to be the "great equalizer" of the Information Age, just as the railroads were for the Industrial Age.

Personal computing systems will continue to grow rapidly in performance while maintaining or reducing current price levels. Today, you can buy a Pentium machine for the same price as a good i386 machine a year or two ago. The power in that Pentium system that you can buy for under $2,000 exceeds the power of a minicomputer only a few short years ago.

With the Internet, you can begin to use the computing power not only in your own home or office (they may increasingly be the same!), you can also function across the city, state, country, or the world. You will do this without an expensive computing staff, and with increasing functionality. This functionality will include easy-to-use desktop video conferencing, higher levels of confidentiality and security than offered today, and the ability to conduct financial transactions without undue concern about theft.

Phases of the Internet

The Internet will look quite different in 1995 and 1996 than it did in 1994 or before. We have witnessed several phases in the evolution of the Internet community, and we are about to enter another.

Pre-Populum Era

The first phase—I call it the "Pre-Populum Era"—started in the late 1960s with the development of the ARPAnet and lasted until 1985. This period saw the basic design work for the Internet occur, including the development of the Transmission Control Protocol/Internet Protocol (TCP/IP) and its underlying tools.

During this period, the Internet was primarily the domain of universities and government scientists, and it was limited mostly to the hard sciences (chemistry, physics, etc.) and computer engineers. There was very little activity in the humanities or for general business purposes.

Supercomputic Era

The Pre-Populum Era was replaced by the "The Supercomputic Era." This period was spawned by Dr. Larry Smarr of the National Center for Supercomputer Applications (NCSA) in Champaign, Illinois.

Smarr was a driving force behind creation of a U.S. "supercomputer center" program. The intention was to establish collaborative research centers for corporate and government use, taking advantage of technology being developed by Cray, Thinking Machines, Control Data Corporation, and others, rather than forcing each corporation that needed such facilities to purchase its own. In many ways, this effort was a response to unified foreign efforts, such as those by MITI (the technology ministry) in Japan.

The Supercomputic Era was launched with implementation of the first National Science Foundation (NSF) network—a 56Kbps-based network service managed by the University of Illinois at Urbana/Champaign. Even with relatively limited access, this network became saturated almost immediately. This led to another NSF procurement for more extensive network services, and in 1987 the Joint Study Partnership of IBM, MCI, MERIT (the state of Michigan research and education network), and the state of Michigan Strategic Fund won the award to implement a T-1 (1.5Mbps) NSFnet program.

As part of this program, the NSF awarded connections to the T-1 "backbone" to eight clusters of universities. These clusters became known as "regional" or "mid-level" networks. They served as the mid-level between the NSFnet backbone and individual universities, government facilities, and business sites.

Documentation from this era refers to the NSFnet as a "supercomputer network." There was considerable reluctance to believe that 1.5Mbps, or the upgrade to 45Mbps (which occurred during 1991), could have been driven by anything other than the need to conduct research and experimentation with supercomputers. After all, it would certainly take an enormous amount of electronic mail or file transfers to need such an expensive endeavor.

Neo-Commercial Era

At the time, supercomputer use was the only application that seemed to justify the effort. For this reason, the Internet remained a mystery to most of the general public and to general business. It wasn't until the "Neo-Commercial Era" that the Internet started to come out of its cloistered existence and to reveal its enormous potential to the global business community.

The Neo-Commercial Era began in earnest in 1990 with the establishment of Performance Systems International (PSI) and the popularization of UUNet Technologies and its Alternet service. By November 1990, the NSF had permitted the establishment of Advanced Network & Services (ANS) as a 501(c)3 not-for-profit company managing the NSFnet. In June 1991, ANS announced the creation of ANS CO+RE Systems Inc. as a wholly owned commercial subsidiary. These three companies marked the emergence of the Neo-Commercial Era.

Following the emergence of the Neo-Commercial Era, many of the mid-level networks spawned by the NSF and those formed to address similar needs at universities began to offer services to businesses as well. This was not entirely a benevolent act, as many viewed this as a "cash cow" that could supplement or replace government funding that was sure to dwindle.

Unfortunately, few of these mid-level networks were businesses themselves, many being a project of a university group. Many of these networks were staffed by individuals who were unfamiliar with the demands of commercial, industrial-strength service offerings, and the result was competition in previously isolated environments from a new breed of Internet entrepreneurs.

Many of these providers thought they had a manifest destiny to serve their particular regions and no other providers—education-related or not—had a right to compete with them. They were wrong.

Bulletin board services or people with technical knowledge and the desire to create an Internet business obtained connections into other Internet service providers—like ANS, Sprint, and UUNet—and became "resellers" of Internet access. During 1993 and 1994 this number grew, and by mid-1994 Internet resellers accounted for more than 25 percent of Internet access revenues in the United States.

By 1995, Internet resellers and the former research and education networks gleaned almost two-thirds of the Internet access revenues in the United States. This indicates that the market has flattened, and rather than a few large organizations capturing substantial market share, the market is divided among many different providers.

Catering primarily to dial-up customers in specific geographic niches, revenues accrued by Internet resellers were growing at a rate of 35 percent per month in 1994. In fact, the rate of growth for Serial Link Internetworking Protocol/Point to Point Protocol (SLIP/PPP) services exceeded 38 percent per month from March 1994 to January 1995.

As an industry, Internet access revenues in the United States grew from an estimated annual rate of $47 million in early 1993 to $120 million by March

1994. U.S. annual revenues are expected to exceed $450 million in 1995, and if you include the portion of Internet access represented by information providers like America OnLine, CompuServe, and others, the U.S. Internet access marketplace is already over $1 billion. Globally, the Internet access marketplace will exceed $2.5 billion by the end of 1995.

Megacorporatic Era

With real revenues from Internet access now apparent, and other revenues likely from hardware, software, education and training, and management services, the Internet entered a new era by December 1994: the "Megacorporatic Era" (Mucho Big Companies).

The Megacorporatic Era will see massive marketing and positioning expenditures from large corporations that want to participate in, and dominate if possible, the Internet market—now that it is finally real.

These companies will come from a variety of backgrounds and have various strengths and weaknesses, but their participation should add both professionalism and financial solidity to the ranks of Internet access providers. I fully expect the Regional Bell Operating Companies will offer Internet access. Ameritech has already announced its Ameritech Advanced Data Service (AADS), and Pacific Bell, NYNEX, and other telephone companies are likely to follow quickly.

Long-distance telephone companies like LCI, Cable and Wireless, and WilTel/LDDS are expected to follow Sprint, MCI, and AT&T by announcing Internet access services.

Information providers, including AOL, CompuServe, GEnie, and Prodigy, now have full Internet services available to their customers. These vendors will probably devote a tremendous amount of effort to marketing and customer solicitation campaigns. It will be interesting to see how well they can retain these customers. Traditional Internet providers will continue to compete aggressively for those customers and ride on the efforts of the information provider community.

Other potential providers of Internet services could include alternative access providers (Metropolitan Fiber Systems and Teleport), smaller local telephone companies, value-added carriers (Advantis and Infonet), and major computing companies (Microsoft and Apple).

With all of these behemoths stomping around in the Megacorporatic Era, holdovers from early periods will evolve so that they can successfully compete, be consumed as part of the "food chain," refocus to provide services to a specific community of interest only, or go away.

Darwinian Era

The Megacorporatic Era will be followed, probably by 1996 or 1997, by the "Darwinian Era." During this timeframe, massive shake-outs, alliances, and mergers are likely to occur, with consumers the ultimate winners. Some of this is beginning to occur with the acquisition of NEARnet, BARRNet, and SURAnet by BBN; the acquisition of ANS by AOL; and the acquisition of The Pipeline by PSI.

Too many powerful players are vying for a share of this market for any one or two to achieve dominance. It is doubtful that even Microsoft can achieve dominance in the near future. All of the viable organizations must focus on identifying and satisfying customer requirements. The most flexible and responsive will be the winners. Those that fail to do so will be the next meal for the strong ones.

The Darwinian Era will be marked by intense competition through innovative value-added services, but it will ultimately reveal a cadre of competent, solid, stable providers. In short, the Internet will make the transition to becoming a true industry.

Conclusion

So what does all this bode for the business user? First, it means that the Internet services industry will look very different in 1996 than it did in 1993 or 1994. Instead of consisting primarily of research and education networks or small (in relative terms) access providers, many large companies will offer general Internet access. Companies like the RBOCs, AOL, CompuServe, Advantis, MCI, and Microsoft will be active contenders.

Strong smaller companies will offer niche-oriented, specialized services. One may cover a single metropolitan area very well, or focus on a particular industry, such as medicine or finance. By offering these kinds of focused services, smaller firms can survive and prosper. It is important, however, that they do not get underfoot of the elephants!

In addition, Freenets and free or low-cost services, such as those offered at Maryland public libraries, will continue to grow. Just as the public libraries did not stop book sales, neither will they erode Internet usage. Rather, they will act as a catalyst for users who want to try it first—if they can wait in line for access—and then obtain their own service from a professional provider.

Because of the tremendous focus on the Internet by both megacorporations and technical entrepreneurs, the Internet will become easier to use as better user interfaces are developed, and more professional as companies compete.

What could go wrong that could kill the Internet as a market? There are several possible answers.

- *A small subset of companies dominates the market and kills off everyone else.* Given the global emergence of the Internet and the large number of organizations that consider it strategically important, it seems unlikely that one company (even AT&T, Microsoft, or IBM) could dominate this market to the exclusion of most others.

- *Government regulations are imposed that "chill" the growth of Internet companies.* Even if this did occur, which I sincerely hope not, the "infection" among potential users has already spread too far. The demand exists and will continue to grow, even if the advent of regulation adversely impacts some of the smaller, more entrepreneurial efforts. The better managed and better financed organizations will prosper, although perhaps at a lower rate of return.

- *This whole thing proves too complicated and the public loses interest.* This may be the greatest potential threat. Given all of the hype and publicity, what happens if our capability to provide good, easy, affordable services fails to please the buying public? Will they stop using these services?

  I believe it is more likely that people will shop for better service rather than give up altogether. Once the personal computer became an integral part of our business lives, it was impossible to take it away, no matter how frustrating it became. I believe the Internet and electronic information services are in the same category.

In short, I cannot foresee anything—technical, marketplace, or regulatory, short of an all-out worldwide war—that could halt this growth.

I believe the Internet holds tremendous promise as a tool of commerce and of learning. As with any tool, however, you must force yourself to understand *how* it can be of value before you buy into it. This alleviates disappointment from unfulfilled expectations and helps you better plan for success.

The Internet gives you the ability to do away with time zones and national boundaries as they relate to communications. It helps you maintain better contact with your own branches, customers, suppliers, and the world at large.

How you use these tools, and how you leverage the tremendous (and growing) number of information resources out there in cyberspace, is entirely up to you.

My sincere hope is that this book has provided enough information to start you on your journey. Every effort has been made to point out many different ways in which the Internet and internetworking could be of value to you, and to enumerate some steps you can take to determine its potential value. Now, it's your turn.

As an exercise, sit down and make a list of all the ways that you communicate with people during a normal business day. Any communications will do. Do you read postal mail? How about the newspaper or trade journals? Do you draft letters? Who types them? How are they transmitted? Do you take telephone calls? Why?

I think you get the idea. If I have motivated you to reconsider how you communicate and to evaluate why you do so in the manner that you do, then I have accomplished most of my objective. The last step is to consider alternative approaches, such as those offered by the Internet.

As a consumer of high-technology services, it is important for you to keep in mind that *you* should be the one in charge of new product or service introductions. Do not let vendors continually introduce products in search of a market. Force them to give you *solutions* to the problems you face!

The Internet and internetworking are wonderful tools. Make them—and their providers—work for you!

I'll see you in cyberspace.

*A*ppendix A

The process of "cost justifying" the procurement of new technologies—including the Internet—requires a clear understanding of existing costs, possible new sources of income, and potential alternatives.

The key to any cost-justification effort is to have a clear understanding of the tasks you are attempting to accomplish, the possible tools, and the investments required to accomplish these tasks. The following worksheet, interspersed with commentary, will assist you in progressing through these tasks.

Directions: Try to answer all parts of this worksheet as accurately as possible, but do not hesitate to make "guesstimates" where needed.

Part One: Status Quo

1. What *business issue* do you want to address? (Examples: reducing courier service or fax costs, reducing telephone tag among employees, finding a better method of software distribution to outlying branches or customers, or gaining greater access to customer prospects).

   It is very important that you understand your business objectives. Without doing so, it will be impossible to set your expectations properly or conduct a reasonable cost-justification exercise. This section answers the question: Why do you want to do this "Internet thing," anyway? It may be important to get the views of several departments or groups within your company. Remember that many applications may cross organizational or budget lines. The true impact of these applications lies across the entire organization, not just one part.

   _____
   _____
   _____
   _____
   _____

2. Specifically *quantify* the annual cost of this issue today. (For example, how expensive are the courier services or fax costs that you wish to reduce? How much revenue is lost by the status quo? How much revenue could you conservatively expect to gain with a small percentage increase?) Estimate the *perceived intangible* impact (enhanced employee morale, etc.).

   This is perhaps the most difficult part of this exercise. First, you need to identify where in your organization the activities impacting this business issue are occurring. How many different departments are sending out faxes? Is one person responsible for this or do all employees send their own faxes? You should be able to capture fax logs that tell where these documents were sent and how many pages were included. This will help us as we begin to explore alternatives. But also try to identify the "people time" also being invested in each activity. Can that time be put to better use? Can the one hour per week that your employees are standing at the fax machine be better used? Consider all of these issues when evaluating the specific, quantifiable impact of this issue on your business.

Once you've determined the quantifiable impacts, look for intangibles, such as the ability to appear more concerned about employee morale, or providing a more rewarding work environment where the employees feel they make a worthy contribution.

_____

_____

_____

_____

_____

3. How frequently does this activity occur?

How many people conduct these activities, such as using the fax machine, on a single day or in a month? When you begin to monitor these activities, you may be surprised how frequently they occur, who is involved, and how much time your organization invests in activities that may be less than appropriate for the people involved. For example, is standing at the fax machine a good investment of the Chief Executive Officer's time?

_____

_____

_____

4. What is the volume of information (number of pages, bytes, visits)?

You can determine the size of computer files or the number of pages of documents that are being distributed. You can check logs, such as for fax transmissions, or you may ask your personnel to become more conscious of the number of pages mailed, physical visits required to complete a task, or the size of computer files.

_____

_____

_____

5. How "mission critical" is this function (time sensitivity)?

Is this particular function critical to the performance of your organization's mission? For example, transferring financial information between banks is a process that could cost or save the banks millions if even a few minutes are lost. This is a "mission critical" application for the bank. Distributing notification of an upcoming seminar may be important to a company, but it is not critical that the information be received within a few minutes. A day or so may be perfectly acceptable, although sooner is certainly better. This would be classified as a "Moderately High" or perhaps even moderately critical application. The announcement of your new vice president is probably not time critical and is intended more for public relations and image purposes, so it does not matter a great deal if the information is received within a few hours or days.

(Circle one)

High   Moderately High   Moderate   Not at all

6. What alternatives (other than the Internet) have been considered to address this issue (leased-line private networks, dial-up directly to each site, etc.)? Why were they not implemented?

It is important that you not assume the Internet is the only solution to your information management issues. This book is not intended as a comprehensive discussion of the many different forms of communication, so it is important for you to consider alternatives such as those mentioned above. Are there ways to accomplish these tasks better than those occurring today without using the Internet? This same cost-justification process applies for other approaches as well. You may still use "internetworking"; it simply may not be provided by the Internet.

_____
_____
_____
_____
_____
_____

Part Two: Internet Alternatives

1. Which Internet access services are most likely to meet your requirements?

Once you have identified your target business applications and their associated information flows, you can estimate the type of Internet connectivity you may need. Methods of preliminary requirements design were covered in earlier chapters. Do you require dial-up service or dedicated access? How many locations do you need to serve? Headquarters? Branch offices? Customer locations? Once you determine your requirements, you can create a document outlining what you think you need (see Chapter Sixteen, "Comparing Apples to Apples") and circulate it to prospective Internet Access Providers (IAPs). They should be able to provide actual costs instead of the estimates listed above, and you can enter these numbers into this part of the form.

(Check one)

__Low-End Dial-Up (Local Access Number)	$240 to $1,200 per yr.
__Host or LAN Dial-Up (Local Access)	$2,300 to $4,600 per yr.
__800 Number Access	Add $700 to $1,300 per yr.
__56Kbps Dedicated Access	$6,000 to $18,000 per yr.
__T-1 (1.5Mbps) Dedicated Access	$18,000 to $47,000 per yr.

2. Additional Fees

The fees paid to your Internet Access Providers (IAPs) may only be the tip of the iceberg. Ask the IAP if you will incur any additional charges from others in order to use the Internet service. These include time-sensitive message units from local telephone companies, additional circuit charges from telephone companies for dedicated access services, and hardware and software. Always ask these questions of your IAP. They should know the answers, and the more helpful and candid with you they are at the beginning, the more likely they will be able to deliver high-quality services throughout your agreement with them. Make the vendors work for you! These additional costs should be entered on the form in this area.

(Check one)

Local Telephone Company Charges

__Message Unit or Timed Unit Charges? $50 per yr.

__Tail Circuit for Leased Lines

__56Kbps $2,000 to $10,000 per yr.

__T-1 $4,000 to $30,000 per yr.

Hardware (Not Included by Provider)

__Router $3,000 to $8,000 one-time

__CSU/DSU $500 to $2,500 one-time

__Software (TCP/IP, Gopher, etc.)   May be free, but may require outside expertise

3. Internal Management Costs

Depending on the applications you select for Internet use, you may need to involve many different people in your organization at a variety of locations. Most IAPs do not provide you with troubleshooting for your organization's internal networks. They do not provide "help desk" services for hundreds of your employees. They normally not provide introductory or continuing training, such as "Internet 101" or how to use the Internet as a research tool, without additional charges. You will should consider whether you need to handle these areas yourself, and at what cost.

A Network Operations Center (NOC) describes a person or group of people responsible for monitoring the technical performance of a network. Most IAPs have NOCs that operate 24 hours per day, 365 days per year. It is important that your services be available whenever your employees need them. The same is true internally. If you have several sites and a variety of network systems, someone must monitor and manage them. The same people now need to take on responsibilities associated with the same tasks in a TCP/IP environment. Do you need to hire additional personnel? Do existing personnel need training? Do you need additional hardware or software? At what costs? Those numbers should be entered here.

Added NOC Costs   _____

The "Help Desk" is an individual or group who provides guidance to your employees on non-trouble issues. "How do I conduct a search on the network?

What are the best search tools for our industry?" "Are there certain news-groups that our customers frequently use?" "How do I do ftp?" "My PCMCIA modem is not functioning properly." All of these are questions that your own Help Desk should answer, especially if you have more than twenty employees using the Internet. At the very least, IAPs will increasingly require organizations to have a "single point of contact" with them. It's costly for the IAP to answer the same question from many employees in your organization, and I suspect that they will soon charge for this

Any personnel costs related to this area should be included here.

Help Desk Function _____

The Internet is a business tool. Your employees will not simply "know" how to use it properly. They need instruction so they do not spend an enormous amount of time "reinventing the wheel" or learning by trial and error. You also need to tell them clearly what they can and should not do with their Internet access. This entails creating a corporate use policy before you broadly implement the Internet within your organization.

Creating use policies, designing an appropriate training environment, and conducting training can involve considerable personnel time and cost. Training should be continuing. Employees will need refreshers. New employees will need training. New techniques and functionality will become available. New applications will present opportunities to save money or reduce expenses. Consider these costs carefully. How well you conduct this phase will impact the success of the entire project.

Continuing Training Program _____

4. Security Costs

Security can be a major hidden expense. As mentioned in earlier chapters, if you worry little about security expenses, you should use only dial-up accounts. Your IAP should have reasonable safeguards in place.

Dedicated access requires significant security consideration.

We have already discussed the need for detailed security planning. Remember that Internet access can be made acceptably secure, as long as you know what that means to your organization. It is impossible to understand this, identify the proper tools to implement your plan, or to clearly communicate your policies to your employees if you have no plan.

Conduct a good network security audit, by internal personnel if they have the experience and skills, or by an independent consulting organization if needed. Either option has associated costs and should be included in your justification report. Remember that no security plan remains effective without regular reviews, updates, and modifications. Security is an ongoing cost that must be considered carefully.

Security Plan Needs to Be Developed _____

Once the security plan is completed, you can begin to determine which tools to use to implement the plan. Contact providers of the various tools to determine potential costs. Remember that the numbers in this discussion are for illustration only. You need precise figures for effective cost justification. Also, these are only a sample of the useful tools. Invest the time to consider which tools you need, then determine their actual costs in your geographic location.

(Check one)

Security Tools
__Route/Packet Filtering $2,000/year (manpower)
__"Firewall" $10,000 one-time
                                      plus $5,000 + manpower
__Applications Layer Gateways $10,000 to $25,000 per yr.

This step should be relatively self-explanatory. You need to accumulate all of the potential costs and investments that make up your conservative estimate of what it will take to implement Internet services.

5. Total Estimated Costs (Add 1 through 4) _____

Part Three: Evaluation and Analysis

1. Describe the likely *quantifiable* impact(s) of your solution on the status quo.

Transfer the monetary value from Part One, Question 2—tangible, quantifiable value—to this portion of the worksheet.

_____

_____

2. Describe the potential *intangible* impact(s) of your solution.

This is an equally important area, although difficult to assess. These are often called "soft savings" and can be very important but hard to use in a mathematical model. Some common intangible benefits are enhanced image, improved employee morale, or greater visibility in your marketplace community. None of these has a specific monetary value, although all can result in significant tangible benefits. Identify these benefits to review and evaluate later, comparing them to the overall investment required for Internet services.

_____
_____
_____
_____

3. Describe the downside(s) if the status quo remains unchanged.

What happens if you fail to change your current methods of operation? Will your measurements become more out of line with your industry? Will you fall further behind your competitors? Is it possible that you could lose market share or influence on the market? Consider these possibilities and determine if action is required.

_____
_____
_____
_____

4. What is the likely potential cost of an Internet solution?

Enter the total costs for the first year, including monthly or annual costs as well as nonrecurring installation fees and equipment costs. (You may amortize these costs over a period of no more than three years. The Internet is changing so rapidly that a longer period is not as meaningful.)

For the second year, omit the one-time costs and anticipate additional expenses (such as personnel) or expense reduction (lower IAP charges). Also, note any changes in the business benefit. For example, if you expect more of your clients to use the Internet for documentation and therefore need fewer paper copies, show those changes here.

First Year: _____
Subsequent Years: _____

5. What is the benefit to cost ratio?

We are now at the point to see if Internet access and services makes sense at a first glance. We have added all of our investment costs and estimated our potential benefit. Assuming that we had a potential savings of $133,000 per year and an investment cost of $97,000, our benefit-to-cost ratio would be 1.37 to 1 ($133,000 divided by $97,000). This shows a slight advantage to using the Internet. We may need to seek other applications to strengthen our case.

First Year: _____

Subsequent Years _____

Part Four: Additional Applications

Remember, this is one potential application. Your investment may be minimal for additional applications.

You may find you can accomplish many different tasks with minimal additional investment in Internet services. For example, perhaps you reduced your courier expenses in your first application. Using the same Internet facilities, you may also reduce costs of distributing press releases and internal sales reports. At the same time, you can enhance sales by increasing your sales organization's efficiency. Each new application should be separately quantified. Then, conduct a revised benefit to cost ratio analysis. In this way, you should gather a reasonably realistic estimate of the Internet's impact on your organization.

Cost justification of Internet access is a lengthy process. It is important to consider all of these factors so you and your management team truly understand the ways the Internet may affect how you conduct business and your opportunities for success.

1. What is the quantifiable value of other applications?

Application _____ Value _____

Application _____ Value _____

Application _____ Value _____

2. What incremental costs will be incurred by these additional applications?

_____

_____

_____

3. Revised benefit to cost ratio

First Year: _____

Subsequent Years: _____

Appendix B

With the proliferation of the Internet, and most notably the World Wide Web, more companies are turning to the Net as a means of enhancing their business operations. The following section is an offering of business-related resources designed to help those conducting research or considering the usefulness of the Net as a business tool.

World Wide Web Sites

Classifieds:

http://www.wanted.com/ads/default2.htm
Use this URL for **wanted.com**'s web site, where you can place ads for online company exposure.

http://cybersight.com/cgi-bin/imi/s?main.gmml
Internet Marketing Inc. offers business deals for companies who want their presence felt on the Information Superhighway.

http://www.net-classifieds.co.uk
Features classifieds for London and the United Kingdom.

http://www.shore.net/olm
On-line Marketing provides Internet advertising for small businesses and individuals.

http://www.imall.com/ads/ads.shtml

At this site you'll find a free classified service provided by **iMall**. It allows users to create new ads, as well as browse and search the current ads.

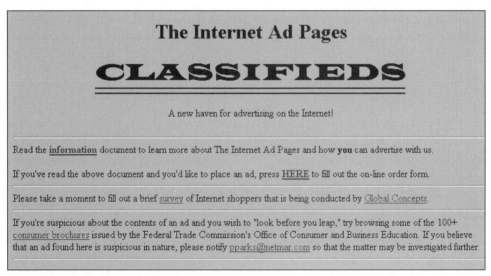

http://netmar.com/mall/ads

The **Internet Ad Pages** provide business opportunities, employment listings, business/service listings, and more.

Consortia:

Welcome to the Center for the Application of Information Technology (CAIT). Our mission is to be a center of learning in the field of information management and to provide our member companies with world-class educational and leadership programs.

For more information about CAIT, please explore the resources listed below. If you would like further information on CAIT online resources, please contact Joe Haspiel at joeh@cait.wustl.edu.

http://www.cait.wustl.edu/cait
The **Center for the Application of Information Technology** is a non-profit consortium that provides training and leadership programs for Information Systems Professionals.

http://www.llnl.gov/fstc
The **Financial Services Technology Consortium (FSTC)** is a group of financial services providers, national laboratories, universities, and government agencies. FSTC sponsors and participates in collaborative research and development on interbank technical projects.

http://www.rt66.com/twl/WWPC.index.html
The **Worldwide Publishing Consortium** provides an international forum for the publishing, graphic arts, communications and multimedia industries. It is designed to promote the exchange of information and the advancement of education.

http://bell.com
The **Alliance for Competitive Communications (ACC)** coordinates the seven Bell telephone companies' effort to open communications markets.

http://www.software.org
The **Software Productivity Consortium Information Server** provides online access to publicly available nonproprietary information. This includes Consortium Membership programs and benefits, descriptions of Consortium technologies, workshops, and more. It is also designed to provide technological and service-based solutions to the many problems inherent in software-intensive systems development.

Economy:

http://www.census.gov/ftp/pub/foreign-trade/www
The site of the **Foreign Trade Division (U.S. Census Bureau)** provides the official statistics of U.S. Trade.

http://ananse.irv.uit.no/trade_law/gatt/nav/toc.html
For details of the Final Act and Agreement Establishing the **World Trade Organization**, visit this site, which includes information on the General Agreement on Tariffs and Trade, Uruguay Round (including GATT 1994).

http://www.jetro.go.jp
The is the site for **JETRO**, or the Japan External Trade Organization, a government organization that encourages international investment and exporting to Japan. The site provides the latest information on Japanese government acquisitions, as well as the Japanese economy and business.

http://www.nar.com/racc
The **Russian American Chamber of Commerce** aims to develop and encourage U.S. trade, investment, and commerce in Russia.

http://www1.usa1.com/~ibnet/icchp.html
The online site of **The International Chamber of Commerce (ICC)** is an organization that aims to serve the business world by promoting trade, investment, and the free market system.

http://rohan.sdsu.edu/dept/worldtc/homepage.html
The **World Trade Center Association/San Diego** offers global access and advantages to its members through affiliation with more than 280 World Trade Center organizations in at least 80 countries around the world. Membership provides access to facilities, services, and contacts with more than 400,000 companies involved in international trade and commerce.

Electronic Commerce:

http://www.commerce.net
CommerceNet is a not-for-profit corporation conducting the first large-scale market trial of technologies and business processes to support electronic commerce via the Internet. CommerceNet is open to public and private organizations that subscribe to CommerceNet's charter "to develop, maintain, and endorse an Internet-based infrastructure for electronic commerce in business-to-business applications."

http://www.ecrc.ctc.com

Backed by government funding, the **Electronic Commerce Resource Center** is designed to provide small- to medium-sized businesses with the resources to develop electronic commerce. Most services are free.

http://gopher.econ.lsa.umich.edu/EconInternet/Commerce.html

This **Commerce on the Internet** site provides a host of links to other commercial web sites that cover topics like network payment systems, protocols for Internet commerce, marketing, and law.

http://www.bizweb.com

This URL will take you to **BizWeb**, an excellent resource site that provides an extensive list of links to companies that are categorized by the goods or services they provide.

Employment/Careers:

http://www.cweb.com

CareerWEB is an interactive online service that offers employers, franchisers and career-related companies the opportunity to reach qualified candidates worldwide, and offers qualified candidates the opportunity to browse various career opportunities.

http://www.careermag.com/careermag

Career Magazine is an excellent online resource designed to meet the various needs of networked job seekers. A "Job Openings" link features indexes of all the job postings from the major Internet jobs newsgroups. The postings are searchable by location, job title, and skills sought.

http://www.ccnet.com/hrcomm
HRCOMM is a free online network for the human resource (HR) community, designed by professionals in the HR field.

http://joblink.com/joblink.html
JobLink is a service provided to companies who hire technical personnel, and is a mechanism for posting available jobs and receiving qualified responses.

Internet Consulting:

http://www.ais.net
American Information Systems, Inc. is a company that offers businesses a variety of Internet connectivity and consulting services.

http://npixi.webmaster.net/info.html
NPiX Interactive designs electronic marketing and communication materials that range from interactive brochures and business cards to World Wide Web site and server construction.

http://www.commerce.net/directories/consultants/consultants.html
This excellent resource takes you to **CommerceNet's** directory, which lists hundreds of Internet consultants specializing in Internet products and services. Users can search the listings alphabetically by specialty or by individual name, and link directly to the relevant WWW site. An excellent resource.

Investments:

http://www.yahoo.com/Economy/Markets_and_Investments
For an extensive source of market and investment information available on the
Web, users should visit **Yahoo** (main URL: **http://www.yahoo.com**) at the
above address. This page features hundreds of links to commercial investment
and financial services, corporate reports, futures and options, mutual funds, and
much more.

References/Directories:

http://www.scbbs.com/~unite-us
At this site, the **African American Business Directory** provides a searchable
and retrievable database plus a 24-hour live operator referral service.

http://www.asia-directory.com/~bruno
The **Asia Business Directories** site features a searchable and categorized
directory of businesses in Asia, and offers a free fax service to listed companies.

http://att.net/dir800
At this site, the **AT&T 800 Directory** allows visitors to browse AT&T's directory of 800 numbers.

http://www.visions.com/netpages
Canada Net Pages provides extensive information on various Canadian business and offers references to finance data available on the World Wide Web.

http://www.directory.net
This site features **Open Market's Commercial Sites Index**, a searchable directory of commercial services, products, and information on the Internet.

http://www.europages.com
This address will take you to the home page of **Europages**, the European Business Directory, which provides company information on 150,000 suppliers from 26 European countries.

a listing of
the 100 largest US companies
on the Web

The World Wide Web is the path most-traveled on the Internet today. For even the smallest of businesses, a Web site has become the corporate vanity plate of the Infobahn.

http://fox.nstn.ca/~at_info/w100_intro.html
The **Web 100** site is a listing of the largest U.S. corporations with presence on the World Wide Web, complete with links to each of their sites. Visitors can also access information on the rapid evolution of business on the Web.

http://www.inetbiz.com/market
The **Wholesaler's Worldwide Marketplace** site provides visitors with information on more than 2,400 wholesalers and manufacturers and includes more than 42,000 businesses.

http://www.yellow.com
The **Worldwide Yellow Pages** site allows users to browse business listings or register their company.

Small Business:

http://www.netaccess.on.ca/entrepr
Entrepreneur On-Line was developed to encourage commercial ventures to provide their information to other entrepreneurs on the Internet.

http://www.fed.org/fed
This **FEDnet** site is a good resource on equity compensation, employee involvement, and other business strategies.

-- Administrator Philip Lader

http://wwwsbanet.uca.edu
The site of the **Small Business Advancement National Center** aims to provide small businesses, entrepreneurs, educators, economic development officers, and small business counselors with the tools needed to further their business and economic goals.

http://www.sbaonline.sba.gov
At this address, users will find the home page of the **U.S. Small Business Administration (SBA)**, whose goal it is "to aid, counsel, assist, and protect the interests of small business concerns to preserve free competitive enterprise and to maintain and strengthen the overall economy" of the United States.

http://www.cqi.com:80/MandA
The site of **World M&A Network** contains hundreds of listings of companies that are for sale, merger candidates, and corporate buyers. The focus is on companies with between $1 million and $100 million in annual revenues.

Business Newsgroups

There are more than 11,000 public newsgroups around the world, so the following list presents only a very small cross-section of business-related sources. Still, these groups will keep you up to date on the latest news and may also put you in contact with people and organizations that can benefit you and your company.

Go to:

alt.business.misc — for general discussions of commerce.

alt.business.multi-level — for information on multi-level (network) marketing businesses.

alt.business.import-export — for discussions of international trade.

alt.business.insurance — for conversations regarding the insurance industry.

alt.business.internal-audit — for discussions of internal auditing.

clari.biz.market.news — for news affecting the financial markets.

clari.tw.aerospace — for aerospace industry and company news.

clari.tw.computers — for computer industry news.

clari.tw.electronics — for electronics manufacturing news.

clari.tw.misc — for general technical industry stories.

clari.tw.new_media — for the latest on online services, multimedia, and the Internet.

clari.tw.stocks — for computer and technology stock prices.

clari.tw.telecom — for information on the telephone, satellite, and telecommunications industries.

clari.nb.business — for Newsbytes, the computer industry's daily news service.

clari.world.americas.canada.business — for Canadian business news.

misc.business.facilitators — for discussions on all types of facilitators.

misc.invest — for news and advice on investing.

Mailing Lists

Here are some business-related mailing lists to subscribe to for information on a variety of topics:

mail to: **majordomo@csn.org** — a mailing list for economic development professionals who aid small business growth.

mail to: **rod@holonet.net** — for details on worldwide markets, product information, advertising, and more.

mail to: **mckinley@holonet.net** — which provides strategic information to help businesses market and advertise more effectively.

mail to: **smi-request@world.std.com** — for stock market commentary.

mail to: **subscribe@xamiga.linet.org** — for information on U.S. foreign trade.

mail to: **Mail-Server@knex.via.mind.org** — a mailing list for people involved in electronic publishing.

mail to: **listproc@online.ora.com** — which provides announcements from Internet publishers O'Reilly and Associates regarding the Net and online publishing.

mail to: **mail-server@rtfm.mit.edu** — to receive a list of Internet mailing lists. Note: The body of the message must read as follows: **send/usenet/news.answers/mail/mailing-lists/***

Internet Access Providers

Nationwide Access Providers

Several companies currently offer nationwide Internet access. Some specialize in Net access alone while others, like America OnLine and CompuServe, are online services that offer connections to the Internet. The following is a list of the major national players:

Alternet: offers access to individuals as well as larger organizations. Alternet can be contacted at (800) 258-9695.

America OnLine: an online service that offers Internet access and provides its own software. AOL can be reached at (800) 827-6364.

CompuServe: another online service that offers Net access. Call (800) 848-8990 for details.

Delphi: offers a text-based menu system and at least one graphical interface. Delphi can be contacted at (800) 695-4005.

The Microsoft Network: software included in the Windows 95 operating environment that promises Internet access. For more information, call Microsoft at (800) 426-9400.

Netcom: local phone numbers for this provider can be found around the United States. Netcom offers its own graphical interface. The company's toll-free number is (800) 501-8649.

Performance Systems International (PSI): another company with local numbers in many states, PSI provides its own software and can be reached at (800) 774-3031.

Prodigy: an online service that also offers Net access. Call Prodigy at (800) 776-3449 for more details.

Local Access Providers

The following is a sample list of local Internet service providers from around the United States. The large access providers are listed first and the local organizations follow, each listed with area code, contact information, and URL if available. Again, this is only a sample list; many more Internet providers are available throughout the country.

Concentric Research Corp.

Area Code:201, 202, 205, 206, 206, 210, 212, 213, 214, 215, 216, 219, 303, 305,
314, 315, 316, 317, 401, 402, 404, 405, 407, 408, 410, 412,413, 414,
415, 419, 501, 502, 503, 504, 505, 508, 510, 512, 513, 516, 517, 518,
601, 602, 606, 612, 614, 615, 616, 617, 619, 702, 704, 706, 708, 713,
716, 717, 719, 801, 803, 804, 805, 810, 813, 816, 817, 901, 904, 910,
915, 916, 918, 919

E-mail for further information: kris@concentric.net
Phone: (800) 745-2747
Modem: (800) 991-2747
Fax: (517) 895-0529
URL: **http://www.cris.com**

Digital Express Group — DIGEX(tm)

Area Code:917, 201, 202, 212, 215, 301, 302, 410, 516, 609, 610,703, 718, 908,
914

E-mail for further information: sales@digex.net
Phone: (800) 969-9090
        (301) 847-5000
Fax: (301) 847-5215
URL: **http://www.digex.net**

Global Connect, Inc.

Area Code: 201, 202, 203, 205, 206, 208, 209, 212, 213, 214, 215,216, 217, 219,
302, 303, 305, 310, 312, 313, 314, 315, 317, 401, 402, 404, 405, 407,
408, 410, 412, 414, 415, 416, 419, 501, 502, 503, 504, 505, 508, 509,
510, 512, 513, 514, 515, 517, 518, 601, 602, 603, 604, 606, 608, 609,
610, 612, 614, 615, 616, 617, 619, 702, 703, 704, 708, 713, 714, 716,
717, 719, 801, 803, 804, 805, 810, 812, 813, 814, 817, 818, 901, 908,
909, 910, 912, 913, 914, 916, 918, 919

E-mail for further information: sales@gc.net
Phone: (804) 229-4484
Fax: (804) 229-6557
URL: **http://www.gc.net**

EMI Communications

Area Code: 914, 201, 202, 203, 212, 215, 301, 315, 401, 516, 518, 607, 617, 716, 800

E-mail for further information: info@emi.com
Phone: (800) 456-2001
Fax: (315) 433-9137
URL: **http://www.emi.com**

I-Link, Inc.

Area Code: 210, 202, 206, 212, 213, 214, 303, 404, 407, 415, 502, 504, 512, 602, 617, 619, 713, 801

E-mail for further information: support@i-link.net
Phone: (512) 388-2393
       (800) ILINK99; (800) 454-6599
Fax: (512) 244-9681
URL: **http://www.i-link.net**

Merit/MichNet

Area Code: 906, 313, 517, 616, 810

E-mail for further information: recruiting@merit.edu
Phone: (313) 764-9430
Fax: (313) 747-3185
URL: **http://nic.merit.edu**

Moran Communications Group

Area Code: 815, 201, 202, 206, 212, 213, 214, 215, 216, 217, 302, 303, 305, 312, 313, 314, 316, 317, 402, 404, 405, 407, 408, 412, 415, 419, 501, 502, 513, 515, 606, 609, 610, 612, 614, 617, 704, 713, 716, 717, 719, 803, 816, 817, 901, 918, 919

E-mail for further information: jmoran@moran.com
Phone: (716) 639-1254
Fax: (716) 636-3630
URL: **http://www.moran.com**

New York Net

Area Code: 201, 203, 315, 516, 518, 607, 609, 716, 718, 914

E-mail for further information: sales@new-york.net
Phone: (718) 776-6811
Fax: (718) 217-9407
URL: **http://www.new-york.net**

NWNet

Area Code: 701, 206, 208, 360, 406, 503, 509, 907

E-mail for further information: melissa@nwnet.net
Phone: (206) 562-3000
Fax: (206) 562-4822
URL: **http://www.nwnet.net/nwnpages**

ONet Networking

Area Code: 807, 416, 519, 613, 905

E-mail for further information: info@onet.on.ca
Phone: (416) 978-4589
        (416) 978-0188
Fax: (416) 978-6620
URL: **http://www.onet.on.ca/onet**

Primenet

Area Code: 208, 209, 213, 419, 520, 602, 612, 714, 715, 816, 818, 909, 915

E-mail for further information: acctinfo@primenet.com
Phone: (602) 395-1010
        (800) 4-NET-FUN
Fax: (602) 870-1010
URL: **http://www.primenet.com**

Synergy Communications

Area Code: 201, 202, 205, 206, 206, 210, 212, 213, 214, 215, 216, 219, 303, 305,
314, 315, 316, 317, 401, 402, 404, 405, 407, 408, 410, 412, 413, 414,
415, 419, 501, 502, 503, 504, 505, 508, 510, 513, 516, 517, 518, 601,
602, 606, 612, 614, 615, 616, 617, 619, 702, 704, 706, 708, 713, 716,
717, 719, 800, 801, 803, 804, 805, 810, 813, 816, 817, 901, 904, 910,
915, 916, 918, 919

E-mail for further information: info@synergy.net
Phone: (402) 346-4638
Fax: (402) 346-0208
URL: **http://www.synergy.net**

A Sampling of
Local Providers by Area Code

Providers are listed under the area code pertaining to their primary area of coverage. Check with each Provider for additional areas of coverage.

201

The Connection
E-mail for further information: support@cnct.com
Phone: (201) 435-4414
Fax: (201) 435-4414
URL: **http://cnct.com**

Carroll-Net
E-mail for further information: jim@carroll.com
Phone: (201) 488-1332
URL: **http://www.carroll.com**

Novasys Interactive
E-mail for further information: info@novasys.com
Phone: (201) 887-2020
URL: **http://www.novasys.com**

Planet Access Networks, Inc.
E-mail for further information: info@planet.net
Phone: (201) 691-4704
Fax: (201) 691-7588

203

Computerized Horizons
E-mail for further information: sysop@fcc.com
Phone: (203) 335-7431
Fax: (203) 335-3007
URL: **http://fcc.com**

CallNet Information Services
E-mail for further information: admin@callnet.com
Phone: (203) 389-7130
URL: **http://www.callnet.com**

NECAnet, Inc.
E-mail for further information: support@neca.com
Phone: (203) 429-2035
Fax: (203) 429-1528
URL: **http://www.neca.com**

204

Magic Online Services Winnipeg Inc.
E-mail for further information: sbrooker@magic.mb.ca
Phone: (204) 949-7777
Fax: (204) 949-7790
URL: **http://www.magic.mb.ca**

205

Cheney Communications Company
E-mail for further information: sales@cheney.net
Phone: (800) CHENEY-1
Fax: (205) 941-0278
URL: **http://www.cheney.net**

interQuest Online Services
E-mail for further information: info@iquest.com
Phone: (205) 464-8280
Fax: (205) 461-8538
URL: **http://www.iquest.com**

206

AccessOne
E-mail for further information: info@accessone.com
Phone: (206) 827-5344
Fax: (206) 827-8792
URL: **http://www.accessone.com**

Northwest CommLink Internet Services
E-mail for further information: gtyacke@nwcl.net
Phone: (206) 336-0103
Fax: (206) 336-2339
URL: **http://www.nwcl.net/homepage.html**

207

Internet Maine Inc.
E-mail for further information: mtenney@mainelink.net
Phone: (207) 780-0416
URL: **http://www.mainelink.net**

208

NICOH Net
E-mail for further information: support@nicoh.com
Phone: (208) 233-5802
Fax: (208) 233-5911
URL: **http://www.nicoh.com**

209

ValleyNet Communications
E-mail for further information: info@valleynet.com
Phone: (209) 486-VNET (8638)
Fax: (209) 495-4940
URL: **http://www.valleynet.com**

210

Texas Networking Incorporated
E-mail for further information: helpdesk@texas.net
Phone: (210) 272-8111
Fax: (210) 272-8222
URL: **http://www.texas.net**

212

Blythe Systems
E-mail for further information: accounts@blythe.org
Phone: (212) 979-0471
URL: **gopher://ursula.blythe.org**

EscapeCom
E-mail for further information: info@escape.com
Phone: (212) 888-8780
Fax: (212) 832-0210
URL: **http://www.escape.com**

Internet Channel
E-mail for further information: access@inch.com
Phone: (212) 243-5200
Fax: (212) 243-3365
URL: **http://www.inch.com**

The New York Web, Inc.
E-mail for further information: nysurf@nyweb.com
Phone: (212) 748-7600
Fax: (212) 608-4494
URL: **http://nyweb.com**

Phantom Access Technologies, Inc.
E-mail for further information: system@phantom.com
Phone: (212) 989-2418
Fax: (212) 989-8648
URL: **http://www.phantom.com**

213

The Loop Internet Switch Co.
E-mail for further information: greg@loop.com
Phone: (213) 465-1311
Fax: (213) 469-2193
URL: **http://www.loop.com/rates.html**

214

Dallas Internet
E-mail for further information: manager@dallas.net
Phone: (214) 881-9595
Fax: (214) 578-6045
URL: **http://www.dallas.net**

On-Ramp Technologies, Inc.
E-mail for further information: sales@onramp.net
Phone: (214) 746-4710
Fax: (214) 713-5400
URL: **http://www.onramp.net**

215

Net Access Internet Services
E-mail for further information: support@netaxs.com
Phone: (215) 576-8669
URL: **http:/www.netaxs.com**

216

EZNet Ohio
E-mail for further information: sales@eznets.canton.oh.us
Phone: (216) 455-7979
Fax: (216) 455-7979
URL: **http://www.eznets.canton.oh.us**

217

Prairienet, The East-Central Illinois FreeNet
E-mail for further information: info@prairienet.org
Phone: (217) 244-1962
URL: **http://www.prairienet.org**

219

Crown.Net Inc.
E-mail for further information: info@crown.net
Phone: (219) 762-1431
Fax: (219) 762-0917
URL: not available

301

EagleNet
E-mail for further information: fwilliam@eagle1.eaglenet.com
Phone: (301) 863-6992
Fax: (301) 863-0453
URL: **http://www.eaglenet.com**

302

Business Data Systems, Inc.
E-mail for further information: admin@bdsnet.com
Phone: (302) 674-2840
Fax: (302) 678-4945
URL: **http://www.bdsnet.com**

The Magnetic Page
E-mail for further information: support@magpage.com
Phone: (302) 651-9753
Fax: (302) 426-9731
URL: **http://www.magpage.com**

303

Colorado Internet Cooperative Association
E-mail for further information: contact@coop.net
Phone: (303) 443-3786
Fax: (303) 443-9718
URL: **http://www.coop.net/coop**

CSDC
E-mail for further information: support@csd.net
Phone: (303) 665-8053
Fax: (303) 443-0808
URL: **http://www.csd.net**

304

Intrepid Technologies, Inc.
E-mail for further information: support@intrepid.net
Phone: (304) 876-1199
URL: **http://www.intrepid.net**

MountainNet, Inc.
E-mail for further information: info@mountain.net
Phone: (304) 594-9075
　　　　(800) 846-1458
Fax: (304) 594-9088
URL: **http://www.mountain.net**

305

BridgeNet, LC
E-mail for further information: chipper@bridge.net
Phone: (305) 374-3031
Fax: (305) 358-4114
URL: **http://www.bridge.net**

Internet Gateway Connections
E-mail for further information: sales@Igc.NET
Phone: (305) 430-3030
Fax: (305) 430-3994
URL: **http://www.Igc.NET**

306

Unibase Telecom Ltd.
E-mail for further information: milton@unibase.unibase.com
Phone: (306) 789-9007
Fax: (306) 761-1831
URL: **http://www.unibase.com**

307

NETConnect
E-mail for further information: scott@tcd.net
Phone: (307) 789-8001
        (800) 689-8001
Fax: (307) 789-5707
URL: **http://www.tcd.net**

309

ICEnet
E-mail for further information: icenet@ice.net
Phone: (309) 454-4638
URL: **http://www.ice.net**

310

Cloverleaf, Inc.
E-mail for further information: sales@cloverleaf.com
Phone: (714) 895-3075
Fax: (310) 420-7255
URL: **http://www.cloverleaf.com**

312

Macro Computer Solutions, Inc. (MCSNet)
E-mail for further information: info@mcs.net
Phone: (312) 248-8649
Fax: (312) 248-9865
URL: **http://www.mcs.net**

Tezcat Communications
E-mail for further information: sales@tezcat.com
Phone: (312) 850-0181
Fax: (312) 850-0492
URL: **http://www.tezcat.com**

313

ICNet
E-mail for further information: ivars@ic.net
Phone: (313) 998-0090
Fax: (313) 998-0816
URL: **http://www.ic.net**

Isthmus Corporation
E-mail for further information: support@izzy.net
Phone: (313) 973-2100
Fax: (313) 973-2117
URL: **http://www.izzy.net**

Msen
E-mail for further information: sales@msen.com
Phone: (313) 998-4562
Fax: (313) 998-4563
URL: **http://www.msen.com**

314

Inlink
E-mail for further information: support@inlink.com
Phone: (314) 432-0149
Fax: (314) 432-2569
URL: **http://www.inlink.com**

Thoughtport
E-mail for further information: human@thoughtport.com
Phone: (800) 477-6870
Fax: (314) 474-4122
URL: **http://www.thoughtport.com**

316

DTC SuperNet
E-mail for further information: info@dtc.net
Phone: (316) 683-1300
Fax: (316) 683-9104
URL: **http://www.dtc.net**

SouthWind Internet Access, Inc.
E-mail for further information: staff@southwind.net
Phone: (316) 263-7963
Fax: (316) 267-3943
URL: **http://www.southwind.net**

317

HolliCom Internet Services
E-mail for further information: sales@holli.com
Phone: (317) 883-4562
        (800) 883-4593
Fax: (317) 883-7669
URL: **http://www.holli.com**

Net Direct
E-mail for further information: kat@inetdirect.net
Phone: (317) 251-5252
Fax: (317) 726-5239
URL: **http://www.inetdirect.net**

318

LinkNet Internet Services
E-mail for further information: webmastr@linknet.net
Phone: (318) 442-5465
Fax: (318) 449-9750
URL: **http://www.linknet.net**

319

Gryffin Information Services, Inc.
E-mail for further information: info@gryffin.com
Phone: (319) 399-3690
Fax: (319) 399-3694
URL: **http://www.gryffin.com**

334

Viper Computer Systems, Inc. (ViperNet)
E-mail for further information: vipersys@viper.net
Phone: (334) 826-1912
(800) VIPER-96
Fax: (334) 826-8727
URL: not available

360

Network Access Services, Inc.
E-mail for further information: sales@nas.com
Phone: (360) 733-9279
Fax: (360) 676-0345
URL: **http://www.nas.com**

Pacific Rim Network, Inc.
E-mail for further information: sales@pacificrim.net
Phone: (360) 650-0442
Fax: (360) 738-8315
URL: **http://www.pacificrim.net**

401

Log On America
E-mail for further information: feedback@loa.com
Phone: (401) 459-6100
Modem: (401) 459-6200 (14.4k)
(401) 459-6216 (28.8k)
Fax: (401) 459-6222
URL: **http://www.loa.com**

402

Internet Nebraska
E-mail for further information: manager@inetnebr.com
Phone: (402) 434-8680
URL: **http://www.inetnebr.com**

MIDnet
E-mail for further information: witts@mid.net
Phone: (800) 682-5550
Fax: (402) 472-0240
URL: **http://www.mid.net**

Probe Technology, Inc., Internet Services Div.
E-mail for further information: info@probe.net
Phone: (402) 593-9800
Fax: (402) 593-8748
URL: **http://www.probe.net**

403

Spots InterConnect, Inc.
E-mail for further information: jason@spots.ab.ca
Phone: (403) 571-SPOT (7768)
Fax: (403) 571-7766
URL: **http://www.spots.ab.ca**

404

Intergate, Inc.
E-mail for further information: sales@intergate.net
Phone: (404) 429-9599
Fax: (404) 429-1018
URL: **http://www.intergate.net**

Internet Atlanta
E-mail for further information: info@atlanta.com
Phone: (404) 410-9000
Fax: (404) 410-9005
URL: **http://www.com/atlanta**

LYCEUM Internet Services
E-mail for further information: sales@mindspring.com
Phone: (404) 248-1733
Fax: (404) 248-1735
URL: **http://www.lyceum.com**

Mindspring

E-mail for further information: sales@mindspring.com
Phone: (404) 888-0725
Fax: (404) 888-9210
URL: **http://www.mindspring.com**

405

IONet

E-mail for further information: support@ionet.net
Phone: (405) 721-1580
Fax: (405) 721-4861
URL: **http://www.ionet.net**

Internet Oklahoma

E-mail for further information: support@ionet.net
Phone: (405) 721-1580
URL: **http://www.ionet.net**

Questar Network Services (QNSnet)

E-mail for further information: info@qns.com
Phone: (405) 848-3228
Fax: (405) 848-9434
URL: **http://www.qns.com**

406

Internet Services Montana, Inc.

E-mail for further information: support@ism.net
Phone: (406) 542-0838
URL: **http://www.ism.net**

407

Florida Online

E-mail for further information: jerry@digital.net
Phone: (800) 676-2599
        (407) 635-8888
Fax: (407) 635-9050
URL: **http://www.digital.net**

Tachyon Communications Corp.
E-mail for further information: scpayne@tach.net
Phone: (407) 728-8081
        (407) 424-6091
Fax: (407) 725-6315
URL: **http://www.tach.net**

408

Bay Area Internet Solutions
E-mail for further information: sales@bayarea.net
Phone: (408) 447-8690
Fax: (408) 447-8691
URL: **http://www.bayarea.net**

409

Cybercom Corporation
E-mail for further information: tech@cy-net.net
Phone: (409) 268-0771
Fax: (409) 260-2652
URL: **http://www.cy-net.net**

410

ABSnet Internet Services, Inc.
E-mail for further information: sales@abs.net
Phone: (410) 361-8160
Fax: (410) 361-8162
URL: **http://www.abs.net**

American Information Network
E-mail for further information: admin@ai.net
Phone: (410) 715-6808
URL: **http://www.ai.net**

412

CityNet, Inc.
E-mail for further information: info@city-net.com
Phone: (412) 481-5406
Fax: (412) 431-1315
URL: **http://www.city-net.com**

Pittsburgh OnLine, Inc.
E-mail for further information: sales@pgh.net
Phone: (412) 681-6130
URL: **http://www.pgh.net**

PREPnet
E-mail for further information: nic@prep.net
Phone: (412) 267-7870
URL: **http://www.prep.net**

413

MAP Internet Services
E-mail for further information: dpignatare@map.com
Phone: (413) 732-0214
       (800) 262-6589
Fax: (413) 732-0254
URL: **http://www.map.com**

Crocker Communications
E-mail for further information: matthew@crocker.com
Phone: (413) 585-1250
       (800) 413-LINE
Fax: (413) 665-1399
URL: **http://www.crocker.com**

414

Green Bay Online
E-mail for further information: staff@online.dct.com
Phone: (414) 431-0088
URL: **http://www.dct.com**

415

Aplatform
E-mail for further information: support@aplatform.com
Phone: (415) 941-2647
Fax: (415) 941-2647
URL: **http://www.aplatform.com**

Sirius Connections
E-mail for further information: admin@sirius.com
Phone: (415) 284-4700
Fax: (415) 284-4704
URL: **http://www.sirius.com**

SlipNET
E-mail for further information: support@slip.net
Phone: (415) 281-3196
        (800) SLIP-NET
Fax: (415) 543-6398
URL: **http://www.slip.net**

ViaNet Communications
E-mail for further information: joe@via.net
Phone: (415) 969-2203
Fax: (415) 969-2124
URL: **http://www.via.net**

416

NSTN Incorporated
E-mail for further information: sales@nstn.ca
Phone: (800) 848-NSTN (6786)
        (902) 481-NSTN (6786)
Fax: (902) 468-3679
URL: **http://www.nstn.ca**

UUNorth International
E-mail for further information: cathie@uunorth.north.net
Phone: (416) 225-8649
URL: **http://www.uunorth.north.net**

417

Woodtech Information Systems, Inc.
E-mail for further information: ej@woodtech.com
Phone: (417) 886-0234
Fax: (417) 886-2170
URL: **http://www.woodtech.com**

419

West Central Ohio Internet Link
E-mail for further information: mike@alpha.wcoil.com
Phone: (419) 229-2645
Fax: (419) 229-2645
URL: **http://www.wcoil.com**

501

IntelliNet, LLC
E-mail for further information: dlaser@intellinet.com
Phone (Little Rock): (800) 290-7677, (501) 376-7676
Phone (Fayetteville): (501) 521-4660
Fax (Little Rock): (501) 375-3063
Fax (Fayetteville): (501) 521-4659
URL: **http://www.intellinet.com**

502

IgLou Internet Services
E-mail for further information: sales@iglou.com
Phone: (502) 966-3848
       (800) I-DO-IGLOU
Fax: (502) 968-0449
URL: **http://www.iglou.com**

503

aracnet.com
E-mail for further information: support@aracnet.com
Modem: (503) 626-6873
Phone: (503) 626-7696
Fax: (503) 626-8675
URL: **http://www.aracnet.com**

InfoStructure
E-mail for further information: allaire@mind.net
Phone: (503) 488-1962
Fax: (503) 488-7599
URL: **http://www.mind.net**

Transport Logic
E-mail for further information: sales@transport.com
Phone: (503) 243-1940
URL: **http://www.transport.com**

504

AccessCom Internet Providers
E-mail for further information: bcolosi@accesscom.net
Phone: (504) 887-0022
Fax: (504) 456-0995
URL: **http://www.accesscom.net**

505

CyberPort Station
E-mail for further information: sales@cyberport.com
Phone: (505) 324-6400
Fax: (505) 325-4995
URL: **http://www.cyberport.com**

New Mexico Internet Access, Inc.
E-mail for further information: accounts@nmia.com
Phone: (505) 877-0617
URL: **http://www.nmia.com**

506

Maritime Internet Services
E-mail for further information: support@mi.net
Phone: (506) 652-3624
Fax: (506) 635-5458
URL: **http://www.mi.net**

507

Internet Connections, Inc.
E-mail for further information: info@ic.mankato.mn.us
Phone: (507) 625-7320
Fax: (507) 625-3551
URL: **http://www.ic.mankato.mn.us**

Millennium Communications, Inc. (Millcomm)
E-mail for further information: info@millcomm.com
Phone: (507) 282-1004
      (612) 338-8666
Fax: (507) 282-8943
URL: **http://www.millcomm.com/millhome**

508

CAPEInternet
E-mail for further information: comments@capecod.net
Phone: (508) 790-1501
URL: **http://www.capecod.net**

FOURnet Information Network
E-mail for further information: info@FOUR.net
Phone: (508) 291-1774
URL: **http://www.four.net**

Internet Exchange Ltd.
E-mail for further information: office@ixl.net
Phone: (508) 647-4726
Fax: (508) 647-4727
URL: **http://web.ixl.net**

UltraNet Communications, Inc.
E-mail for further information: mitch@ultranet.com
Phone: (508) 229-8400
    (800) 763-8111
Fax: (508) 229-2375
URL: **http://www.ultranet.com**

509

Cascade Connections, Inc.
E-mail for further information: carrie@cascade.net
Phone: (509) 663-4259
URL: **http://www.cascade.net**

NCWNet
E-mail for further information: info@ncw.net
Phone: (509) 664-9004
    (800) 407-0002
Fax: (509) 662-0712
URL: **http://www.ncw.net**

510

Beckemeyer Development
E-mail for further information: sales@bdt.com
Phone: (510) 530-9637
Fax: (510) 530-0451
URL: **http://www.bdt.com**

512

Open Communications, Inc.
E-mail for further information: Help@easy.com
Phone: (512) 250-5765
Fax: (512) 250-5765
URL: **http://www.easy.com**

OuterNet Connection Strategies
E-mail for further information: support@outer.net
Phone: (512) 345-3573
Fax: (512) 206-0345
URL: **http://www.outer.net**

513

The Dayton Network Access Co. (DNACo)
E-mail for further information: support@dnaco.net
Phone: (513) 237-6868
Fax: (513) 236-5790
URL: **http://www.dnaco.net**

EriNet Online Communications
Area Codes: 513
E-mail for further information: support@erinet.com
Phone: (513) 291-1995
Fax: (513) 436-1466
URL: **http://www.erinet.com**

Internet Access Cincinnati
E-mail for further information: sales@iac.net
Phone: (513) 887-8877
         (513) 333-0033
Fax: (513) 887-2085
URL: **http://www.iac.net**

514

NetAxis of Montreal
E-mail for further information: info@NetAxis.qc.ca
Phone: (514) 482-8989
Fax: (514) 483-6718
URL: **http://www.NetAxis.qc.ca**

Connection MMIC inc.
E-mail for further information: michel@connectmmic.net
Phone: (514) 331-6642
Fax: (514) 332-6642
URL: **http://www.connectmmic.net/homemmic.html**

515

Des Moines Internet, Inc.
E-mail for further information: brentf@dsmnet.com
Phone: (515) 270-9191
Fax: (515) 270-8648
URL: **http://www.dsmnet.com**

516

Long Island Information, Inc.
E-mail for further information: support@liii.com
Phone: (516) 248-5381
URL: **http://www.liii.com**

Network-USA
E-mail for further information: office@netusa.net
Phone: (516) 543-0240
Fax: (516) 543-0274
URL: **http://www.netusa.net**

518

AlbanyNet
E-mail for further information: sales@albany.net
Phone: (518) 465-3294
URL: **http://www.albany.net**

Klink Net Communications
E-mail for further information: admin@klink.net
Phone: (518) 725-3000
(800) KLINK-123
Fax: (518) 725-3152
URL: **http://www.klink.net**

520

Opus One
E-mail for further information: sales@opus1.com
Phone: (520) 324-0494
Fax: (520) 324-0495
URL: **http://www.opus1.com**

601

Datasync Internet Services
E-mail for further information: support@datasync.com
Phone: (601) 872-0001
(601) 452-0011
URL: **http://www.datasync.com**

InterSys Technologies, Inc.
E-mail for further information: support@inst.com
Phone: (601) 949-6992
(800) 701-3472
URL: **http://www.inst.com**

602

Crossroads Communications
E-mail for further information: sales@xroads.com
Phone: (602) 813-9040
Fax: (602) 545-7470
URL: **http://www.xroads.com**

RTD Systems & Networking, Inc.
E-mail for further information: sales@rtd.com
Phone: (602) 318-0696
Fax: (602) 322-9755
URL: **http://www.rtd.com**

603

The Destek Group, Inc
E-mail for further information: inquire@destek.net
Phone: (603) 635-3857
Fax: (603) 635-7314
URL: **http://www.destek.net**

Empire.Net, Inc.
E-mail for further information: sales@empire.net
Phone: (603) 889-1220
Fax: (603) 889-0366 (call before faxing)
URL: **http://www.empire.net**

MonadNet Corporation
E-mail for further information: info@monad.net
Phone: (603) 352-7619
Fax: (603) 358-2870
URL: **http://www.monad.net**

NETIS Public Access Internet
E-mail for further information: info@netis.com
Phone: (603) 437-1811
Fax: (603) 437-1811
URL: **http://www.netis.com**

604

auroraNET, Inc.
E-mail for further information: jcryer@aurora.net
Phone: (604) 294-4357 x101
Fax: (604) 294-0107
URL: **http://www.aurora.net**

605

Dakota Internet Services, Inc.
E-mail for further information: service@dakota.net
Phone: (605) 371-1962
URL: **http://www.dakota.net**

RapidNet LLC
E-mail for further information: gary@rapidnet.com
Phone: (605) 341-3283
Fax: (605) 348-1031
URL: **http://www.rapidnet.com**

607

Art Matrix - Lightink
E-mail for further information: homer@lightlink.com
Phone: (607) 277-0959
Fax: (607) 277-8913
URL: **http://lightlink.com**

608

SupraNet Communications, Inc.
E-mail for further information: sales@supranet.com
Phone: (608) 836-0282
Fax: (608) 836-0283
URL: **http://www.supranet.com**

WiscNet
E-mail for further information: wn-info@nic.wiscnet.net
Phone: (608) 265-6761
Fax: (608) 262-4679
URL: not available

609

NetK2NE (K2NE Software)
E-mail for further information: vince-q@k2nesoft.com
Phone: (609) 893-0673
URL: **http://k2nesoft.com**

New Jersey Computer Connection
E-mail for further information: support@pluto.njcc.com
Phone: (609) 896-2799
Fax: (609) 896-2994
URL: **http://www.njcc.com**

610

Enter.Net
E-mail for further information: info@enter.net
Phone: (610) 366-1300
Fax: (610) 391-9508
URL: **http://www.enter.net**

612

gofast.net
E-mail for further information: info@gofast.net
Phone: (612) 647-6109
URL: **http://gofast.net**

Minnesota MicroNet
E-mail for further information: help@mm.com
Phone: (612) 882-7711
URL: **http://www.mm.com**

613

Channel One Internet Services
E-mail for further information: admin@sonetis.com
Phone: (613) 236-8601
Fax: (613) 236-8764
URL: **http://www.sonetis.com**

Cyberus Online Inc.
E-mail for further information: info@cyberus.ca
Phone: (613) 233-1215
Fax: (613) 233-0292
URL: **http://www.cyberus.ca**

Information Gateway Services
E-mail for further information: info@igs.net
Phone: (613) 592-5619
         (800) 268-3715
Fax: (613) 592-3556
URL: **http://www.igs.net**

614

GANet
E-mail for further information: bradb@ganet.net
Phone: (614) 799-3720
URL: **http://www.ganet.net**

615

The Telalink Corporation
E-mail for further information: bill@telalink.net
   ted@telalink.net
Phone: (615) 321-9100
Fax: (615) 327-4520
URL: **http://www.nashville.net/telalink**

The Tri-Cities Connection
E-mail for further information: oper@tricon.net
Phone: (615) 378-5355
Fax: (615) 378-0117
URL: **http://www.tricon.net**

616

Iserv
E-mail for further information: info@iserv.net
Phone: (616) 281-5254
Fax: (616) 281-2268
URL: **http://www.iserv.net**

617

Blue Sky, Inc.
E-mail for further information: marketng@bluesky.net
Phone: (617) 270-4747
Fax: (617) 270-4754
URL: **http://www.bluesky.net**

Channel 1
E-mail for further information: support@channel1.com
Phone: (800) 745-2747
       (617) 864-0100
URL: **http:/www.channel1.com**

Cyber Access Internet Communications, Inc.
E-mail for further information: sales@cybercom.net
Phone: (617) 396-0491
Fax: (617) 396-0854
URL: **http://www.cybercom.net**

North Shore Access
E-mail for further information: info@shore.net
Phone: (617) 593-3110
Fax: (617) 593-6858
URL: **http://www.shore.net**

Pioneer Global Telecommunications
E-mail for further information: sales@pn.com
Phone: (617) 375-0200
Fax: (617) 375-0201
URL: **http://www.pn.com**

Plymouth Commercial Internet eXchange
E-mail for further information: sales@pcix.com
Phone: (617) 741-5900
Fax: (617) 741-5416
URL: **http://www.pcix.com**

618

On-Line Information Access Network, SSI Communications
E-mail for further information: sysop@oia.net
Phone: (618) 692-9813
Fax: (618) 692-9874
URL: **http://www.oia.net**

619

CTSNET
E-mail for further information: support@cts.com
Phone: (619) 637-3637
Fax: (619) 637-3630
URL: **http://www.cts.com**

LightLink Internet Access Services
E-mail for further information: jskains@lightlink.satcom.net
Phone: (619) 337-2641
Fax: (619) 337-2641
URL: **http://www.satcom.net**

701

Red River Net
E-mail for further information: lien@rrnet.com
Phone: (701) 232-2227
URL: **http://www.rrnet.com**

702

Access Nevada, Inc.
E-mail for further information: info@accessnv.com
Phone: (702) 294-0480
Fax: (702) 293-3278
URL: **http://www.accesssnv.com**

NevadaNet
E-mail for further information: braddlee@nevada.edu
Phone: (702) 784-6861
Fax: (702) 784-1108
URL: **http://www.scs.unr.edu**
     http://www.nevada.edu

703

Capital Area Internet Service
E-mail for further information: support@cais.com
Phone: (703) 448-4470
URL: **http://www.cais.com**

MediaSoft Corporation
E-mail for further information: Support@mediasoft.net
Phone: (703) 777-9475
Fax: (703) 777-9475
URL: **http://www.mediasoft.net**

Monumental Network Services
E-mail for further information: mns@mnsinc.com
Phone: (703) 631-3600
Fax: (703) 631-0748
URL: **http://www.mnsinc.com**

NetRail, Inc.
E-mail for further information: sales@netrail.net
Phone: (703) 524-4800
Fax: (703) 534-5033
URL: **http://www.netrail.net**

704

Internet of Shelby
E-mail for further information: parks@vnet.net
Phone: (704) 480-1801
Fax: (704) 480-8455

Cybernetx, Inc.
E-mail for further information: info@cybernetx.net
Phone: (704) 561-7000
Fax: (704) 527-3727
URL: **http://www.cybernetx.net**

705

MCD*Net
E-mail for further information: office@mcd.on.ca
Phone: (705) 523-0243
URL: **http://www.mcd.on.ca**

706

Znet
E-mail for further information: support@znet.augusta.ga.us
Phone: (706) 722-2175
Fax: (706) 736-9120
URL: **http://www.znet.augusta.ga.us**

707

Northcoast Internet
E-mail for further information: info@northcoast.com
Phone: (707) 443-8696
Fax: (707) 441-0321
URL: **http://www.northcoast.com**

CASTLES Information Network
E-mail for further information: mking@sparc1.castles.com
Phone: (707) 422-7311, (800) WEB-ME-NOW
Fax: (707) 422-5265
URL: **http://www.castles.com**

708

Sun Valley SoftWare, Ltd.
E-mail for further information: ken@svs.com
Phone: (708) 983-0889
Fax: (708) 983-2584
URL: **http://www.svs.com**

WorldWide Access
E-mail for further information: support@wwa.com
Phone: (708) 367-1870
Fax: (708) 367-1872
URL: **http://www.wwa.com**

709

NLnet
E-mail for further information: support@nlnet.nf.ca
Phone: (709) 737-4555
Fax: (709) 737-3514
URL: **http://www.nlnet.nf.ca**

713

Black Box
E-mail for further information: mknewman@blkbox.COM
Phone: (713) 480-2684
URL: **http://www.blkbox.com**

InfoCom Networks
E-mail for further information: pancamo@infocom.net
Phone: (713) 286-0399
URL: **http://www.infocom.net**

Info-Highway International, Inc.
E-mail for further information: lorell@infohwy.com
Phone: (713) 447-7025
Fax: (713) 447-8526
URL: **http://www.infohwy.com**

714

Gordian

E-mail for further information: uucp-info@gordian.com
Phone: (714) 850-0205
Fax: (714) 850-0533
URL: **http://www.gordian.com**

KAIWAN Internet Access

E-mail for further information: sales@kaiwan.com
Phone: (714) 638-2139
Fax: (714) 638-0455
URL: **http://www.kaiwan.com**

Liberty Information Network

E-mail for further information: sysadmin@liberty.com
Phone: (714) 996-9999
        (800) 218-5157
Fax: (714) 974-9484
URL: **http://www.liberty.com**

Network Intensive

E-mail for further information: info2@ni.net
Phone: (800) 273-5600
Fax: (714) 450-8410
URL: **http://www.ni.net**

716

E-Znet, Inc.

E-mail for further information: support@eznet.net
Phone: (716) 262-2485
Fax: (716) 262-3766
URL: **http://www.eznet.net**

ServiceTech, Inc.

E-mail for further information: ddewey@servtech.com
Phone: (716) 263-3360
Fax: (716) 423-1596
URL: **http://www.servtech.com**

Vivanet
E-mail for further information: sales@vivanet.com
Phone: (716) 272-9101
        (800) VIVA-SKY
Fax: (619) 457-0888
URL: **http://www.vivanet.com**

717

Keystone Information Access Systems
E-mail for further information: office@yrkpa.kias.com
Phone: (717) 741-2626
URL: **http://yrkpa.kias.com**

718

SILLY.COM
E-mail for further information: root@silly.com
Phone: (718) 229-7096
URL: **http://www.silly.com**

719

OldOlo Company
E-mail for further information: dave@oldolo.com
Phone: (719) 636-2040
        (719) 528-5849
Modem: (719) 632-4111
Fax: (719) 528-5869
URL: not available

Rocky Mountain Internet, Inc
E-mail for further information: support@rmii.com
Phone: (800) 900-RMII
        (719) 576-6845
URL: not available

801

DirecTell LC
E-mail for further information: kathy@ditell.com
Phone: (801) 647-5838
Fax: (801) 647-9868
URL: **http://www.ditell.com**

Infonaut Communication Services
E-mail for further information: info@infonaut.com
Phone: (801) 370-3060
Fax: (801) 229-1579
URL: **http://www.infonaut.com**

802

SoVerNet
E-mail for further information: sales@sover.net
Phone: (802) 463-2111
Fax: (802) 463-2110
URL: **http://www.sover.net**

803

South Carolina SuperNet, Inc.
E-mail for further information: good@pces.com
Phone: (803) 748-1207
Fax: (803) 748-1227
URL: **http://www.scsn.net**

804

Widomaker Communication Services
E-mail for further information: bloyall@widomaker.com
Phone: (804) 253-7621
Fax: (804) 229-4458
URL: **http://www.widomaker.com**

805

Lightspeed Net
E-mail for further information: ampy@lightspeed.net
Phone: (805) 324-4291
Fax: (805) 324-1437
URL: **http://www.lightspeed.net**

SLONET Regional Information Access Network
Phone: (805) 781-3666
Fax: (805) 549-9336
URL: **http://www.slonet.org**

SmartLink Networking
E-mail for further information: admin@smartlink.net
Phone: (805) 294-1273
Fax: (805) 294-8188
URL: **http://www.smartlink.net**

WestNet Communications, Inc.
E-mail for further information: help@west.net
Phone: (805) 892-2133   (805) 289-1000
Fax: (805) 892-2135
URL: **http://www.west.net**

808

Hawaii OnLine (HOL)
E-mail for further information: support@aloha.net
Phone: (800) 207-1880
          (808) 533-6981
Fax: (808) 534-0089
URL: **http://www.aloha.net**

Pacific Information eXchange (PixiNet)
E-mail for further information: query@pixi.com
Phone: (808) 596-7494
Fax: (808) 483-4147
URL: **http://www.pixi.com**

809

Caribbean Internet Service, Corp.
E-mail for further information: webmaster@caribe.net
Phone: (809) 728-3992
Fax: (809) 726-3093
URL: **http://www.caribe.net**

810

Michigan Internet Cooperative Association (MICA.net)
E-mail for further information: tbenner@coop.mica.net
Phone: (810) 355-1438
URL: **http://www.mica.net**

812

Evansville
E-mail for further information: heck@evansville.net
Phone: (812) 479-1700
Fax: (812) 479-3439
URL: **http://www.evansville.net**

813

CFTnet
E-mail for further information: sales@cftnet.com
Phone: (813) 980 1317
Fax: (602) 985 1995
URL: **http://www.cftnet.com/access.html**

Intelligence Network Online, Inc.
E-mail for further information: greg@intnet.net
Phone: (813) 442-0114
Fax: (813) 448-0949
URL: **http://www.intnet.net**

PacketWorks, Inc.
E-mail for further information: mitchell@packet.net
Phone: (813) 446-8826
Fax: (813) 447-1585
URL: **http://www.packet.net**

816

Interstate Networking Corporation
E-mail for further information: staff@interstate.net
Phone: (816) 472-4949
Fax: (816) 472-0627
URL: **http://www.interstate.net**

Tyrell Corporation
E-mail for further information: support@tyrell.net
Phone: (816) 459-7584
         (800) TYRELL-1
Fax: (816) 452-5483
URL: **http://www.tyrell.net**

817

DFWNet
E-mail for further information: sales@dfw.net
Phone: (800) 2DFWNet
Fax: (817) 870-1501
URL: **http://www.dfw.net**

Texas Metronet, Inc.
E-mail for further information: sales@metronet.com
Phone: (214) 705-2900
Fax: (817) 267-2400
URL: **http://www.metronet.com**

818

KTB Internet Online
E-mail for further information: help@ktb.net
Phone: (818) 240-6600
Fax: (818) 246-8856
URL: **http://www.ktb.net**

Lightside, Inc.
E-mail for further information: support@lightside.com
Phone: (818) 858-9261
Fax: (818) 858-8982
URL: **http://www.lightside.com**

852

LinkAGE Online Limited
E-mail for further information: help@hk.linkage.net
Phone: (852) 2331-8123
Fax: (852) 2795-1262
URL: **http://www.hk.linkage.net**

901

Magibox, Inc.
E-mail for further information: lmarcus@magibox.net
Phone: (901) 757-7835
Fax: (901) 754-6438
URL: **http://www.magibox.net**

902

internet services and information systems (isis) Inc.
E-mail for further information: sales@isisnet.com
Phone: (902) 429-4747
Fax: (902) 429-9003
URL: **http://www.isisnet.com**

903

RapidRamp
E-mail for further information: root@rapidramp.com
Phone: (903) 759-0705
URL: not available

904

Gateway Telecommunications/VectorNet
E-mail for further information: support@vectornet.com
Phone: (800) 375-8658
          (904) 375-8658
Fax: (904) 378-9607
URL: **http://www.vectornet.com**

Polaris Network
E-mail for further information: staff@polaris.net
Phone: (904) 878-9745
URL: **http://www.polaris.net**

905

HookUp Communications
E-mail for further information: accounts@hookup.net
Phone: (905) 847-8000
Fax: (905) 847-8420
URL: **http://www.hookup.net**

IGS Oshawa (Information Gateway Services)
E-mail for further information: ike@osha.igs.net
Phone: (905) 723-2750
Fax: (905) 723-2199
URL: **http://www.osha.igs.net**

907

ImagiNEt, Inc.
E-mail for further information: coppick@imagi.net
Phone: (907) 455-9638
Fax: (907) 455-9640
URL: **http://www.imagi.net**

Internet Alaska
E-mail for further information: support@alaska.net
Phone: (907) 562-4638
Fax: (907) 562-1677
URL: **http://www.alaska.net**

908

Castle Network, Inc.
E-mail for further information: request@castle.net
Phone: (800) 577-9449
         (908) 548-8881
Fax: (908) 548-7605
URL: **http://www.castle.net**

910

Red Barn Data Center
E-mail for further information: postmaster@rbdc.rbdc.com
Phone: (910) 774-1600
Modem: (910) 768-8700
Fax: (704) 798-5433
URL: **http://www.rbdc.com**

913

Databank, Inc.
E-mail for further information: support@databank.com
Phone: (913) 842-6699
Fax: (913) 842-8518

914

epix
E-mail for further information: karndt@epix.net
Phone: (800) 374-9669
URL: **http://www.epix.net**

Mnematics, Incorporated
E-mail for further information: service@mne.com
Phone: (914) 359-4546
Fax: (914) 359-0361
URL: **http://www.mne.com**

916

CalWeb Communications
E-mail for further information: admin@calweb.com
Phone: (916) 641-WEB0 (9320)
Fax: (916) 381-5848
URL: **http://www.calweb.com**

Lloyd Internetworking
E-mail for further information: human-emailinfo@lloyd.com
Phone: (916) 676-1147
Fax: (916) 676-3442
URL: **http://www.lloyd.com**

919

Interpath
E-mail for further information: helpdesk@interpath.net
Phone: (919) 890-6300
        (800) 849-6305
Fax: (919) 890-6319

Nando.Net
E-mail for further information: sysop@nando.net
Phone: (919) 836-2808
Fax: (919) 836-2814
URL: **http://www.nando.net**

970

Frontier Internet, Inc.
E-mail for further information: jbd@frontier.net
Phone: (970) 385-4177
Fax: (970) 385-6745
URL: **http://www.frontier.net**

International Access Providers

The following list is a sample of foreign Internet access providers. Again, many other overseas providers exist, and more arrive on the scene all the time, so this list is by no means complete.

Africa

Egypt

RitseCom
Area Code: +20
E-mail for further information: tkamel@ritsec.com.eg
Phone: 20 2 3403538
Fax: 20 2 3412139
URL: **http://ritsec_www.com.eg**

Ghana

Chonia Informatica
Area Code: +233
E-mail for further information: info@osagyefo.ghana.net
Phone: +233 21 669420
Fax: +233 21 669420
URL: **http://rzunextbet1.unizh.ch**

South Africa

Commercial Internet Services
Area Code: +27
E-mail for further information: info@cis.co.za
Phone: +27 12 841-2892
Fax: +27 12 841-3604
URL: **http://www.cis.co.za**

Internetworking Africa (Pty) Ltd
Area Code: +27
E-mail for further information: info@iafrica.com
Phone: +27 21 683-4370
          0800 020003 (Domestic)
Fax: +27 21 683-4695
URL: **http://www.iafrica.com/iafrica/home.html**

Zambia

ZAMNET Communication Systems Ltd, Lusaka, Zambia
E-mail for further information: sales@zamnet.zm
Phone: +260 1 290358
          +260 1 293317
Fax: +260 1 290358
URL: **http://www.zamnet.zm**

Asia/The East

Hong Kong

Hong Kong Supernet
Area Code: +852
E-mail for further information: info@HK.Super.NET
Phone: (852) 23587924
Fax: (602) 23597925
URL: **http://www.hk.super.net**

India

Live Wire! BBS
Area Code: +91
E-mail for further information: support@f1.n606.z6.fidonet.org
support@lwbom.miqas2.fidonet.org
Phone: (91-22) 577-1111
Fax: (91-22) 578-7812
      (91-22) 579-2416

Japan

Global OnLine Japan
Area Code: +81
E-mail for further information: sales@gol.com
Phone: +81-3-5330-9380
Fax: +81-3-5330-9381
URL: **http://www.gol.com**

RIMNET (Rapid Information Systems)
Area Code: +81
E-mail for further information: question@st.rim.or.jp
Phone: +81-3-5489-5655
Fax: +81-3-5489-5640
URL: **http://www.st.rim.or.jp**

Korea

KORNET (Korea Telecom)
Area Code: +82
E-mail for further information: helpme@kornet.nm.kr
Phone: +82 2 766 5900~2
Fax: +82 2 766 5903
URL: **http://www.kornet.nm.kr**

Kuwait

Gulfnet Kuwait
Area Code: +965
E-mail for further information: info@kuwait.net
Phone: +965 242 6728
Fax: +965 243 5428
URL: **http://www.kuwait.net**

Malaysia

Jaring Net—Malaysia
Area Code: +60
E-mail for further information: noc@jaring.my
Phone: (603) 254-9601
Fax: (603) 253-1898
URL: **http://www.jaring.my**

Pakistan

Brain Computer Services
Area Code: +92
E-mail for further information: basit@brain.com.pk
Phone: +92 42 541-4444
Fax: +92 42 758-1126
URL: **http://singnet.com.sg/~brains**

Philippines

InFoCom Technologies
E-mail for further information: pars@mnl.sequel.net
Phone: 632-635-2359
Fax: 632-635-2360
URL: **http://www.sequel.net**

Singapore

Singapore Telecom
Area Code: +65
E-mail for further information: sales@singnet.com.sg
Phone: +65 730-8079
Fax: +65 732-1272
URL: **http://www.singnet.com.sg**

Sri Lanka

Lanka Internet Services, Ltd.
Area Code: +94
E-mail for further information: info@lanka.net
Phone: +94-71-30469
Fax: +94-1-343056
URL: **http://www.lanka.net**

Taiwan

Institute for Information Industry
Area Code: +886
E-mail for further information: service@tpts1.seed.net.tw
Phone: 733-6454
        733-8779
Fax: 737-0188
URL: **http://www.seed.net.tw**

Vietnam

NetNam Telematic Services, Vietnam National Institute of Information Technology
Area Code: +84
E-mail for further information: admin@netnam.org.vn
Phone: +84-4 346-907
Fax: +84-4 345-217
URL: in development

Australia

APANA (ACT Region)
Area Code: +61
E-mail for further information: act@apana.org.au
Phone: (06) 2824328
Fax: (06) 2824328
URL: **http://www.act.apana.org.au**

InterConnect Australia Pty Ltd
Area Code: +61
E-mail for further information: sales@interconnect.com.au
Phone: +61 3 9528 2239
Fax: +61 3 9528 5887
URL: **http://www.interconnect.com.au**

Planet Internet
E-mail for further information: rael@planet.net.au
Phone: (03) 9205 0300
Fax: (03) 9819 0533
URL: **http://www.planet.net.au**

World Reach Pty Ltd
Area Code: +61
E-mail for further information: info@wr.com.au
Phone: (02) 436 3588
Fax: (02) 436 3998
URL: **http://www.wr.com.au**

New Zealand

Internet Company of New Zealand
Area Code: +64
E-mail for further information: ikuo@iconz.co.nz
Phone: 64-9-358 1186
Modem: 64-9-303 0088
Fax: 64-9-300 3122
URL: **http://www.iconz.co.nz**

Lynx Internet
Area Code: +64
E-mail for further information: info@lynx.co.nz
Phone: (+64) 3 3790 568
Fax: (+64) 3 3654 852
URL: **http://www.lynx.co.nz**

Europe/Eastern Europe

Austria

LINK-ATU / Medienzentrum der Hochschuelerschaft an der TU Wien
Area Code: +43
E-mail for further information: sysop@link-atu.comlink.apc.org
Phone: +43 1 586 1868
Modem: +43 1 586 0409
Fax: +43 1 569 154

Belgium

Interpac
Area Code: +32
E-mail for further information: info@interpac.be
Phone: 32 2 646 60 00
Fax: 32 2 640 36 38
URL: **http://www.interpac.be**

Bulgaria

EUnet Bulgaria
Area Code: +359
E-mail for further information: postmaster@Bulgaria.EU.net
Phone: +359 52 259135
Fax: +359 52 234540
URL: **http://www.eunet.bg**

Croatia

CARNet
Area Code: +385
E-mail for further information: helpdesk@CARNet.hr
Phone: +385 1 461-431
Fax: +385 1 461-469
URL: **http://www.CARNet.hr**

Czech Republic

EUnet Slovakia
Area Code: +42
E-mail for further information: info@Slovakia.EU.net
Phone: +42 7 725 306
Fax: +42 7 728 462
URL: **http://www.eunet.sk**

Finland

Clinet Ltd
Area Code: +358
E-mail for further information: clinet@clinet.fi
Phone: +358-0-437-5209
Fax: +358-0-455-5276
URL: **http://www.clinet.fi**

France

Calvacom
Area Code: +33
E-mail for further information: scom1@calvacom.fr
Phone: 33 - 1 - 34 63 19 19
Fax: 33 - 1 - 34 63 19 48
URL: **http://www.calvacom.fr**

Internet-Way
Area Code: +33
E-mail for further information: info@iway.fr
Phone: + 33 1 41 43 21 10
Fax: + 33 1 41 43 21 11
URL: **http://www.iway.fr**

Germany

bbTT Electronic Networks GmbH

Area Code: +49

E-mail for further information: stefan@b-2.de.contrib.net

Phone: +49 30 817 50 99

Fax: +49 30 817 69 76

URL: **http://www.bbtt.com**

EUnet Germany

Area Code: +49

E-mail for further information: sales@Germany.EU.net

Phone: +49 231 972 00

Fax: +49 231 972 1111

URL: **http://www.Germany.EU.net**

Greece

FORTHnet

Area Code: +30

E-mail for further information: pr@forthnet.gr

Phone: +30 81 391200

Fax: +30 81 391201

URL: **http://www.forthnet.gr**

Hungary

EUnet Hungary

Area Code: +36

E-mail for further information: info@Hungary.EU.net

Phone: +36 1 2698281

Fax: +36 1 2698288

URL: **http://www.eunet.hu**

Ireland

Ireland On-Line
Area Code: +353
E-mail for further information: sales@iol.ie
Phone: +353 1 8551739
Fax: +353 1 8551740
URL: **http://www.iol.ie**

Israel

DataServe Internet services
Area Code: +972
E-mail for further information: register@datasrv.co.il
Phone: +972-3-647-4448

Italy

CSP/ALPcom Internet Services
Area Code: +39
E-mail for further information: info@alpcom.it
Phone: +39 11 3187407
Fax: +39 11 4618 ext 212
URL: **http://www.alpcom.it**
      http://www.csp.it

I.NET S.p.A.
Area Code: +39
E-mail for further information: c-staff@inet.it
Phone: +39 2 26162261
Fax: +39 2 26110755
URL: **http://www.inet.it**

NETTuno service
Area/Country codes: +39
E-mail for further information: staff@nettuno.it
Phone: +0039 51 6599423 / 6599411
Fax: +0039 51 6592581
URL: **http://www.nettuno.it**

TIZETAnet, Tizeta Informatica srl
Area/Country codes: +39
E-mail for further information: staff@tizeta.it
Phone: +39 51 346-346
Fax: +39 51 346-346
URL: **http://www.tizeta.it**

Latvia

Versia, Ltd.
Area Code: +371
E-mail for further information: postmaster@vernet.lv
Phone: +371 2417000
       +371 2428686
Fax: +371 2428937
URL: **http://www.vernet.lv**

Lithuania

State Enterprise InfoCentras
Area Code: +370
E-mail for further information: postmaster@lira.lt
Phone: +370 7 706952
Fax: +370 7 706952

Luxembourg

Europe Online S.A.
Area Code: +352
E-mail for further information: inet-sales@eo.net
Phone: +352 40 101 226
Fax: +352 40 101 201
URL: **http://www.eo.net**

The Netherlands

Hobbynet
Area Code: +31
E-mail for further information: info@hobby.nl
Phone: +31 36 5361683
Modem: +31 20 6657152
URL: **http://www.hobby.nl**

Internet Access Foundation - The Netherlands
Area Code: +31
E-mail for further information: info@iaf.nl
Phone: +31 15 566108 (Dutch)
      +31 5982 2720 (English)
Fax: +31 15 566108
URL: **http://www.iaf.nl**

Norway

Oslonett
Area Code: +47
E-mail for further information: oslonett@oslonett.no
Phone: +47 22 46 10 99
Fax: +47 22 46 45 28
URL: **http://www.oslonett.no**

PowerTech Information Systems Inc.
Area Code: +47
E-mail for further information: post@powertech.no
Phone: +47 2220 3330
Fax: +47 2220 0333
URL: **http://www.powertech.no**

Portugal

EUnet Portugal (run by PUUG)
Area Code: +351
E-mail for further information: info@Portugal.EU.net
info@puug.pt
Phone: +351 (1) 294 2844
Fax: +351 (1) 295 7786
URL: **http://www.Portugal.EU.net**
   http://www.puug.pt

Romania

EUnet Romania SRL
Area Code: +40
E-mail for further information: info@Romania.EU.net
Phone: +40 1 312.6886
Fax: +40 1 312.6668
URL: **http://www.Romania.EU.net**

Spain

Goya Servicios Telematicos—EUnet Spain
Area Code: +34
E-mail for further information: info@world.net
Phone: +34 1 413 4856
Fax: +34 1 413 4901
URL: **http://www.eunett.es**

Sweden

Bahnhof Internet Access
Area Code: +46
E-mail for further information: bahnhof-info@bahnhof.se
Phone: +46 18 100899
Fax: +46 18 103737
URL: http://www.bahnhof.se

TerraTel
Area Code: +46
E-mail for further information: info@netg.se
Phone: 46-(0)31-280373
URL: **http://www.netg.se**

Switzerland

Internet ProLink
Area Code: +41
E-mail for further information: info@iprolink.ch
Phone: +41 22 788 8555
Fax: +41 22 788 8560
URL: **http://www.iprolink.ch**

Ukraine

Communication Company Lucky Net Ltd., Kiev, Ukraine
Area Code: +380
E-mail for further information: goo@lucky.net
Phone: +44 290-04-38
Fax: +44 290-04-38
URL: **http://www.lucky.net**

Small Venture DKT Ltd
Area Code: +380
E-mail for further information: postmaster@rocket.kharkov.ua
Phone: +380 572 445-708
Fax: +380 572 431-677

Cycle PF
Area Code: +380
E-mail for further information: rezgs@oreh.dp.ua
Phone: +380 562 46-5171
Fax: +380 562 47-4665
URL: **http://oreh.dp.ua**

United Kingdom

Aladdin
Area Code: +44
E-mail for further information: info@aladdin.co.uk
Phone: +44 (0)1489 782221
Fax: +44 (0)1489 782382
URL: **http://www.aladdin.co.uk**

Demon Internet Ltd
Area Code: +44
E-mail for further information: sales@demon.net
Phone: +44-(0)181 371 1234
Fax: +44-(0)181 371 1150
URL: **http://www.demon.co.uk**

Foobar Internet
Area Code: +44
E-mail for further information: sales@foobar.co.uk
Phone: +44 116 2330033
Fax: +44 116 2330035
URL: **http://www.foobar.co.uk**

GreenNet
Area Code: +44
E-mail for further information: support@gn.apc.org
Phone: +44 (0)171 713 1941
Fax: +44 (0)171 833 1169
URL: **http://www.gn.apc.org**

PC User Group/WinNET Communications
Area Code: +44
E-mail for further information: info@win-uk.net
Phone: +44 181 863 1191
Fax: +44 181 863 6095
URL: **http://www.ibmpcug.co.uk**

Total Connectivity Providers Ltd
Area Code: +44
E-mail for further information: sales@tcp.co.uk
Phone: +44 (0)1703 393392
Fax: +44 (0)1703 393392
URL: **http://www.tcp.co.uk**

Russia

GlasNet Computer Network Users Association
Area Code: +07
E-mail for further information: alexz@glas.apc.org
Phone: +07 095 262-7079
Fax: +07 095 207-0889
URL: **http://www.glas.apc.org**

Relcom/EUnet
Area Code: +07
E-mail for further information: noc@relcom.EU.net
Phone: +7 095 9434735
        +7 095 1941995
Fax: +7 095 194-33-28
URL: **http://www.relcom.EU.net**
     http://www.kiae.su

Tambov Center of New Information Technologies
Area Code: +07
E-mail for further information: postmaster@tixm.tambov.su
Phone: +7 0752 220735
Fax: +7 0752 471313
URL: **http://www.tixm.tambov.su**

South/Central America

Argentina

SiON Online Services
Area Code: +54
E-mail for further information: info@sion.com.ar
Phone: +541 656-9195
        +541 469-1335
Fax: +541 469-1334

Chile

RdC S.A. — CHILE, Latin America
Area Code: +56
E-mail for further information: info@rdc.cl
Phone: +56 2 686-2484
Fax: +56 2 635-1132
URL: **http://mailnet.rdc.cl**

Ecuador

Ecuanex, (Quito, Ecuador)
Area Code: +593
E-mail for further information: intercom@ecuanex.ec
Phone: 593-2-227-014
Fax: 593-2-227-014

Mexico

Mundo Internet
Area Code: +52
E-mail for further information: webmaster@kin.cieamer.conacyt.mx
Phone: 81-29-60 Ext. 227, 228
Fax: 81-29-23
URL: **http://w3mint.cieamer.conacyt.mx**

CMACT
Area Code: +52
E-mail for further information: info@mail.cmact.com
Phone: 378-0636
Fax: 378-0696
URL: **http://www.cmact.com**

Nicaragua

UniComp
Area Code: +505
E-mail for further information: computo@uni.ni
yadira@uni.ni
Phone: (505)(2) 783142
Fax: (505)(2) 673709
URL: not available

Paraguay

Digital Electronics Laboratory (L.E.D.)
Area Code: +595
E-mail for further information: info@ledip.py
Phone: +595 21 334 650
Fax: +595 21 310 587
URL: not available

Peru

Red Cientifica Peruana
Area Code: +51
E-mail for further information: operador@rcp.net.pe
Phone: +511 445 5168, +511 445 9286, +511 445 5797
URL: **http://www.rcp.net.pe**

Venezuela

NetPoint Communications, Inc.
Area Code: 305, +58
E-mail for further information: rjc@netpoint.net
Phone: 305-891-1955
Fax: 305-891-2110
URL: **http://www.netpoint.net**

*G*lossary

A B u s i n e s s

G l o s s a r y   t o

I n t e r n e t   T e r m s

This glossary is designed for business people interested in incorporating the Internet into their daily business lives. Terms in *italics* are defined elsewhere in the glossary. For more detailed technical explanations, please consult many of the other publications mentioned in the Bibliography.

AIX
IBM's version of *UNIX*, a popular server operating system.

Anonymous FTP
A type of FTP *server* set to receive requests from anyone on the Internet without a specific password. The user logs into the site using "anonymous" as the name and normally enters his or her *e-mail* address as the password. The site then grants that user access to public files. See also *FTP*.

Application
Software that accomplishes a particular task, such as a word processor or a spreadsheet; also a tool used to accomplish a specific task or set of tasks. For example, on the Internet, e-mail is an application.

Applications Layer Gateway
A sophisticated *firewall* designed as a single unit rather than a system of *routers* and a workstation. Also known as a Bastion Host, the Applications Layer Gateway normally contains more features than a firewall and can establish a true session, ensuring better performance and assurance of security.

Archie
A *server*-based system used to find files that are available using *Anonymous FTP*. Archie does the identification; FTP allows you to actually gain access to them.

Authentication
The capability to ensure that a user is who he or she purports to be on the Internet. Electronic authentication is accomplished through the use of user-specific qualities: something only the user knows—a password, for example; something the user has—such as a *smart card*; or something specific about the user as a physical entity, authenticated through the use of biometric scanners, which include voice prints, fingerprints, or retinal scans.

Bits
An abbreviation for binary digits. These are the building blocks for digital data communication. Eight bits in a byte.

Bits Per Second (bps)
The speed at which *bits* are transmitted over a communications medium, such as telephone lines, fiber-optic facilities, or satellites.

Browser
Software program that permits the user to browse the *World Wide Web* or other Internet server facilities. *Mosaic* and *Netscape* are examples of the most popular and widely used browsers.

BTW
Internet shorthand for "by the way."

CERT
Computer Emergency Response Team, the group responsible for issuing security alerts to the Internet community. They assist in security issues but are not the Internet Police Force. There is no one organization responsible for law enforcement on the Internet.

Chat
See *Internet Relay Chat*.

CIX
Commercial Internet eXchange, a nonprofit Internet trade association that permits *Internet Access Providers* to exchange customer communications among its members. CIX members include networks from every continent except Antarctica.

Client
A software *application* that works on the user's behalf to interface with a *server* elsewhere on the network. Your telephone acts as a client to the telephone company central office switch client.

DECnet
A set of proprietary data networking *protocols* developed and used by Digital Equipment Corporation operating systems in lieu of *TCP/IP*. DECnet is carried across the Internet encapsulated in TCP/IP *packets* but not in its native form.

Dedicated Line
A permanently connected private telephone line between two locations. Dedicated lines (also known as private lines or leased lines) are typically used to connect a medium to very large local area network (*LAN*) to the nearest point on an *Internet Access Provider's* backbone network.

Dial-up
The process of connecting a computer and its associated *modem* to the Internet using a standard telephone line. Dial-up also refers to a type of Internet access service requiring the use of a modem and telephone line. It can also mean a port that accepts dial-up connections.

Dumb Account
Also known as *shell* or *terminal emulation*, a dial-up Internet access service that requires the use of a standard communications software package (e.g., ProComm Plus, Crosstalk, Microphone), and provides limited graphical capabilities. These are traditionally less expensive than smart *SLIP/PPP* accounts.

DNS
Domain Name System, a distributed database system for translating numerical Internet addresses (i.e., 198.27.36.4) into recognizable names (such as maloff.com.us) and vice versa. DNS permits you to use the Internet without the need to remember long strings of numbers. It also permits organizations to use their domain names as a form of advertising. DNS can identify the name of your organization (The Maloff Company), the type of organization (commercial is identified by .com), and perhaps even the country (United States is identified by .us).

E-Mail
Electronic mail, the capability to send written messages to someone else using a computer connected to a computer network.

Encapsulation
Within an Internet environment, it is possible to wrap *TCP/IP* around other forms of information to make them usable across the Internet. *DECnet* from Digital Equipment can be encapsulated in TCP/IP *packets* and distributed across the Internet. At the destination end, the TCP/IP packets are then unwrapped permitting the DECnet information to continue traveling as needed. The opposite of encapsulation is Native Mode, in which the information is sent in its original form.

FAQ
A Frequently Asked Question, also referring to a list of such questions and their answers. Many *newsgroups*, *LISTSERV* lists, and other Internet discussion groups maintain FAQs so that participants are not bothered with answering the same questions over and over again as new people join the discussions.

Firewall

A system designed to provide network security for *servers* on your local area network (*LAN*). It normally consists of two *routers* and a *Unix* workstation placed between an organization's LAN and the external access to the Internet.

Flame

An often personal written attack against the author of a *newsgroup posting* or other public message. These attacks can be seemingly unprovoked and out of proportion to the alleged infraction. To minimize flaming and ensure that they are participating in Internet discussions according to the standards at the time, *newbies* should silently get to know a discussion group (known as lurking) before posting messages. There are no concrete rules, just common sense and observation.

Flamer

One who *flames* others regularly. These people often develop a negative reputation and are normally ignored once they become known. They can still be unpleasant even when their reputations precede them.

Freenet

Organizations that provide free Internet access to people in specific geographic regions, often through public libraries or chambers of commerce. Information provided by Freenets concerning a particular city or town can be quite useful. The quality of their services is as good as the specific volunteers who offer the access.

FTP

File Transfer Protocol, a *protocol* that defines how files are copied from one computer to another. Also refers to any *application* program that moves files using that protocol.

FYI

Internet (and generally used) shorthand for "For Your Information."

Gopher

A menu-based, text-oriented system for exploring the Internet; also a *server* system that allows external users to access resources that you wish to make available across the Internet.

Graphical User Interface (GUI)

Pronounced "gooey," a graphical user interface enables an Internet user to see graphics, hear sounds, and view movies without using other tools. A GUI on the Internet is similar to using a Windows environment rather than a simple text-based DOS one.

Hackers

People who try to use computer networks such as the Internet to break into other computers for the simple joy of it or for more sinister purposes. Also refers to software engineers and Internet tinkerers who like to hack code together.

HTML

HyperText Markup Language, the coding language used to create *World Wide Web* documents.

Hypermedia

Term referring to collections of document and data files that utilize both *hypertext* and multimedia.

Hypertext

Documents that contain links to other documents. Selecting a link will automatically navigate the user to another document. On the Internet's *World Wide Web*, documents can link to files on other computers.

IMHO

Internet shorthand for "In My Humble Opinion;" used, more often than not, when the user has not exhibited much in the way of humility.

Infobot

An automated *e-mail* response to a specific e-mail address (i.e., info@maloff.com).

Internet

When not capitalized, indicates any collection of distinct networks operating as one. When capitalized, the term refers to the worldwide network of networks that interconnect with each other using the *TCP/IP protocol* suite as well as other similar protocols. Internet also refers to the shared information utility consisting of databases and human resources originating anywhere globally, as well as the worldwide community of people who use *Internet Access Providers* to communicate for business, pleasure, and education.

Internet Access Provider

Also known as IAP, an organization that offers Internet connection services to end users. Services include *dial-up* or *dedicated line* access.

The Internet Adapter

Also known as TIA and similar to SlipKnot, software tools to permit users with *dumb*, *terminal emulation*, or *shell accounts* to have the appearance and functionality of a *graphical user interface* like *SLIP*.

Internet Relay Chat

A service permitting large numbers of users to communicate in writing via the Internet in real time rather than in a delayed fashion such as occurs with *mail*.

ISDN

Integrated Services Digital Networks, a digital telephone service used instead of standard telephone service. Where provided by the local telephone company, ISDN can be used as a less expensive alternative to *dedicated access lines*.

ISOC

The Internet Society, a membership organization involved in helping to provide guidance to the evolution of Internet and its technical standards.

Jughead

A *gopher* service similar to *Veronica*, used to undertake keyword searches of gopher menus at specific sites.

Knowbot

Short for "Knowledge Robot," an experimental information retrieval tool. Knowbots have not been perfected, although some of the newer search tools are heading in the right direction.

LAN

Local Area Network, a system that links computers within a single building or local physical area. Commonly, LANs are connected using wires or infrared signals.

LISTSERV

Similar to netnews, a LISTSERV is an electronic discussion on a given topic. Thousands of LISTSERVs are in operation. As compared to *Usenet*

Newsgroups, you subscribe to a LISTSERV by sending an *e-mail* message. All *postings* to this list are then sent to the e-mail boxes of the list's *subscribers*. LISTPROC is the same as LISTSERV except that it is hosted on a *Unix* machine rather than LISTSERV IBM mainframes. A form of LISTSERV, called LISTSTAR, is hosted on Macintosh machines.

Lurker

A person who subscribes to and reads the *postings* on an Internet discussion group but who does not post messages. It is important to lurk for awhile to become familiar with the character of a group before posting messages.

Mail Reflector

A special *e-mail* address used to send a single message to multiple users. E-mail sent to marketing@ans.net would then be forwarded to all twenty *subscribers* to this reflector. Mail reflectors are very useful for distributing information internally or externally.

Modem

A computer peripheral used to connect a computer to a data transmission line (normally a telephone line). Most modems are now operating at 9600 or 14,400 *bits per second*. Increasingly, *Internet Access Providers* are beginning to support 28.8 kbps transmission speeds (28,800 bits per second). To take advantage of large graphics, sound files, or video clips while using the Internet, use the fastest modem that you can afford.

MOO

An object-oriented MUD. See *MUD*.

Mosaic

A popular *World Wide Web browser* originally developed at the National Center for Supercomputer Applications in Illinois, it is now included in many commercial packages, including those from Spyglass and CompuServe's Internet group (formerly Spry Corporation). The original developers of Mosaic are also building *Netscape*.

MUD

Multi-User Dungeon or Dimension; originally a series of role-playing games modeled after the Dungeons and Dragons games. MUDs are increasingly being used by businesses as a way to interact electronically with their customers or as a tool to enhance remote training of employees.

Netscape

The most prominent of the *World Wide Web browsers*, noted for its enhanced capability to accommodate a variety of graphic design techniques.

Newbie

A new Internet user; one who is inexperienced in Internet culture.

Newsgroups

Also known as netnews or *Usenet News*, this is an informal and somewhat anarchic group of systems that exchange users' messages. The systems are similar to bulletin boards. More than 12,000 newsgroups cover a seemingly infinite range of specific topics and interests. You must subscribe to newsgroups and use a news reader to access them. They may contain text messages, graphics files, sound files, video files, or software programs.

NIC

Network Information Center; any organization responsible for supplying information about any network. An NIC acts as the "institutional librarian" in an organization, tracking useful information and helping users find it when needed. The Defense Data Network (DDN) NIC plays an important role in coordinating the Internet with other NIC organizations throughout the world, while the InterNIC coordinates Domain Name and Internet Address assignment.

NOC

Network Operations Center, a group responsible for day-to-day network management. Each *Internet Access Provider* has an NOC of some sort. Most large companies also have an NOC. It is important to know whether your access provider's NOC operates 24 hours a day, 365 days a year. Users never know when the network will malfunction in the midst of an important information transfer.

NSFnet

The National Science Foundation Network; the NSFnet is not the Internet. It was established in the mid-1980s to connect universities, government laboratories, and commercial research facilities. The NSFnet today is in the process of returning to its research roots as the growing commercial Internet takes hold around the world.

Operating System

Computers operate with two general types of software: systems software and applications software. *Applications* software are the programs that do something for you—word processors, spreadsheets, databases, etc. Systems software is what makes a computer run. DOS is a systems software, as is *Unix*. Systems software is also referred to as the operating system for a particular computer platform (Sun, IBM, HP, etc.).

Packet

A bundle of data; a "communication envelope" containing information. On the Internet, information is broken into small chunks, called packets, and sent out across the network. Each packet may take a different path from its predecessor ("packet switching"), thus making the best use of available network facilities rather than congesting one path while others remain unused. *TCP/IP* is a packet switching *protocol*.

Ping

A *Unix* diagnostic utility used to measure whether a remote computer can be reached and the length of time that it takes for the round trip.

Posting

An individual message or article sent to a *newsgroup*; also the act of sending a message to an Internet discussion group.

POTS

Plain old telephone service, that is, a standard telephone line.

PPP

See *SLIP/PPP*.

Protocol

The set of instructions that defines how computers act when exchanging information. Protocols designate everything from how bits are transmitted across wires to the structure of an *e-mail* message. As a protocol suite, *TCP/IP* permits computers using different protocols to communicate with one another.

RFC

Request for Comments. A set of papers in which Internet standards, proposed standards, descriptive information, and generally agreed-upon ideas are stored.

Router

A hardware system that assists in the transfer of data between two networks that use the same *protocol*. Popular manufacturers of routers include Cisco Systems, Bay Networks, and Shiva.

Server

Software that allows a computer to perform a specific function for another computer. Other computers contact the server program by using matching *client* software. *The World-Wide Web* and *gopher* are systems run on server software programs. Server also refers to the computer on which the server software is operating. Most servers on the Internet today are *Unix* systems, although larger computers are in use, as well as some Macintoshes and larger 486 machines.

Service Provider

See *Internet Access Provider*.

Session

When interfacing directly with a computer, you are said to have established a session. *Telnet* requires establishing a session, as do video conferencing or Internet voice applications. A session can be thought of as a through connection between a user and a computer.

Shell Account

A shell account is a terminal-style account on a computer that you access from a computer running *terminal emulation*. They are called shell accounts because when you connect as a terminal to a standard *Unix* system, you are giving commands to the Unix shell, or interface structure.

SLIP/PPP

Serial Line Internet Protocol (SLIP) is a *protocol* that allows a computer to use Internet protocols and become actually connected to the Internet (as compared to using a *dumb account*). In comparison with dumb accounts, SLIP/PPP would replace ProComm Plus or Microphone as the communications software. Point to Point protocol (PPP) is a newer standard that is replacing SLIP, but you will see them both in use and referred to interchangeably.

SlipKnot

See *Internet Adapter*.

Smart Account
See *SLIP/PPP.*

Smart Cards
Used as an *authentication* tool, these come in several varieties: cards containing a computer chip and requiring a card reader, cards containing a digital clock and requiring the user to enter the displayed number (it changes every sixty seconds and produces a new random number), or a device containing an optical strip that generates a random pass code directly to the computer monitor screen.

Smileys
Known more officiously as emoticons, keyboard-based expressions of emotion used to illustrate and enliven text-only Internet messages. When sending a written message or *posting*, users indicate that they are joking or not entirely serious by the use of smileys such as :-) (You need to look at it sideways!).

Sniffer
A software tool used by *hackers* to capture user pass codes, thus breaching the security of the Internet user or system.

Subscribers, List
Members of a *LISTSERV* or LISTPROC who are required to ask that they be included—subscribed—on any messages that are posted to a particular list.

TCP/IP
Transmission Control Protocol/Internetworking Protocol, the suite of computer languages that helps to define the Internet as a network capable of transmitting data from one computer to another. It is through TCP/IP that many different networks around the world using different computer systems can communicate.

Telnet
An Internet tool that allows a user to log into a remote computer as if he or she were physically using that remote computer. *Internet Relay Chat* uses Telnet to permit users to interact in real time with others.

Terminal Emulation
Not too long ago, there were no personal computers. All computer users interfaced with computers using a terminal—an associated computer workstation. With the advent of personal computers, we needed a way for PCs to communicate directly with mainframe computers. This was accomplished by

having the PC "pretend" to be a computer terminal. A VT100 terminal is used to interface with DEC VAX computers. Today, you may see software programs asking you if you wish to use VT100 emulation. This is a relic of the past and may become unimportant in the near future.

Timeout

A suspension of connection between two computers when one computer fails to respond to the commands of the other after a preset period of time has elapsed. Timeouts prevent computers from continuously trying to communicate with each other when one has stopped responding.

Unix

A popular operating system, important in the evolution of the Internet. Most of the servers on the Internet operate on Unix platforms. Some of the more popular Unix systems are manufactured by Sun, IBM, Hewlett-Packard, and DEC.

Usenet

Also known as netnews or *newsgroups*, an informal and somewhat anarchic group of systems that exchange Internet messages on a wide variety of specific topics. These systems are similar to bulletin boards and covered more than 12,000 subjects at the time of this publication. Users must subscribe to specific newsgroups and use a news reader to access them. Newsgroups may contain text messages, graphics files, sound files, video files, or software programs.

UUCP

Unix-to-Unix Copy Program, a software facility that copies files between *Unix* systems so mail and news services can transfer between computers. UUCP has been largely replaced by other Internet tools.

Veronica

The Very Easy Rodent-Oriented Net-wide Index to Computerized Archives, developed at the University of Nevada at Reno as a response to the problem of identifying resources in a rapidly expanding universe of *gopher servers*. Similar to *Archie*, Veronica allows users to search all gopher sites for files, directories, and other related resources.

WAIS

Wide Area Information Servers, a *client/server*-based system of searching for information in databases spread across computers connected to the Internet.

WAIS was developed by the Thinking Machines Corporation, became an independent company (WAIS, Inc.), and has recently been acquired by America OnLine.

White Pages
Lists of Internet user addresses categorized by individual or name of organization rather than by topic or area of interest. There are a variety of white page services evolving, including *Whois.*

WHOIS
An electronic *White-Pages* tool used to identify individuals by name or affiliation. There are a variety of Whois (pronounced who is) *servers* being run by organizations around the world. It is expected that Whois will be replaced by new and better approaches in the next several years.

World Wide Web
A *hypertext*-based system to find and access Internet resources. The WWW or Web uses the Hypertext Transport Protocol to link documents between sites.

Yahoo
An Internet-based directory and search tool of World Wide Web sites. Yahoo, which stands humorously for Yet Another Hierarchical Officious Oracle, identifies Internet resources by subject category (i.e., business, education, recreation) or by using keywords in a search of the more than 40,000 Web sites accessible globally.

Yellow Pages
Lists of Internet user addresses categorized by topic or area of interest rather than by individual or organizational name. There are several printed Internet Yellow Pages, including *Mecklermedia's Official Internet World Internet Yellow Pages*. Such printed directories of resources help focus any Internet search session. Because the Internet is evolving so quickly, however, it is best to supplement a search of printed directories with online searches using *WAIS, Veronica, Yahoo,* or other similar Internet-based search tools.

Bibliography

For business people looking to become familiar with the Internet, a variety of printed resources can be useful. Each of these has its own strengths and weaknesses. In addition, they can also be divided into a variety of categories. These include Internet Business, Internet Resource Guides and Directories, Internet Reference Books and Manuals, and Magazines and Newsletters.

Internet Business

Cronin, Mary, *Doing Business on the Internet*, Van Nostrand Reinhold, New York, NY, 1994.

Cronin, Mary, *Doing More Business on the Internet*, Van Nostrand Reinhold, New York, NY, 1995.

Resnick, Rosalind and Dave Taylor, *The Internet Business Guide*, Sams Publishing, Indianapolis, IN, 1994.

Janal, Daniel S., *Online Marketing Handbook*, Van Nostrand Reinhold, New York, NY, 1995.

Sullivan-Trainor, Michael, *Detour: The Truth About the Information Superhighway*, Programmers Press, IDG Books Worldwide, Inc., Braintree, MA, 1994.

Internet Resource Guides and Directories

Cady, Glee Harrah, and Pat McGregor, *Mastering the Internet*, Sybex, Alameda, CA, 1995.

Dern, Daniel P., *The Internet Guide for New Users*, McGraw-Hill, Inc., New York, NY, 1994.

Estrada, Susan, *Connecting to the Internet*, O'Reilly & Associates, Inc., Sebastopol, CA, 1993.

Godin, Seth, ed., *Best of the Net*, Programmers Press, IDG Books Worldwide, Inc., Braintree, MA, 1995.

Kehoe, Brendan P., *Zen and the Art of the Internet—A Beginner's Guide*, PTR Prentice-Hall, Englewood Cliffs, NJ, 1993.

Krol, Ed, *The Whole Internet User's Guide and Catalog*, O'Reilly & Associates, Inc., Sebastopol, CA, 1994.

Lane, Elizabeth S., and Craig Summerhill, *An Internet Primer for Information Professionals: A Basic Guide to Networking Technology*, Meckler Corp., Westport, CT, 1992.

LaQuey, Tracy, and Jeanne C. Ryer, *The Internet Companion: A Beginner's Guide to Global Networking*, Addison-Wesley, Reading, MA, 1993.

Peal, David, *Access the Internet*, Sybex, Alameda, CA, 1994.

Sullivan-Trainor, Michael, *Detour: The Truth about the Information Superhighway*, Programmers Press, IDG Books Worldwide, Inc., Braintree, MA, 1994.

Internet Reference Books and Manuals

Breeding, Marshall, *Mecklermedia's Official Internet World World Wide Web Yellow Pages*, Programmers Press, IDG Books Worldwide, Inc., Braintree, MA, 1996.

Dougherty, Dale, and Richard Koman, *The Mosaic Handbook for Microsoft Windows*, O'Reilly & Associates, Inc., Sebastopol, CA, 1994.

Dougherty, Dale, Richard Koman, and Paula Ferguson, *The Mosaic Handbook for X Window Systems*, O'Reilly & Associates, Inc., Sebastopol, CA, 1994.

Dougherty, Dale, and Richard Koman, *The Mosaic Handbook for the Macintosh*, O'Reilly & Associates, Inc., Sebastopol, CA, 1994.

Hahn, Harley, and Rick Stout, *The Internet Yellow Pages*, Osborne McGraw-Hill, Berkeley, CA, 1994.

Liu, Cricket, Jerry Peek, Russ Jones, Brian Buus, and Adrian Nye, *Managing Internet Information Services*, O'Reilly & Associates, Inc., Sebastopol, CA, 1994.

Newby, Gregory B., *Mecklermedia's Official Internet World Internet Yellow Pages*, Programmers Press, IDG Books Worldwide, Inc., Braintree, MA, 1996.

Magazines and Newsletters

Boardwatch Magazine
7586 West Jewell Ave., Suite 200
Lakewood, CO 80232

Inter@ctive Week
100 Quentin Roosevelt Blvd.
Garden City, NY 11530

Internet World
Mecklermedia Corporation
20 Ketchum Street
Westport, CT 06880

Internet Business Report
A CMP Publication
600 Community Drive
Manhasset, NY 11030
NetGuide
A CMP Publication
600 Community Drive
Manhasset, NY 11030

Wired
520 Third St.
Fourth Floor
San Francisco, CA 94107

Index

C

Software Productivity
  Consortium Information
  Server, 264
Software Publishers
  Association, 138
Solaris, 157, 159
Sony Online, 38
South Africa, 50, 194,
  321-322
South America, 104, 183,
  187-188, 337-339
South Carolina SuperNet,
  312
Southeastern Banking and
  Finance Company,
  210-215
South Pacific, IAPs in,
  overview of, 190-193
Southwest Airlines, 38, 118
SouthWind Internet Access,
  287
Sovan Teleport, 190
SoVerNet, 312
Soviet Union, 50. *See also*
  Russia
Spacenet GmbH, 188
Spain, 333
speech synthesizers, 40
sponsorship, of cybermall
  sections, 121
Spots InterConnect, 289
Sprint, 5, 131, 163, 165, 218
  the history of the Internet
    and, 244, 245
  as an IXC, 169-170
  recent developments at,
    171-172
  SprintLink, 158, 171
  SprintMail, 21
SprintNet, 199, 219
Spry Corporation, 38, 208,
  348
Spyglass, 38, 348
SQL*Net, 159
Squire, Sanders, & Dempsey,
  55
Sri Lanka, 325
SSI Communications, 306
SSL (Secure Socket Lock), 78
Stanford University, 115
Star Trek: Generations
  (script), 66
Star Wars (film), 20
Starwave Corporation, 38

State Enterprise
  InfoCentras, 331
status quo, cost-justification
  and, 206, 250-251,
  256-257
steamship travel, 238, 241
Stefferud, Einar, 76
Stein, Lee, 76
Sterling Software, 199
Stoll, Clifford, 231
SunFlash, 10
Sun Microsystems, 9-10, 39,
  87
SunSoft, 159
Sun Valley SoftWare, 309
supercomputers, 11, 47, 141,
  142, 243
Supercomputic Era, 243
Supernet, 163
SupraNet Communications,
  302
SURAnet (Southeastern
  University Research
  Association
Network), 115, 163, 167, 246
Sweden, 50, 190, 333-334
Sweeps Vacuum and Repair
  Center, 120
Switzerland, 32, 334
Sybase, 39
Symantec Corporation, 137
Synergy Communications,
  277
SynOptics Communications,
  86
Syracuse University, 45
System 7 Pro, 158
system problems, public dis-
  cussion of, subscribing
  to, 110-111

T

T-1 lines, 71, 148, 209, 243,
  253, 254
Tachyon Communications
  Corporation, 291
tail circuits, 207, 209, 212,
  254
Taiwan, 192, 325
Tambov Center of New
  Information
  Technologies, 336
Tandem Computers, 81
tariff offerings, 172

Taylor, Dave, 121
TCP/NG (Transmission
  Control Protocol/Next
  Generation), 227
TCP/IP (Transmission
  Control
  Protocol/Internet
  Protocol), 21, 52, 154, 227
  basic description of, 352
  CIX and, 185
  cost-justification analysis and,
    208, 254
  DECnet and, 343
  encapsulation and, 344
  ftp and, 26
  the history of the Internet
    and, 242
Technet, 192
TechWeb, 34
Telalink Corporation, 304
Telebroker, 52
Tele-Comm, 39
"telecommuting," 44, 61, 206
"telemedicine," 45-49,
  142-144, 176
telephone(s)
  800-number service, 9, 212,
    253
  bills, reducing, 15, 16, 82-83,
    87-89
  invention of, 241
  as "invisible tools," 60
Teleport, 173, 245
telex services, 242
telnet, 20, 49, 91, 352
  basic description of, 26-27
  sites, of special interest, 27
Templar, 144
Terisa Systems, 39
terminal emulation
  accounts, 65
TerraTel, 334
Texas, 30, 176, 278, 315
Texas Metronet, 315
Texas Networking
  Incorporated, 280
text files, transfer of, 21,
  25-26. *See also* ftp (file
  transfer protocol)
text-to-speech converters,
  40
Tezcat Communications, 285
Thailand, 50
Theslof, Gene, 47

internet
WORLD™

A New Series from Internet World and IDG Books!

GET THE NET

GET ON.

Mecklermedia's Official Internet World 60-Minute Guide to the Internet Including the World-Wide Web

Get on the 'Net now! Internet World Editor Andrew Kantor gets you browsing the Internet in 60 minutes or less, downloading news, business data, games, sounds, and a whole lot more! BONUS disk includes browser software, connection utilities and lots of other cool stuff from Mecklermedia.

Mecklermedia's Official Internet World 60-Minute Guide to the Internet Including the World-Wide Web
By Andrew Kantor
ISBN: 1-56884-342-9
$19.99 USA / $26.99 Canada

GET PROTECTION.

Mecklermedia's Official Internet World Internet Security Handbook

Learn what works — and what doesn't. Author William Stallings has written more than a dozen books and several technical papers on data communications and security issues. His successful consulting business has managed top security projects for a variety of companies. Learn his best tips and techniques regarding firewalls, encryption, cybercash, and minimizing hacker risk.

Mecklermedia's Official Internet World Internet Security Handbook
By William Stallings
ISBN: 1-56884-700-9
$29.99 USA / $42.99 Canada

GET PAID.

Mecklermedia's Official Internet World net.profit: Expanding Your Business Using The Internet

Anyone can send e-mail, transfer files, and download software. But do you know how to use the Internet as a strategic business tool? There are more than 20 million potential clients on the Internet today — and lots more to come. Author Joel Maloff will teach you how to explore the Internet for opportunities in business innovation and cost reduction.

Mecklermedia's Official Internet World Net.Profit:Expanding Your Business Using The Internet
By Joel Maloff
ISBN: 1-56884-701-7
$24.99 USA / $34.99 Canada

IDG BOOKS
WORLDWIDE

For more information or to order, call 800-762-2974

For volume discounts and special orders, please call Tony Real at 415-655-3048

Here's Your Chance to Start a No-Risk Trial Subscription to Internet World . . .

The Only Magazine Focused Exclusively on Helping You Navigate the Internet

FREE TRIAL ISSUE!

Here's your chance to send for a No-Risk Trial Subscription to Internet World, the only magazine focused exclusively on helping you navigate the Internet. Whether you're new to the Internet or a seasoned user, Internet World gives you all the information you need to make the most of your time on the Internet. Each issue brings you:

- tips on using the Internet's various search and retrieval tools.
- expert commentary on new services and resources.
- interviews with Internet luminaries and exciting coverage of technical, legal, commercial, and social aspects of the Internet.

For advanced users, Internet World brings a compelling blend of news, features, columns, tips, how-to articles and personality, and vendor profiles. For beginners, there's the Entry Level column aimed at helping "newbies" connect to the Internet and navigate its resources.

Mail the attached TRIAL SUBSCRIPTION voucher today and take advantage of this risk-free offer!

RETURN TODAY

TRIAL SUBSCRIPTION VOUCHER

☐**Yes**, please enter my risk-free trial subscription to Internet World! If I'm not completely satisfied with my first issue, I'll write "cancel" across your first invoice, return it and owe nothing at all. Otherwise, I'll pay just $19.97 for a one-year (12 issues) subscription— an incredible 66% savings off the annual newsstand cost.

   ❏ 1 year (12 issues) only $19.97 ($39.43 off the newsstand costs.)
   ❏ 2 years at only $39.94 (Double my savings!)

Name ❏ **Mr.** ❏ **Mrs.** ❏ **Ms.** _____
Address _____
City/State/Zip _____
_(City/Province/Postal Code)

E-mail address _____
_(optional)

   ❏ **Payment enclosed**   ❏ **Bill me later**
Rate in the Americas (other than U.S.) $44.00 (includes postage and Canadian GST).
Allow 6-8 weeks for delivery of first issue.

AIDG95

internet WORLD

Master the Internet with Internet World

The Most Widely Read Magazine Devoted Entirely to the Internet

Despite all you've read and heard about the Internet, there's only one magazine focused exclusively on helping you navigate the Internet—*Internet World*. And now you can save 66% on the magazine that everyone's talking about:

> **"Recommended."**
> *PC Magazine, March 1994*

> **"A regular infusion of Internet ideas. The magazine covers a full range of Internet services..."**
> *The New York Times, June 1994*

> **"You'll most likely want to subscribe..."**
> *Information Today, June 1994*

Whether you're new to the Internet or a seasoned user, INTERNET WORLD gives you all the necessary information to make the most of your time on the Internet—tips on using the various search and retrieval tools, expert commentary on new services and resources, exciting coverage of technical, legal, commercial, and social aspects of the Internet. So subscribe today!

IDG BOOKS WORLDWIDE REGISTRATION CARD

RETURN THIS REGISTRATION CARD FOR FREE CATALOG

Title of this book: Internet World net.profit: Expanding Your Business Using the Internet

My overall rating of this book: ❏ Very good [1]   ❏ Good [2]   ❏ Satisfactory [3]   ❏ Fair [4]   ❏ Poor [5]

How I first heard about this book:

❏ Found in bookstore; name: [6] _____
❏ Advertisement: [8] _____
❏ Word of mouth; heard about book from friend, co-worker, etc.: [10] _____

❏ Book review: [7] _____
❏ Catalog: [9] _____
❏ Other: [11] _____

What I liked most about this book:
_____
_____

What I would change, add, delete, etc., in future editions of this book:
_____
_____

Other comments: _____
_____

Number of computer books I purchase in a year: ❏ 1 [12]   ❏ 2-5 [13]   ❏ 6-10 [14]   ❏ More than 10 [15]

I would characterize my computer skills as: ❏ Beginner [16] ❏ Intermediate [17] ❏ Advanced [18] ❏ Professional [19]

I use ❏ DOS [20] ❏ Windows [21] ❏ OS/2 [22] ❏ Unix [23] ❏ Macintosh [24] ❏ Other: [25]_____
(please specify)

I would be interested in new books on the following subjects:
(please check all that apply, and use the spaces provided to identify specific software)

❏ Word processing: [26] _____
❏ Data bases: [28] _____
❏ File Utilities: [30] _____
❏ Networking: [32] _____
❏ Other: [34] _____

❏ Spreadsheets: [27] _____
❏ Desktop publishing: [29] _____
❏ Money management: [31] _____
❏ Programming languages: [33] _____

I use a PC at (please check all that apply): ❏ home [35] ❏ work [36] ❏ school [37] ❏ other: [38] _____

The disks I prefer to use are ❏ 5.25 [39] ❏ 3.5 [40] ❏ other: [41]_____

I have a CD ROM: ❏ yes [42]   ❏ no [43]

I plan to buy or upgrade computer hardware this year: ❏ yes [44]   ❏ no [45]

I plan to buy or upgrade computer software this year: ❏ yes [46]   ❏ no [47]

Name: _____ Business title: [48] _____ Type of Business: [49] _____

Address (❏ home [50] ❏ work [51]/Company name: _____)

Street/Suite# _____

City [52]/State [53]/Zipcode [54]: _____ Country [55] _____

❏ **I liked this book!** You may quote me by name in future
IDG Books Worldwide promotional materials.

My daytime phone number is _____

IDG BOOKS

THE WORLD OF
COMPUTER
KNOWLEDGE

❑ YES!

Please keep me informed about IDG's World of Computer Knowledge.
Send me the latest IDG Books catalog.